Chris R Korte is a lifelong practicing Christian. Through years of study, he found that Christianity and the Bible do not always have consistent and plausible answers to many of life's questions. Consequently, he began studying *A Course in Miracles* (ACIM) over fifteen years ago, which answered all of those tough questions. By applying ACIM in his daily life, he has attained a more peaceful, loving, and forgiving existence. Chris' main passion is as a spiritual seeker, with a lifetime of experiences.

This book is dedicated to my three children. May this work help you find truth in this world and realize the love I have for you.

Chris R Korte

There Must Be a Better Explanation

God, Jesus, Christianity, Life, and Death

AUSTIN MACAULEY PUBLISHERS™

LONDON * CAMBRIDGE * NEW YORK * SHARJAH

Ordering Information
Quantity sales: Special discounts are available on quantity purchases by corporations, associations, and others. For details, contact the publisher at the address below.

Publisher's Cataloging-in-Publication data
Korte, Chris R
There Must Be a Better Explanation

ISBN 9798891550834 (Paperback)
ISBN 9798891550858 (ePub e-book)
ISBN 9798891550841 (Audiobook)

Library of Congress Control Number: 2023922473

www.austinmacauley.com/us

First Published 2024
Austin Macauley Publishers LLC
40 Wall Street, 33rd Floor, Suite 3302
New York, NY 10005
USA

mail-usa@austinmacauley.com
+1 (646) 5125767

20240408

I would like to acknowledge Helen Schucman, Bill Thetford, Ken Wapnick, and Gary Renard. They were presented with something that seemed new and different which they gifted to the world. Although I may not have learned my lessons fully, I am moving forward and growing in this life the best I know how because of their dedication to the truth.

Table of Contents

Introduction

The average Christian is trying to live a good life and has staked their eternal life on God's word in the Bible, the interpretation of the Bible, and the teachings of their Christian Church. But what if the lessons we have been taught are not totally correct? What if the Christian interpretation of the Bible and Jesus are not totally right? What if the life, death, resurrection, and teachings of Jesus were misunderstood? My intention is to show that we are mistaken about our life and there were many misunderstandings about God and Jesus' message, and there is a better explanation.

Christianity tries to answer questions like: Why are we here? What is the purpose of life? Is there a Heaven and hell? Is there a loving, caring God? What was Jesus' real message about life? Is the Bible the inspired, inerrant word of God? Why is there so much suffering? How can I be happy and at peace? Is the belief in Jesus' death and resurrection the way to Heaven? Why is Christianity the answer? I personally have operated on faith that Christianity was the answer to all of these questions, yet there are so many problems, contradictions, mysteries, and errors with which we are left. I will do my best to lay out some of them and offer what the true answers are to all of these questions. This book does not specially answer all of the questions, however when it doesn't, it points to the answer. We all must be seekers and this book is written for me first as I am a seeker not a saint.

The first part of the book looks at the Old Testament and some of the problems with God, His Law, and the Prophets. I end chapters with a newer revelation that corrects the Old Testament teachings. The second part reviews the New Testament and Jesus' life and teachings. I end most chapters with my understanding of the topic based on *A Course in Miracles*. I will offer practical and helpful ways to understand the Bible and Jesus with the goal of a better way to live and get to Heaven.

This book is not intended for scholars but for average Christians who are either searching for truth or looking to strengthen what is true in Christianity.

- I will repeat ideas throughout the book as they overlap between topics and that is what helps me to understand a complex issue. Besides, repetition is the mother of remembrance.
- CE is used as Common Era instead of AD.
- Certain words that call for respect are capitalized.
- The Apostles are specifically the original twelve and the disciples are all followers of Jesus.
- Consistent with the Bible, I use masculine pronouns, although feel free to substitute what makes you comfortable. Using he or she for the divine is not right either as gender pronouns cannot define Spirit, but label is what we humans do.
- I use Apologist or religious leaders to denote a wide array of Christians that typically promote orthodox Christianity. Their titles could be Preacher, Minister, Clergy, Priest or Academic. By using Apologist, I present a general opposing view while not criticizing specific individuals. Biblical scholars and historians are used as neutral experts.
- For simplicity and brevity, I use Jewish people or the Jews to also cover the Israelites, Hebrews and tribes of Abraham.
- Some biblical verses are abbreviated to enhance the reading.
- Lessons from influential people are used, however, if they are not verbatim or originally from that person, they are impactful statements nonetheless.
- Many words are used interchangeably with their synonyms such as Spirit and soul, names for Heaven, hell, the devil, etc.
- The Church is the original body of believers and all Christian organizations thereafter.
- All biblical quotes are from the New King James version unless otherwise noted.
- *A Course in Miracles* is abbreviated as the Course or ACIM and quotes are from the Foundation for Inner Peace version.

- I do my best to convey my understanding of Christianity, the Bible, and *A Course in Miracles.*
- In referencing God, Jesus, the Holy Spirit and some biblical figures, I will use the Bible's characterizations even though I believe some of the qualities and words attributed to them are not true of these deities and principals.
- I do my best to communicate ideas, but if there are mistakes, try to learn from the general theme and overlook the specific blunder.

It is not my intention to degrade anyone's belief or shake anyone's faith, but to strengthen the understanding of what is real and true. My overarching question throughout the book is: how do you know which interpretation of Christianity is true? *A Course in Miracles* is deep and I will only touch the surface here.

From the Course,

I am here only to be truly helpful.
I am here to represent Him Who sent me.
I do not have to worry about what to say or what to do, because He Who sent me will direct me.
I am content to be wherever He wishes, knowing He goes there with me.
I will be healed as I let Him teach me to heal. (T-2.V.18:2–6)

1. Is Christianity the Best Explanation of the Evidence?

As a lifelong Christian, I have reverence and respect for the 2000-plus-year history and tradition of Christianity. I also respect Judaism's long history as the root of Christianity. Immersing myself in the Bible and what the religious leaders say about Christianity, I have come to the conclusion that Christianity is inconsistent, contradictory, doesn't always make sense, and is not the best explanation for the evidence of this life. After studying Christianity and the Bible, concentrating on the New Testament, I have identified many problems and conflicts that have led me to important, yet unanswered questions. If Christianity as written in the Bible is true, which of the thousands of different Christian denominations are teaching the truth?

My yardstick for evaluating Christianity is twofold. Does Christianity help me here on earth, not to get ahead or make my life easier, but to be more loving, peaceful, and a good person? And more importantly, will being a Christian get me to Heaven? With regard to peace in this life, the Bible does say that we will have troubles; however St. Paul says that through Jesus Christ we can have the peace which passeth understanding. Is there peace, even among Christians? Can anyone have peace with so much suffering? Additionally, the Bible advances eternal punishment which overshadows any feeling of peace. With regard to Heaven, the basic theological tenets of Christianity do not demonstrate that its doctrine is the path to Heaven.

In the following chapters, I will delve into the problems, contradictions, and unanswered questions. I'll list a few questions here and then describe what I have found based on *A Course in Miracles* that answers the question of Heaven while helping me on earth. Christianity cannot truly and completely answer these questions to the satisfaction of many Christians, me included.

1) If God is perfect love and loves us, would He kill His own children as the Bible says?

2) Could an all-powerful, all-loving, all-caring God create a world where such suffering is possible?

3) Jesus said ask and it will be given you. Why doesn't that work for everyone at all times or even sometimes?

4) Given the thousands of Christian denominations, which one has the correct theology?

5) Why do so many of God's Old Testament laws contradict Jesus' command to love your neighbor?

6) Since Jesus' own Apostles didn't understand his message, do we know what Jesus actually said and meant?

7) If salvation is belief in Jesus, what about people born before Jesus or born to a different culture/faith?

The traditional answers to these questions given by the Bible and Apologists are explored in this book but come up wanting. They're answered by well-meaning Christians because they must be answered to maintain the faith, although they don't always make sense. One of the problems with the answers given by Apologists is that they will quote Scripture to prove Scripture. If the reliability of Scripture is in question, then quoting more Scripture will not help to validate itself. Is the reliability of the Bible supported by life, nature, or outside evidence?

Fortunately, there is a newly revealed teaching that explains all of life and answers all of these questions. It is a book from Jesus called *A Course in Miracles*. I was open to a new way of looking at everything because Christians historically believe in changing theologies. In the Bible, there was one monotheistic religious belief called Judaism and then Jesus came and basically transformed God's religion to a new monotheistic religious belief called Christianity. The new religion had a lot of the same actors, except the theology was different. Apologists will say that Christianity is the fulfillment of Judaism, but if that was the case, wouldn't all Jews have become Christians?

I know that introducing a new interpretation of Christianity sounds like some new-age gibberish, but if you continue on this journey with me, I will lay out the argument for why traditional Christianity does not necessarily bring peace to our lives and get us to Heaven. If you are not at peace in this chaotic world and are somewhat confused about what it takes to get to Heaven, then this book will point you in the right direction. If you have questioned whether your interpretation of the Bible is true, then this book will give answers to many of the interpretation questions. You will be presented with a unifying message about God and Jesus. Even if you don't agree with the message, you will learn something new that may help you in your life and heavenly quest.

A Course in Miracles, often abbreviated as ACIM or the Course, was given by Jesus as a voice in the mind of a woman in New York over a seven-year period from 1965 to 1972. It is a three-volume work where Jesus gives his true teachings and even corrects the Bible when it has erred. It is not a new religion because you personally study and practice with guidance from the Holy Spirit, who along with Jesus is the only authoritative teacher. The Course uses Christian terminology since that is what Jesus taught during his incarnation here, and it references the King James Bible over eight hundred times. The main difference between traditional Christianity and these teachings is that God is only perfect love, and the historical Jesus is only love, peace, and forgiveness.

The Course is similar to the biblical teachings of Jesus where he teaches us to repent, as in change our minds, and become like him through the constant practice of forgiveness. True unconditional forgiveness was practiced by Jesus toward everyone for everything as evidence of his love. The Course does not attempt to teach the meaning of love because that cannot be taught; it does, however, aim at removing the blocks to love's presence, which is our natural spiritual state. The Course is over 1,500 pages long and it says that it is simple but not easy.

I have studied the Course for over fifteen years and although not an expert, I will do my best to relay the main concepts to answer the questions, problems and contradictions I have found in Christianity. The information I will provide may astound, confuse, or dishearten you, or it may gladden and relieve you. You might not believe all of it because of your years of orthodox Christian practice and conditioning, but you will hear truths that you can use to build on what you already believe.

This book will demand an open mind from you, just as the early Jewish Christians had to realize that there was a new teaching and they had to move on from their Jewish religion to a new theology. You will come away with a renewed understanding of God, Jesus, Christianity, the world, why you are here, how to have peace in this hectic world, and the true way to get to Heaven.

The previous seven questions will be answered in detail throughout the book using my understanding of *A Course in Miracles*. This book will also illustrate how the problems and contradictions of Christianity can be plausibly and practically answered by ACIM. I do not revel in pointing out the flaws of Christianity, as it has been my religious practice all my life, but you must first empty your cup before you can fill it with the truth. Depending on where you are in your faith and spiritual journey, you may have been looking for these answers all your life, or you may not be ready to hear them just yet.

I promise two things from this book – peace and salvation. Given our short tenure on this earth and the prospect of eternity in the next, salvation is probably the main reason to be a Christian. Therefore, I'll briefly expound on the seventh question, which is examined in detail in chapter nineteen. The main tenant of Christianity is the belief in Jesus as salvation or the only way to Heaven. Although the New Testament describes several ways to get to Heaven, I will focus on the Christian teaching that salvation is by grace through faith in Jesus.

If God wills that none shall perish as the Bible states, then belief in Jesus as the only way to Heaven would exclude about three-fourths of all humanity, including the Jews, who remain faithful to the God of the Old Testament. To analyze this more deeply I would like to do a quick thought experiment to see if belief in Jesus is the way to Heaven. We must begin by defining Heaven as the home of God having only God's attributes of love, peace, and joy. In a word, Heaven is perfect. Even though you believe in Jesus and know that he died for your sins, are you perfect love and peace? How will you fit into a place of perfect love and peace if you still have judgment, anger, envy, fear, and guilt in your heart, or as part of who you currently are? Jesus himself, or belief in Jesus, cannot violate your free will and change you unless you change yourself and become love. Even if your sins are forgiven, you will defile the perfectness of Heaven if you are not perfect.

Your purification needs to be done by you while you are on earth in a body. Jesus became perfect love and peace while on earth and his life and teachings were the way, the truth, and the life. The Course does not say you have to be perfect to get to Heaven, it says you have to practice perfect forgiveness, and that forgiveness removes all those negative characteristics. Once you remove all negatives, love is the only thing left and is what you are.

I realized deep in my heart that belief in the perfect human Jesus, though it might make me be a better person, left me unsure of what Jesus was asking me to do. How can I join God's perfection in Heaven if there are biblical contradictions on the subject? If you came this far, then get ready to experience theological answers that you may never have been exposed to.

First, you need a broader understanding of the similarities and differences between the traditional teachings of Christianity and *A Course in Miracles*. Throughout the book I will do my best to explain my understanding of both Christianity and ACIM to answer all the questions that I present. I will only focus on Christianity, although Course teachings that are from an eternal, unchanging deity, apply to everyone, everywhere, at all times. Here are some of the similar beliefs in a rough comparison.

<u>Similarities between Christianity and *A Course in Miracles*, i.e. both believe are true</u>

The Trinity – The Father, Son, and Holy Spirit
Monotheism – there is only one true God, who is perfect love
God created everything that is real
The Holy Spirit is our guide and comforter, leading us to Heaven
There is a state of Heaven, and it is our home
Jesus was a person who was a Son of God and a savior of the world
Jesus died, was resurrected, and ascended into Heaven
Jesus' two great Commandments are love God and love your neighbor
We are all children of God
There is a negative force which Christians call the devil and the Course calls the ego
Miracles are real

<u>Differences between Christianity and *A Course in Miracles*</u>

<u>Christianity</u>	<u>ACIM</u>
We as bodies are made in God's image	God only creates exactly like him
God created the world	God only creates what is eternal

Salvation is through belief in Jesus	Salvation is by thinking with the Holy Spirit
We are all bodies	We are all one Spirit
God is judgmental but a just ruler	God only extends love to His creation
The Bible is the inerrant word of God	The Bible was written by man and is inspired
We are all sinners and have original sin	We have only missed the mark and are innocent in eternity

If these main tenets of Christianity along with others are opposed to the teachings of the Course and as such are not the truth, then I need to define truth. For this book, I use true, truth, real, and reality interchangeably, because they are usually synonyms and have each other in their definitions. The use of real is usually about the material world or everything solid, as in reality. When I talk about the spiritual world and Heaven or the unseen world, it is understood as not solid or in physical existence although real in a different way. The dictionary definition of truth is that which is in accordance with the actual state of affairs, conforming to reality, or consistent with facts.

As an example, you could say a water bottle is real and true because it is a physical object and corresponds to its intended purpose as a water bottle. We think the water bottle is true but only based on our confined perspective and for a limited time. The water bottle can be used for many other things. Also, before it was shaped into a water bottle it was plastic pellets, and before that a petroleum substance, and before that maybe a dinosaur or vegetation, and so on. After its temporary use as a water bottle, it can then be recycled into Aunt Edna's shower cap.

This example of a water bottle being true is only limited and short term. Religion and spirituality are unlimited and timeless; therefore, they must be true for all time, in all situations and locations, and for all people.

A more appropriate, unlimited, and eternal definition for real and true is: *That which never changes.* If something changes, then it can't be true because it is not the same as it was before or for all time. It was something and then changed to something else. If it is true, then it cannot change or be changed or it was or will be something different. The water bottle might be relatively true but not absolutely true. When we are talking about truth regarding God, Spirit, and theology, we are talking about the unchangeable and eternal. When we are talking about deities and eternal life in Heaven, the definition must be absolute, permanent, eternal and objective.

Hopefully, you had the first of the big ah-ha's and realized that according to this definition, everything in the physical universe probably has changed or will change in the billions of years of the universe's existence. Therefore, pursuant to my precise and comprehensive definition, nothing in the physical world is true or real. We only think the physical world is real because of our limited perspective and for us, that's all we know.

However, the Holy Spirit, our guide in this life, knows that only God and His Kingdom are real. His only function is to teach us this most crucial lesson. The only thing that is true on this earth or in the universe of form is the thoughts we think with God or Spirit. The only absolute truth is "God is." This is also the understanding of perfect oneness. If we are talking about God and spirituality and even the religion that explains them, we can't use time and space bound definitions because God and His Kingdom are outside of time and space. We will get into this conundrum later, but for now realize that we have to think bigger and rely on the Holy Spirit to begin to understand God and His Kingdom. One of the shortcomings with humans and man-made religion is we cannot really grasp or understand God and Heaven by ourselves.

For the religion of Christianity to be real and true, it must be eternal and never change. Since Christianity includes the Old Testament and Christianity has changed God's plan from the Jews and the Law to belief in Jesus, then that part of Christianity cannot be true. In a nutshell, either the biblical accounts are wrong, or we greatly misunderstood them. I like to be positive so I'm going to say we've misunderstood God's plan. I will present the plan Jesus communicated in *A Course in Miracles* and introduce things that may seem wild and far out, but I assure you they're quite realistic once you look at them from a divine point of view and then let it sink in.

When I realized Christianity didn't make sense to me and started studying ACIM, I had doubts though I gave myself some latitude because I already believed some biblical views that were wild and far out. I know atheists laugh at some of our beliefs like there's an invisible all-powerful God who controls a world which has so many problems. Or God sent Jesus to die for us as the only way for us to be saved as a sacrifice to Himself. There are many more unbelievable stories in the Bible that we believe because that's how we were raised, and most Christians believe them.

In the pursuit of truth, we must be open and realize that just because everyone believes something does not make it true, and just because no one believes it does not make it false. The one thing I do know is that I don't know everything, and we as a species don't know everything, which is why we need the Holy Spirit. We learn new things to expand our understanding but only if we are open to new ideas. We then keep what works and discard what doesn't.

About five hundred years ago, Martin Luther started the Protestant Reformation by asking questions and pointing out inconsistencies and problems in orthodox Christianity. If the devil has sway over the world as the Bible says, then everyone would be wise, as Martin Luther did, to question everything in religion. Learning the Course requires the willingness to question every value that you hold. The mark of an open, learning mind is being more committed to truth and understanding than to our convictions. The goal of learning is not to shield old views from new facts; it is to revise old views to incorporate new facts. Christianity and *A Course in Miracles* are directed to the same ends, it is the means which are very different.

I want to apologize in advance for my sometimes direct and severe insights. It is not my intention to degrade or attack the views held by others or any organized religion. With this work, I am actually elevating God to only perfect love. The beauty of what I'm going to present is, you don't have to believe all of it for it to help you. You can continue to believe what you always have and still grow in love and peace. You can continue to worship in the way you are accustomed, as love, gratitude, and fellowship are always beneficial. However, if you begin to love a little more, you will be on your way home.

I will try to demonstrate that the historical Jesus believed in the teachings of the Course and that you don't need to totally change your life if you don't want to. I know that if you begin to change your mind about the world, your life will follow. My objective is to point out what I have learned, inform those who are seeking truth, and help everyone become more peaceful and eventually return to our home in Heaven – at least for those who choose to listen. I only want to be helpful, and I will let the Holy Spirit lead me and do the real work.

This book can be summed up fairly easily: Jesus was love, peace, and forgiveness. God is love, peace, and joy. Anything in religion or the world that does not conform to these attributes is not of them or even real and true.

Note: There are other attributes that apply to Jesus such as kindness, patience, and goodness, although all come from love.

2. A Course in Miracles

It is essential that you have an open mind and be comfortable with questioning some of the teachings that you have known all your lives as you explore the questions and answers about Christianity. Before I try to summarize a teaching that encompasses what mere humans cannot fully understand, I want to summarize the Allegory of the Cave by Plato. He told this story thousands of years ago relating it to the search for knowledge. This may be what it will be like when we realize that what we thought was true is not true and what we think of as unreal is, in fact, real.

Summary of Plato's Cave

There were several men who had been imprisoned in a cave for as long as they could remember. They were separately chained to a low wall facing the back of a cave. They were chained so tightly that they could not move their heads to look around, they could only see what was on the back wall. The cave entrance was on the other side of the low wall behind them. The light from a fire outside the cave showed through the cave entrance and reflected shadows on the large back wall that they looked at all day.

As people walked by the cave entrance, their shadows along with whatever they were carrying reflected on the large back wall. The prisoners also heard voices and grew to know that the shadows and voices were the reality of the world. After decades in this predicament, one of the captives broke free and made his way to the cave entrance. When he looked outside, he saw that people were walking and carrying objects in front of the cave entrance and this was casting shadows on the back cave wall. He realized the shadows themselves were not real but were made by real people walking by, contrary to what he and his fellow prisoners had thought their entire lives.

In excitement, the freed prisoner went back into the cave to tell the other prisoners what he had discovered. The chained prisoners did not believe him because their limited knowledge of shadows constituting reality was all they knew, and they could not envision or comprehend a different reality. They were so adamant in their beliefs that the shadows were real, they wanted to kill the freed prisoner rather than believe that what they knew was wrong.

Although this was written about 2500 years ago, human nature still prevents some of us from opening ourselves up to new and different ways of thinking. This allegory could have been written about Jesus, who being born a Jew, was teaching something different from what all of Judaism steadfastly held on to. Jesus was literally killed for blasphemy against their religion even though his miracles demonstrated that he had the authority to confront the way things always were. So why would Jesus wait two thousand years to explain and correct his teachings in *A Course in Miracles*? The short version is that people were not ready until now for a radical new understanding of life as we have known it for several millennia. In the twenty-first century, we are much more open to new ideas and have a more accepting and inquisitive Christian community as evidenced by the thousands of Christian denominations. Coincidentally, several major religions that are much older than Christianity have believed some of the concepts explained in ACIM for thousands of years.

Here is my thumbnail understanding of *A Course in Miracles'* explanation of why we think we are here.

In the beginning and throughout eternity, there is God, and we as Spirit, are part of God in Heaven. We are one with God and everything created is exactly like God and one with God. Everything is perfect. Then something appears to happen; a thought from God's creation in the form of a tiny idea of what it would be like to be different from God. It is a thought that only lasts for a nanosecond and God does not respond to it because the idea is not of God. Since we are like God in Heaven, our spiritual mind in Heaven has immense power. Because this idea is an ungodly thought, the illusory universe is created from it, along with the people, in what is known as the big bang.

Scientists are able to trace our origins back to the big bang but will never be able to go past that because it is the beginning of physical creation. Since this thought of separation from God and the resulting creation of the universe of time and space are not of God, it cannot be real and did not happen. It seems real because of the divine power of our minds. In essence, we humans are dreaming that we are living material lives in a body away from God in Heaven.

The Course says that all of our time is spent dreaming and our waking and sleeping dreams only have different forms. In fact, we are at home in God's loving grasp dreaming that we are here, yet able to awaken to our home in Heaven at any time. The world and our physical existence are an illusion, although our existence as Spirit is still real. This is what Jesus meant in Luke 17:21, when he said, "For indeed the kingdom of God is within you." To illustrate that this is true is by agreeing that most Christians believe that God is perfect. The classical and biblical definition of perfection is that it is complete, or it is lacking nothing. Therefore, for God to be complete, He cannot lack us, His children, otherwise He would not be complete and perfect. Nonetheless, the Bible is based on the precept that most of humanity is not and will not be in Heaven with God, being eternally separated from God based on His salvation plan. If God does not include everyone, then He is incomplete and cannot be perfect. Therefore, either He is not perfect, or we are indeed with Him in Heaven and this life that we think is real must be something other than our reality.

I know this might be alien and is a lot to take in. It took me a while to wrap my mind around it, but I knew there had to be another explanation because what we have been taught does not work. Even atheists have many questions that can't be answered. My hope is that if this explanation resonates at all as true for you, then you will realize that it eliminates so many of the problems we have with God and this suffering existence, because He didn't create any of it. This line of thought is not as farfetched as you might think as other major religions have similar beliefs. Hindus believe in Maya, the physical and mental limited reality of our everyday lives which is illusory. Buddhists believe in impermanence, that nothing in the world will last and everything changes, concluding that the world is not real and is a world of illusion. This isn't a surprise because the eastern religions have always been more mystic, and the western religions have been more materialistic.

Albert Einstein, the great theoretical physicist, is quoted as saying, "The illusion that we are separate from one another is an optical delusion of our consciousness." He also said, "The distinction between past, present, and future is only a stubbornly persistent illusion." Einstein theorized that time and space was not fixed and immutable but circumstantial and relative. Another physicist, Niels Bohr, said everything we call real is made of things that cannot be regarded as real. Looking at things from the quantum level, he also said that those who are not shocked when they first come across quantum theory cannot possibly have understood it.

Physicist Erwin Schrödinger addressed consciousness in reality when he said, "The total number of minds in the universe is one. In fact, consciousness is a singularity phasing within all beings." He was just scratching the surface to understand the mind because it is like an iceberg with most of its substance underwater where you can't see it. The great minds of today like Elon Musk and Neil deGrasse Tyson ruminate, using computer terminology, that we might be living in some kind of computer simulation.

Elon pronouncing, "We're most likely in a simulation." Regarding time and space from a theoretical scientific view, Einstein and other scientists understood some of the illusion, although they did not comprehend the whole picture. The bottom line is that life on earth is not real and only our life in Heaven with God is real.

To continue the story, when this error of thought occurred, the Holy Spirit was put into the mind of the dreamer in order to remind us of who we are and to slowly and gently wake us up from that false reality. If you really think about it, what is the role of the Holy Spirit? God is sovereign and works in the world and Jesus said I will be with you always and is our salvation back to Heaven. The answer is the Holy Spirit came into existence to make sure we woke up. This is why everyone will eventually be saved or will wake up to Heaven, because in reality, we never left Heaven. We just need to become aware of our dreaming state. God did not react to the thought of separation; he merely gave the answer. Although He does know that His communication channels are not fully open.

It is slightly more technical and complicated than this but you don't need to understand the reason as much as how to get back to Heaven. There are many places in the Bible where the writers touched on this cosmic story because they did have inspiration from the Holy Spirit, although they did not understand enough to give a complete picture of how and why this happened.

It is with hesitation that I describe Jesus because he is worshipped as the pinnacle of Christian theology. As we will see, even his story in the Bible does not add up to who he was and why he died. Jesus was a man just like the rest of us. He is God's Son, just like all of us. Jesus was in the illusion and at one time thought he was a body. The difference was Jesus learned his lessons and was the first to awaken while on earth in the dream. He knew that his real life was in Heaven with his Father and spent his ministry teaching what he could about the Kingdom of Heaven given the current political and religious environment. He didn't try to change the world because he knew it was an illusion and taught forgiveness as a way to remove the blocks to love and peace so our minds could fit back into Heaven. His death and resurrection were not demanded by God as a price Jesus had to pay for our salvation.

It was a forgiveness lesson that he wanted to teach as part of his ministry. The lesson is the body is not real and there is no death. Jesus spent much of his time listening to the Holy Spirit. That guidance is how he could perform miracles and know that his mission on earth was to teach about God in Heaven and how to get there. Unfortunately, Jesus was not as open and specific as many require, as he taught in vague parables and what he did teach is often misunderstood. Ultimately, he knew that all of us would awaken when we are supposed to and so he learned his lessons, taught what he could and left the rest in the hands of the Holy Spirit.

This is a very high-level account of what happened and why, and we will explore in more detail the questions regarding the teachings of Christianity as it relates to our life. The Course says that its curriculum is to know who you really are. This is not a new age "getting in touch with yourself." This is know your real self in Heaven and awaken to it. Jesus knew that vicarious salvation cannot work because only you can change your mind about who and whose you are to save yourself.

3. Why Is There So Much Suffering in the World?

Many people look at the beauty in the world and say that God created a beautiful world. What this really means is that it is a beautiful world for them at that time. For every person appreciating the beautiful things of this world, there might be an equal number of people suffering. Taken in totality, the world could be a 50-50 proposition. Half the people in the world have it pretty good at times while the other half is really struggling. Then circumstances might flip, and the other half suffers. The world is one of duality, which means that everything has an opposite, such as good and bad, happy and sad, right and wrong, pleasure and pain, etc.

The bottom line is everyone suffers at some time in their life, whether from disease, natural disasters, old age, starvation, loss, depression, isolation, physical harm, disappointment etc. If you are living a good life, things are going your way, you are financially sound and you are in good health, you will still die, and everyone you know and love will die. Furthermore, if you are a decent human being, you will feel for and even suffer with the millions of people who are suffering.

This raises the question: what kind of God creates a world where virtually everyone suffers? I'm not asking the question of why God allows evil because that is too easily dismissed by Apologists as man's evil nature. Instead, I am focusing on the suffering that is not due to man's inhumanity to man, only on the natural and unavoidable conditions of life on earth.

The Bible, purported to represent God's revelation and promises to His people, is full of stories of tremendous suffering. The disturbing thing is, a good amount of the suffering is caused by God as punishment for His children's actions or inactions. God commanded and caused suffering on His

Chosen People, the Jews, for their disobedience. God also directed suffering at His other children, the Pagans, in defense of or to elevate His Chosen People.

Some examples in the Bible of God directly causing suffering are Noah and the flood, destroying Sodom and Gomora, leaving the Jews as Egyptian slaves for over four hundred years, letting armies defeat the Jews when they were not faithful, helping the Jews defeat other armies when they were faithful, and killing the firstborn of every Egyptian. An estimate of the number of people God directly and indirectly killed in the Old Testament is over one million people killed. Expand that number to the ones who suffered as a result of God's intervention and it is clear that multi-millions have suffered as a direct result of God's biblical work. Suffering is so prevalent that it has become the way things are. Everyone with a body suffers at some point. This message is not preached much during Sunday service because it's hard to worship a God who we believe is all-loving and yet the world and the bodies He created and His actions cause so much suffering.

A book in the Bible that discusses the topic of suffering is the Old Testament book of Job. In summary, the book of Job relates the story of God and the devil testing the faithfulness of Job through intense suffering. There are no reasons given for this suffering other than God is the Almighty and cannot be questioned. If the story of Job is true, God agreed with or even encouraged the devil to attack the righteous Job causing him great suffering. If the devil is currently at work in the world and has been throughout time, and God is in control of the world, is it fair to say that God has allowed or even encouraged the devil to attack, tempt and make us suffer in order to test our faithfulness? Does God's sovereignty dictate that He can do the same to us and we cannot question His actions? How do we know that God is not repeating the scenario of Job now in any of us? The book of Amos even says the people of God will suffer because God is punishing them for their sins.

Rabbi Harold Kushner's book on suffering is titled, *When Bad Things Happen to Good People.* It is not titled *Why* bad things happen to good people. This is because it is self-evident the world is full of suffering for the good and the bad, the followers of God and Jesus, and all non-believers. In essence, misery is poured out on everyone in one form or another. Why? Kushner's answer to all the seemingly random suffering is summarized as: God is a God of judgment and not of power, a compassionate God but powerless to overcome the evil in the world.

Apologists really don't have a good answer for suffering, yet they try to explain it in a positive and practical way. One of the main reasons given for our pervasive suffering from a theological viewpoint is the fall of man or original sin. They say God created the world perfect for Adam and Eve in the Garden of Eden and Adam's disobedience caused them to be kicked out of the garden to live a life of suffering, along with the rest of humanity. If God is all-knowing and He made man, then He knew what we would do even if we had free will. He knew we would sin and as a consequence we would suffer naturally and by His hand for our entire existence. That is in essence how God set it up and those are His rules. If free will is the underlying cause and God gave us free will and told us there are certain things we can't do or we would suffer, then is that really free will?

Another explanation by Apologists of why we have suffering is that God has not acted to defeat evil and suffering YET. This gives credibility to the precept that God is all-powerful and all-loving and will flex His sovereign muscle in the future. We too cry out like the Psalmist, "How long, O Lord? Will you forget me forever?" If Apologists are right and God will abolish suffering eventually, can we really say He is all-loving for the ones that must endure to their end? God is all-powerful so He could intervene at any time.

Most faithful do believe God is all-loving but can't explain suffering. If God allows suffering and even builds it into His system, His world, then we must question what all-loving really means when it comes to God. It was reported that there is an inscription on a barrack wall in Auschwitz that said, "If there is a God, He will have to beg for my forgiveness." Would a loving God abandon His children in this life and the one to come?

Apologists will counter this paradox with their reasons why God allows and uses suffering to keep his omniscience intact. Here are some reasons given that God would allow suffering:

- God allows suffering to prepare us for the trials and complexities in life.
- God uses suffering to take our attention off the world and draw us closer to Him.
- God uses suffering to remind us of the reality of sin.
- God uses suffering to increase our faith.
- God uses suffering to help us grow in community with others.

Although these offer different ways to understand suffering, these reasons sound like backend explanations for a God who could have created a perfect world with no suffering if He was all-powerful and all-loving. If God knew that no one would continue to be perfect and He allowed and even instituted suffering because of it, then He put conditions on his love. Could He have let us continue to live in paradise with our imperfections?

If suffering originally started with Adam and Eve as a punishment for sin, and Jesus' death freed God's people from the bondage of sin, why do we still suffer? Telling people that God is a loving and compassionate God and He has the power to cure illness, relieve suffering and help people in need, although He does not, leaves people less likely to believe in and trust God. When you suffer, you are rightfully suspect of the proclamation that He has a loving plan for your lives. The story of the fall of man had to be in the Bible as a way to justify the suffering in God's world. If you didn't have the story of the fall, how could you explain an all-powerful, all-loving being creating a world with so much suffering?

When it comes to the creation story and its description of original sin as the cause of suffering, it's hard to imagine the story being true. It doesn't explain why we have to suffer for the actions of Adam and Eve or why animals suffer. St. Augustine, an influential early Church Father, said original sin was basically passed down from human to human through concupiscence by male sperm. This is a strange explanation of the how of suffering but not the why.

There is a proposition about God's qualities which display contradicting truths. It says that all four pillars of God and His relationship to the world cannot be true together. The pillars are:

God is all-Powerful

God is all-Loving

God is all-Knowing

There is suffering

Knowing we would suffer, either God is not all-powerful or God is not all-loving. If God is all-loving and we suffer, then He is not all-powerful. If God is all-powerful and all-loving and we suffer, He may not know of it. These types of arguments about God's limitations are hard to overcome so there must be a better explanation.

An Explanation of Suffering from *A Course in Miracles*

ACIM claims that God is perfect love, being only love. There is suffering in the world because God did not create the world and it is the domain of the ego/devil and not God. God would not will His children to suffer; therefore, His children cannot suffer. This means there must be another explanation to why we feel like we suffer. The answer to the four pillars is that we only think or appear to suffer in the dream that we are dreaming, and that is all. Our spiritual selves are real and do not suffer or change because they're eternal and are in Heaven. Our bodies and everything in the physical world are not real and will one day cease to exist. We are dreaming that we are here and God does not recognize the dream since it is not real. Therefore, God is not responsible for or the cause of our suffering in the world and neither is our sin.

When we had the thought of what it would be like to be different from God, the universe of form was made and because we felt guilty for thinking that thought, we became fearful of God's punishment. We followed the ego's/devil's plan to escape from God's assumed punishment by punishing ourselves or causing our own suffering. We unconsciously hoped to mitigate the punishment of God through our suffering. Jesus knew this and instead of alleviating everyone's suffering, he tried to teach us to seek the Kingdom of Heaven and not worry about the world. If the cause of the world and all its suffering is that we are dreaming that we are separate from God, then the answer is to wake up from the dream and reunite our Spirit with God.

The answer is not for God to eliminate suffering or answer our prayers to relive our suffering, it is to eliminate the cause of suffering and that cause of suffering is the dream of separation. God did help by sending the Holy Spirit into the dream with us to remind us that this is not real. This life, this world, and all of our suffering is an effect of our thought of separation. Jesus said to seek the Kingdom as the answer to everything, and seeking the Kingdom is merely to focus our full attention on it. The cause of our suffering is our dreaming and the effect is the suffering. The effect (suffering) can only be eradicated by removing the cause. When we change our thinking or mind, we will awaken to our home in Heaven with God, then our imagined suffering will be over and forgotten.

The knowledge that we are at home in God's loving grasp, dreaming that we are here is the beginning of peace on earth for us. You can still look at the world as beautiful by knowing that all thoughts and expressions of love are true and from God; rightly giving Him glory here on earth as still all-loving, powerful, and knowing.

4. Is God Ruling Over the World?

Christianity is based on the fact that God is sovereign, created the world, rules the world, is active in the world, and has a plan for us. His sovereignty is overwhelming in the Old Testament and carried into the New Testament. Apologists claim that the whole Bible is one story about a sovereign and righteous God redeeming His imperfect people. If you believe God is sovereign and in control of the world and has a plan for your life, you may be one of the many who say, *Thank God* when things are going well for you. You may also be one of the many who say they are *Blessed*, or one who feels God performs good works for them. Gratitude is always good. However, if you are someone who expresses gratitude to God for your good fortune, then you also have to admit that when things don't go your way, a God in charge should also bear the responsibility.

Most people experience pain and suffering even though they're good and faithful. Everyone who has prayed for a miracle for themselves or others, or has many people praying for them, knows the heartache and feelings of abandonment when that miracle does not come about. If God is given credit for the good, should God also be blamed when bad things happen? If God is all-powerful, should He be held responsible for turning a deaf ear to our prayers for help?

Apologists say we don't know the mind of God, that there are reasons for our suffering, and God has a plan that we can't understand. That may all be true; however, if He is praised for His goodness, shouldn't He be blamed for His negligence? There are bad things that do happen to us because of the evil of others, our bad choices, or our free will; but that only accounts for some of our pain, sorrow, and failures. We are surely not responsible for natural disasters, childhood diseases, terminal illnesses, random accidents, and the inevitability of death.

If, as the Bible says, in all things God works for the good of those who love Him, why do the faithful suffer? Things do not always work in our favor and in looking at God's actions in the Old Testament, it shows us that God is selective, arbitrary, not always actively helping, and at times punishing. When we fervently pray and nothing happens or something bad happens, we are told that God is mysterious and unknowable. If God is unknowable, how do we know He is in charge? If God is the source of miracles and they appear to be random, are we doing something wrong, are we not righteous enough, do we not have enough faith, or can there be another explanation?

We are taught to love God continually, but does God love us continually if He only occasionally shows up to help in the world and in our lives? In Matthew 7:11, Jesus said a loving Father gives good gifts to those who ask Him. It doesn't say sometimes, but when you ask. This dichotomy is a big reason so many people have a problem with a God who we are told cares, has the power to help, but seems to be inactive in the world. The God of the Old Testament promised to help His Chosen People, while apparently ignoring the rest of the world.

With the randomness of God's actions in the world, could it be that God has abandoned us or we are not good enough? Surely that is how it occurs in the story of Cain and Abel, where God only liked one of their offerings and not the other. If God is selective, then is He all-loving? Could it be that He is only a cheerleader on the sidelines and doesn't actually intervene on our behalf? John is the last prophet after Jesus and since then we haven't added to the Bible in over two thousand years. Should we assume that all of God's major interventions for us have ended?

Another question about God's sovereignty in the world is the question of the devil's role with humankind. There are many biblical references and a general understanding that the devil is also active in the world. Some would say that the world is the devil's domain. 1 John says the whole world lies under the sway of the wicked one. Do God and the devil compete in the world, or is one dominant and one subordinate? Did God abandon the world to the devil? How can God be sovereign if the devil has sway over the world? Job demonstrates that God is observing the world and He grants the devil freedom to act.

In Genesis, when God made the world, he said it is good, although the devil being present in the beginning makes you conclude that it was not good and never has been. God allowed the devil to initiate the fall of Adam and Eve. Apologists say the world was created good and perfect and that man's disobedience spoiled it. God knew there was a supernatural being that tricked Eve into disobedience. Therefore, evil in the form of the serpent was using his sway on humans before Adam and Eve sinned. Would a loving Father kick His naive and trusting children out of paradise for one disobedient act after being duped by a preternatural being? If Adam and Eve did not sin, would there be suffering, would we live forever in paradise on earth and not suffer death, and would we still be trying to get to Heaven? Would Jesus have forgiven the whole thing?

Jesus answered the question of God's sovereignty in this world when he said numerous times that God was in Heaven. At least twenty times in the Gospels, Jesus refers to his Father being in Heaven, and therefore not in the world. It's odd that Jesus didn't have a more earthly relationship and more one-on-one personal contact with God than Moses or Adam and Eve. The reason is that Jesus knew God was in Heaven. He taught it subtlety so as not to raise the ire and further condemnation from the Jewish leaders, which may have resulted in his earlier death for blaspheming God.

The most well-known prayer from the Bible is the Lord's Prayer. Jesus says that God is in Heaven as it begins, "Our Father who art in Heaven." The first time I noticed this curiosity, I was climbing a local mountain with my wife and friends. We were ascending and the group decided to turn back, nevertheless, I wanted to go to the very top. Like many, I wanted to be near the heavens and get close to God to feel a special connection. Many religious believe in the power and holiness of objects, people, and places, and I was no different. I revered certain churches, relics, holy objects, martyrs, and, of course, the Bible. I got to the top alone, and the view was magnificent. I started to pray the Lord's Prayer and I had an epiphany where Jesus was saying that God was really in Heaven and as a loving Father, could not be part of or the creator of this suffering world.

I had previously never dwelled on the specific words of the prayer, except this time it hit me as odd that Jesus would say this when we all believe God is everywhere. I had a knowing that Jesus was telling me that what we thought about God was not true, and I should pray about it to get clarification.

Other biblical passages that confirm Jesus' message that God is in Heaven are, John 14:12 when Jesus says, "[...] because I go to my Father." And

Matthew 10:32–33, "I will also confess before My Father who is in heaven" and "I will also deny before my Father who is in heaven." Matthew 16:17, "[…] but My Father who is in heaven." And Matthew 12:50, "For whoever does the will of my Father in heaven." The Gospel of Matthew has Jesus saying over a dozen times that his Father is in Heaven. Everyone concedes that God is in Heaven and everywhere, so why does Jesus specifically say only Heaven?

Furthermore, why does Jesus need to tell his Father in Heaven about believers on the earth if God is working the plans for our good? The answer is exactly what Jesus was saying: God is in Heaven because this is a dream. God does not recognize the dream because it is not real. God is in Heaven with our spiritual selves and thus will not respond to our earthly pleas for help. Ask and you shall receive pertains to the Holy Spirit's answering our prayers by giving us guidance.

Another interesting point regarding God being in Heaven is the opening of the Old Testament. The very first statement in Genesis is, "In the beginning God created the heavens and the earth." If God's dwelling place is Heaven, where did He dwell before He created Heaven? Moses, who is supposed to have written Genesis, lived about 2500 years after Adam and Eve. Are we confident that the story is recounted accurately? Can we be assured he understood the complexity or immenseness of creation to explain it even generally? If, as Jesus said, Heaven is the holy dwelling place of God, how can things like certain geographical lands, churches, or relics be revered as holy? According to the Course, there can be no places or things that are holier than others because they are all the same, being untrue. Holiness is only found in a relationship where God's love is extended to us and by us. His creations in Heaven are one and when you realize your brother is one with you, you will also be holy indeed.

Apologists use God's moral authority to justify the atrocities committed in the Old Testament as just and moral because they came from God. Because God is sovereign in the world, what God commands must be morally right. Therefore, when God commanded the Jews to slaughter the Amalekites, it became intrinsically good because a good God commanded it. If God is sovereign, unchanging, and His actions and commands are eternal, why aren't all of His commands applicable to us today?

If God is active and sovereign in the world, then what was and is the role of the Holy Spirit? Jesus said the Holy Spirit would come to the Apostles when he returned to the Father. This is another reference to the Father being in Heaven and then putting the Holy Spirit in charge of the welfare of the faithful. If Jesus and the Father are one as he says, then Jesus would still be communing with the Apostles and all people after he left his earthly existence. Jesus now says the Holy Spirit will guide the people. Why did Jesus say he would send the Holy Spirit when the Holy Spirit has been interacting with the Old Testament Jews for thousands of years? Did God give up his sovereignty and command of the world to the Holy Spirit?

The Apostles' Creed says Jesus was conceived by the Holy Spirit, which makes it sound like the Holy Spirit is also active in the world. When Jesus says he will send the Holy Spirit to the Apostles, it appears to elevate the Holy Spirit to the intercessor between man on earth and God in Heaven. This confirms God being in Heaven and not sovereign.

ACIM's View of God's Sovereignty

Jesus' explanation of God's sovereignty and control of the world based on *A Course in Miracles* is that God is and always was in Heaven and Jesus knew it to be true. He also knew God did not create the world and as such was not in control of the physical universe or watching over our actions. God did not let the devil torment Job to see if Job would still be faithful to God if he lost everything. What loving Father would do that and still be called loving? All of the stories about God intervening to either help or punish us came from the fear and guilt of our ego mind.

Although there is not a creature known as the devil, the Course does say that there is a wrong thought in our minds competing with the right thoughts of the Holy Spirit. This wrong thought is called the ego and is somewhat comparable to the Bible's devil. This wrong thought of who we are convinced us to separate from the oneness of God, which resulted in the formation of the world and the loneliness that we feel. When Jesus said ask and you shall receive, he was not speaking of God being involved in the world, he was saying the Holy Spirit will always answer your prayers with guidance, comfort and love.

The love of the Holy Spirit may provide secondary physical benefits, known as physical miracles, if that is what is best for you, but they come from our minds with the power of the Holy Spirit's love. The Holy Spirit is the still small voice who came into the mind at the time of the seeming separation and reminds us of our true home in Heaven and who we are in reality. God is kind, compassionate, merciful, and patient, not in this world, but by sending the Holy Spirit into the dream with us to gently awaken us.

As with suffering, knowing that God is not in control or running the world answers so many questions about why a loving God would not intercede to help us. It overturns the thought of a capricious God who interacts with some people and not us. The world is not of God and you cannot believe and invest in the world and know God. We all need to overcome the world as Jesus did. God is everywhere that is real, although the world is not real. God is Spirit, however the world is form. Form is the body and the universe and they are an illusory dream in our minds as we continue to live on in Heaven with God. Knowing that God and Heaven are real, the world is not real, and knowing that God is not arbitrarily controlling our lives or neglecting our needs is the beginning of peace in our lives.

5. God's Image and Chosen People

Although we sometimes think of God as an older gentleman with white hair, beard, and flowing white robes, we know He is actually Spirit and does not have a body. He is nonmaterial, invisible, infinite, Spirit. We are none of those, so what does it mean to be created in God's image and likeness? Apologists say we have Godly aspects in our human nature that are not shared with any other life form, such as the ability to love, create, choose good and truth, and exercise free will. Or it could refer to the immaterial part of humanity such as the moral and social faculties that we also share with God. Some say we are reflections of God not reproductions of God. My question when reading the Bible is, did God create us in His image or did we create God in our image? Voltaire said, "If there were no God, it would be necessary to invent one." This is a completely plausible statement given that every society throughout history has had some type of God to worship and to explain how and why things work the way they do. If these gods had different names and were depicted and understood differently, and there is only one God, then they were all made in the people's image.

With so many different gods, are all societies wrong about God except one? Another indicator that we made God in our image is the deity that you worship is usually dependent on where you live. Although some nations have a mixture of religions each with their own God, most have a dominant religion with their God and you can be known by your religion instead of your nationality. A definition could be, God is a contrived system of control depicted differently depending on your geographical location. Ultimately, we have endowed God with our characteristics.

It is clear that God refers to an image of a Father or creator in relation to the image of ourselves. In most cases, individuals have simply absorbed the dominant faith and understanding of who God is from their family and society based on where they grew up. Currently, it is estimated that the people of this world worship hundreds if not thousands of different gods. If there is only one God in Heaven and we all see Him differently, that is proof we make Him up in our creative minds rather than who He really is. If God only revealed himself in the Bible, then only about a quarter of humanity would know about Him. We were certainly not made in God's image and likeness regarding our physical form and attributes; however, we were made in God's image and likeness regarding our spiritual nature.

If we are made in God's image, which is pure Spirit, why do we have a body and make it so important when form is not an attribute of Spirit? We are told in the Bible that in the end times we will be transported to Heaven in our glorified bodies. Heaven is not a physical place; therefore our bodies will turn to dust, nonetheless our Spirit is what lives on. The notion of a glorified body was partially derived from Luke 24:14, when Jesus ascended into Heaven and the Apostles saw him float bodily into the sky. Jesus did not enter the realm of Heaven in a body. It's only natural that we humans are fixated on the body, it is literally the thing we think we are. Everything we do is either for our body or someone else's body.

Unfortunately, we look at our situation backward. We think we are human beings having a spiritual experience but we are actually Spirit having a human experience. The second Commandment says not to make false idols. Haven't we made the world and the body into a false idol? We have indeed made the body an idol, calling it at times the altar of God when in fact it is nothing and will disappear at its end. Our true nature as Spirit never ends and because it is immaterial, it will not deteriorate. God as Spirit is so different from us that we could not be created in His image and likeness in our form on earth. Confirmation is that we all must die, although God or Spirit never dies.

If God knew us before we were formed, we must have a spiritual nature and were Spirit before we came to earth. Do we then spend our earthly existence trying to get back to Heaven? Why did we even come to earth in the first place? If we have free will, did we have a choice whether to come to earth or stay in Heaven? If we didn't have a choice, then why were we sent by God knowing that more than three-quarters of all humanity won't make it back to Heaven given His Christian requirements?

If Adam and Eve were made perfect, why did God give them a Commandment to follow? Even with free will, perfection does not need rules to follow, it is just perfect. Additionally, if Adam and Eve were made in God's image, why weren't they and their offspring God's Chosen People? The Jewish nation as God's Chosen People began long after Adam with Abraham and his covenant with God. This covenant would make a great nation and all families on the earth would be blessed. God said in several Old Testament passages that I will be your God and you will be my people. How did a changeless God later change His Chosen People from Jews to Christians? The Bible says the reason for God's Chosen People was to bring forth the Messiah as foretold by the prophets. The problem is that God's own Chosen People, the Jews, did not recognize Jesus as the Messiah or Savior and rejected him as the Son of God. They even used God's Mosaic Law to justify the killing of God's only begotten Son. It's hard to say how many Jews converted to Christianity but most of the early Christians were probably Pagan converts.

The foundational document of Christianity is the Old Testament, the story of God's Chosen People. According to Christianity's salvation by grace through faith and belief in Jesus, God's Chosen People may not make it into Heaven because they don't believe in Jesus. What about the fate of people on the planet before Abraham? Did God not want to commune with them, did He not want to reveal Himself to anyone who wasn't Jewish? There were large civilizations such as the Chinese dynasties before Jesus that had never heard of the God of the Jews. 2 Peter 3:9, says God is, "[…] not willing that any should perish but that all should come to repentance."

Does the ALL in that declaration mean all those who were not the Chosen People or believers in Jesus? If it does include everyone, how did God communicate that to them? If God is almighty and sovereign, then His will should be known to all. Did God have a different plan for salvation before Jesus, a separate plan for the Jews and some other plan for the Pagans or Gentiles? If God had a Chosen People and only communicated His salvation to them, does that make some of God's children more special than others? This exclusive agreement would seem to negate the biblical statement that God wills that none shall perish.

Christianity is based on John 3:16 saying, "For God so loved the world that he gave his only begotten Son, that whoever believes in Him should not perish but have everlasting life." If that was the Almighty God's plan, then two thousand years later, about a quarter of the seven billion people are Christian and many more than seven billion have died not knowing about or believing in Jesus. John 14:6, Jesus says, "No one comes to the Father except through me." Doesn't this statement nullify the relationship and salvation of God's own Chosen People? No one knows the mind of God or the hearts of people, still, if believing in Jesus is His plan, a success rate of saving about twenty-five percent of everyone who lived is not a very effective plan.

Jesus says with men it is impossible but with God all things are possible. Does God have other plans so everyone will have the opportunity to not perish? One other explanation of the plan is that God might retroactively go back and save people of faith. But then why do we need to be a Christian?

St. Paul declared that it is not through the Law of Moses that you are saved. He deemed the Law important because he would not have known sin except through the Law. The unfortunate part is all the guilt, fear, and suffering the Law brought on the Jews that the Gentiles did not have to go through. They can just follow Jesus without following the Mosaic Laws. It's interesting that the Gentiles had multiple gods, who controlled the rain, crops, fertility, battles, etc. The Jews had God performing a similar function of taking care of them, and the only difference is that it was just one God instead of many.

In essence, God made tremendous demands on the Jews that they struggled to keep. Moses said that if the Jews are obedient, God would set them above others, and if disobedient, they would suffer and serve others. God had a Chosen People, and instead of loving them unconditionally, He put conditions on them. The Jews suffered like all societies, so what was the advantage of keeping those arduous laws if Jesus is the way? Furthermore, why did the Jews fall away from God so often if his message was clear, direct and helpful? Was it because they were just human and created to falter like the rest of us? Or was it that the Jews didn't feel the presence of God since He instilled fear and only seemed to communicate with kings and outcast prophets? Or was it that their personal lives were full of misery and suffering like everyone else's and God's promised blessings didn't always make a difference?

Apologists say if you sin against an infinite and eternal God, the penalty is infinite and eternal punishment. And so, it was with God's Chosen People as they suffered throughout history, and since they're not Christians, may continue to suffer into eternity. God's Chosen People had many difficulties and were enslaved in Egypt for over four hundred years, not to mention the unimaginable suffering of the Holocaust. What kept God away for four centuries if these were His people and He was to set them above others? The

Jews today still celebrate the Passover when God's angel killed all the firstborn of the Egyptians to convince Pharaoh to let His people go.

Was God being vengeful for Pharaoh killing the firstborn of the Jews? The Exodus is one of the greatest stories of all time, but how many Jews lost faith and died in the many generations while they prayed and waited for their God? There are numerous biblical scholars who don't think the Exodus happened as recorded given the scant archeological evidence or written records depicting over one million Jews fleeing Egypt and setting up camp elsewhere. If it did happen, then God purposely let His Chosen People suffer and die in those four hundred years.

We are indeed made in God's image and likeness in our real existence in Heaven. We are Spirit and as such are like our Father in Heaven. Jesus taught in John 17:23, "I in them, and You in Me; that they may be made perfect in one." You are one with God because you are an extension and expression of God. As with a good portion of the Bible, it was inspired and the writers had a vague notion of the truth but misunderstood much of the message. Case in point, the general creation story has some validity although it mistakenly produced the world of form and the existence of sin.

As told in the Bible, Adam and Eve were created perfect and lived in the garden of paradise. God gave the command to not eat of the fruit of the tree of knowledge of good and evil, but they were tricked by the serpent and were subsequently kicked out of the garden by God. They were relegated to a life of hard work and suffering and were separated from God never to return to the garden on earth. The story either came to Moses in a vision or was handed down through the generations to him. Either way the story was produced by a mind riddled with fear and guilt because a loving God would not abandon or kick out His children. The story was made up because we feel distanced from God and it invented a plausible reason for all the suffering on earth.

ACIM's Take on God's Image and Chosen People

What actually happened that caused the creation of form? We were happy in Heaven and everything was a garden paradise, but we had the thought of what it would be like to be different from God. This is impossible because God is everything. Because we are like God, we are unimaginably powerful and this thought resulted in the creation of the universe of time and space, which we call the big bang. Now, instead of the perfection of oneness, we think we have twoness or duality, where everything has an opposite. This is why the tree in the garden was called the tree of good and evil, because good and evil are opposites or two different states.

The oneness in Heaven does not have an opposite; therefore anything other than Heaven is unreal. Adam and Eve eating of the tree of good and evil was analogous to them leaving Heaven or oneness and experiencing duality, which is not of God. Moses was wrong when he said we were kicked out of the garden. We left Heaven in our minds of our own accord because of our free will to think thoughts other than God. Except God is everything, and it is impossible for that thought to become reality. The thought caused an extremely short blip in Heaven that was over in a nanosecond, but long enough to split our minds and create the universe that we dream we are in. There is no original sin or sin at all because we are still in Heaven dreaming that we are here. In Genesis, Adam was put to sleep, but nowhere in the Bible does it say that he woke up. According to the Bible then, we are still sleeping as descendants of Adam.

The thought that I am a body is the original sin, although it is not a sin against God. It is only us forgetting what and who we really are. Salvation is remembering who we are and waking up from the dream. This is what Jesus did, not dying for our sins, only playing his part to teach a lesson to help us wake up. The lesson is that death is not real just as life on earth is not real. Is there death in Heaven? Reality is only in Heaven with God, anything else is not real. We chose to think differently from God and then listened to the ego to escape what we thought would be God's punishment. We suffer on earth because we are afraid of God's punishment and we punish ourselves in lieu of God's retribution. God does not punish and is only love. God still loves and communicates with us in Heaven, although His communication is not full. Therefore, He welcomes our return to full communication. The creation story is an allegory for what seemed to happen in our minds. The story is not factual; rather, it represents the writer's understanding of how we got here.

Most importantly, there is no world. We are reviewing what has already happened in a dreamlike state and can wake up to our home in Heaven at any time. You cannot see Spirit or Heaven with the body's eyes, but it is all there is in reality, so it is everywhere and can be awakened to. This is what Jesus meant when he said the Kingdom of God is at hand. The Kingdom is accessible now. Jesus awoke first and teaches everyone how to do it. In the story of the fall, in our minds we choose the ego instead of God. Because we think we are here, we are continually making that choice every day we believe we are bodies. Is it more arrogant to think that we are made perfect by a perfect God and are still perfect in Heaven, or is it more arrogant for us to think that a perfect God could make something that is not perfect?

God did not have a Chosen People because all of God's children are in Heaven and are one in Spirit. God does will that none shall perish, through our waking up from the dream of separation from Him. Since we believe we are here on earth, God placed the Holy Spirit in our split minds at the time of the seeming fall or separation. The Holy Spirit gently reminds us of who we really are. At times, we mistake the voice for God who guides and comforts as a voice telling us that we are special to God, more special than others, especially those heathens. Any voice that demands, controls, punishes, or makes us more special than someone else is the voice of the ego and not God.

The thoughts in our minds that say we are special to the exclusion of others or that we should suffer, sacrifice, attack or blame our brothers is not from God. The love of the Holy Spirit sometimes causes miracles, which could explain why some people think they're special if they experience miraculous works. The Jews have a prayer, Hear O Israel: The Lord our God, the Lord is one! This is the truth and if there is only God and all is one then everyone must be part of that oneness, not in form on earth, but in Heaven where all is one. The Jews didn't understand that everyone and everything is one and most likely thought this prayer meant that they were special to their God. Could God love only some of His children and still be called loving?

6. God's Nature

We are told that we know about God through several sources: by creation and the natural world, as revealed to us in the Bible, how He works in our lives, and by going inside to hear and feel Him. We are taught that God is perfect, loving, just, merciful, holy, divine, and Spirit. God is described by the Omnis: Omniscient – all-knowing; Omnipotent – all-powerful; Omnipresent – everywhere at once; and Omnibenevolent – all-loving. If we look at each one of these with a critical eye, we can see disparities between what we are taught, what nature is like, what God does in the Bible, and what we experience.

On the one hand, the world can be a wonderful place. If you delve into the statistical improbability of humanity living on this planet, it is indisputable that some higher power, divine creator, or master designer had his hand in setting the balance of factors just right for our habitation. Scientists call us the Goldilocks' planet. This represents the unbelievably exacting conditions needed for life. Such as: the perfect amount of oxygen, the tilt of the earth, the amount of water on the surface, the constants of gravitational force, the speed of light, the strong and weak nuclear forces, the location of the moon and sun, the placement of our galaxy in the solar system, etc. The confluence of these ingredients is a very convincing argument, but it does not preclude a different type of life other than humans existing on one of the billions of planets in the universe.

Some scientists predict there are billions of planets in each galaxy, like our Milky Way galaxy and there are billions of galaxies. With the mind-boggling size of the universe, it lends even more credence to the theory of an intelligent designer, and the possibility that we may not be alone or even the apple of God's eye.

When we look at how God reveals himself through the natural world, our living conditions are not ideal most of the time. There are natural disasters, toxic chemicals, and environmental hazards that kill us. Many people succumb to starvation related death, or the extremes of freezing or dying of dehydration. We have to eat to stay alive, which means working and competing for our food, not to mention killing millions of animals to slake our hunger. The will to stay alive is innate in all animals, requiring them to battle the elements and avoid predators. Even trees use their roots to battle other trees' roots for underground water.

At times, our own bodies are beautiful machines that grow and function well, but sickness is always a concern and everybody will eventually die. The conclusion is that the world that God supposedly created is wonderful and also awful at the same time. The world is hard and life is hard. Creation and the natural world point to a creator, but is it an Omni-God who created and sustains this deadly place? Was it really perfect in the beginning, and then Adam and Eve spoiled it for us? Going from perfect to not perfect is not an attribute of a perfect God. What is the nature of a loving creator who would create such difficult living conditions and put His children through them?

The second way we know the nature of God is through the Bible. Two ways to look at how God is revealed in the Bible: what the Bible says about God's nature, and His actions in the Bible. We must also compare what the Bible says about God and the way human existence plays out.

In the Bible, God is described with many positive attributes, both by His word and by the Bible writers, including the aforementioned Omni's. There are also negative characteristics of God in the Bible such as judgmental, wrathful, and vengeful. Coincidentally, many of these are also the positive and negative characteristics of mankind, lending credence to the belief that we created God in our image. The Old Testament writers attributed our positive human characteristics to God, although His actions are often contrary to these positive traits. Again, in reality, God is outside of time and space and cannot be defined by time and space definitions.

A major message throughout the Bible is to repent. However, God killing or commanding the killing of His own children is not loving if it denies them the chance to repent. Would a loving God even put His children in a position where their own destruction is possible? Apologists say that free will to obey or turn from God is the reason for our damnation, but again, would a loving God create a world, a scenario, an existence where His own children's destruction was possible? Even more disturbing, is the fact that the laws that result in eternal justice are created by God and are not some outside uncontrollable force. With humans, being disobedient to your parents does not make you a non-child, or result in death, or lifelong separation. You will always be your parents' child and will most likely be welcomed back into a relationship with them. With the God of the Bible, it's one and done. If you don't get it right this life, you are forever separated from God.

God is said to be the author of all the laws and Commandments given through Moses. These laws would not only put you to death in this life but relegate you to eternal punishment. Apologists say God still loves you but you have turned your back on Him and He does not send you to hell, you choose it. Again, what loving Father would put his children in a position where eternal punishment is possible? If hell is a place as the Bible says, and God made everything, then He made hell as part of creation. There is much debate about the existence of hell as a state or an actual place, yet the Bible is certainly full of colorful references to it.

There are many reasons that we reject God: we grew up with a different religion, we grew up an atheist, we were hurt by religious leaders, we denied God because of extreme suffering, or we believed being a good person was enough. The Bible is still unmistakable that we will be subjected to eternal punishment for our natural or God given inclinations.

Apologists say all sin is committed against an eternal and infinite God; therefore, the just penalty for our sin is also eternal and infinite. It seems to me this reasoning is backing into the fact the Bible says hell is eternal. Wouldn't annihilation be preferable to everlasting punishment, and shouldn't our free will give us that choice? Would a merciful God subject us to everlasting punishment instead of annihilation? Hell is like the psychopath keeping you alive so he can torture you and annihilation is the merciful psychopath who gives you a quick death. The problem with a loving God creating hell is probably why the Catholic Church developed purgatory. People couldn't fathom a loving, forgiving, merciful God separating from us for all eternity. Atheists might ask if you believe in a God who loves you so much that He created hell in case you don't love him back. Is this the same God who said, "I will never leave you nor forsake you?" No, God being eternal, would wait for all of eternity until we come back to Him, and in reality, He does.

Here are some of God's Old Testament's laws that would have to be loving if God is all-loving. Most of these verses are preceded by something like, *Then the Lord spoke to Moses,* or *The Lord said to me.* They are usually directed at certain people. They are summarized but are close to the actual law. Please look them up in their entirety and context. They are in order of the books except for the last one.

- Kill a child who strikes his parents (Exodus 21:15)
- Kill a child who curses his parents (Exodus 21:17)
- Kill all sorceresses (Exodus 22:18)
- Kill all who lie with an animal (Exodus 22:19)
- Kill everyone who profanes the Sabbath (Exodus 31:14)
- Kill anyone who works on the Sabbath (Exodus 31:15)
- Kill all Adulterers (Leviticus 20:10)
- Kill all Homosexual males (Leviticus 20:13)
- Kill all mediums (Leviticus 20:27)
- Kill anyone who blasphemes God (Leviticus 24:16)
- Kill outsiders who come close to the tabernacle (Numbers 1:51)
- Kill those that commit harlotry (Numbers 25:4)
- Kill those that serve other gods (Deuteronomy 13:13)
- Kill all males that you battle (Deuteronomy 20:13)
- Kill all males of cities God gives you as inheritance (Deuteronomy 20:16)
- Kill sons who are stubborn and rebellious (Deuteronomy 21:20)
- Kill any bride who is not a virgin (Deuteronomy 22:21)
- Kill all who do not seek the Lord (2 Chronicles 15:13)
- Kill children for the iniquity of their fathers (Isaiah 14:21)
- Kill false prophets (Zechariah 13:3)
- Kill all who Kill any man (Leviticus 24:17)

These laws command men to kill men, women, and children. Psalm 19:7 says, "The Law of the Lord is perfect, converting the soul." You cannot convert your soul or repent if you have been stoned to death. What it creates is fear and a distanced relationship with God. Christians do not follow these laws because St. Paul said Jesus fulfilled the Law and the non-Jews that were converting to Christianity would probably have never joined a religion with such drastic and harsh laws. Even though we don't follow these laws now, they speak to the nature of the Old Testament God as one who would have His Chosen People put to death their own family, friends and community.

Would following these laws make you holy as God says in Leviticus 11:45, "You shall therefore be holy, for I am holy?" Would Jesus as God incarnate follow any of these laws even though he lived in the same Jewish community that these laws were being followed? Jesus would not affirm a law that called for death. These laws resemble the religious honor killings that we abhor today. If you review the above laws, how many reflect the two great Commandments that Jesus said all the Laws and the Prophets hang on? Jesus' Commandments say nothing about killing, punishing, judging, or excluding. They only speak of love. These laws are not based on love rather on judgment and punishment. Is the God of love, mercy, forgiveness, goodness, righteousness, and patience, the same one who gave these commands? Is this the same God who gives good things to His children when they ask? Is this the same God who wills that none shall perish?

We don't have to follow those laws because Christianity says we have a new covenant. How do we know there won't be a new covenant in the future? If God is unchanging, then why did salvation switch from following the Old Testament laws to salvation by grace through faith in Jesus? Moses privately received these laws, why do we trust a single source who so blatantly contradicts Jesus' teachings of love and forgiveness? In the Gospels, there were multiple writers and numerous eyewitnesses; however Moses is alone with God when he had these conversations. Additionally, the writings of the creation story by Moses launched the biblical concept of sin and punishment. It's interesting that many Christians refute Mormonism because it relies on one person's receiving and interpreting the golden plates used to write the book of Mormon. Moses' revelations follow a similar pattern but are considered fact.

The Bible says God directly or indirectly kills his own children. It's estimated that the number of people killed directly by God or from the direction of God is over one million. Estimates are difficult because we don't know exactly how many people were on earth when God's flood killed everyone except for Noah and his family. We don't know how many first-born Egyptians or soldiers there were in Egypt; or how many men, women, and children were in the town of Amalek; or how many inhabitants of Sodom and Gomorrah were vaporized; or how many perished under the sword from God's command to destroy the Hittites, Amorites, Canaanites, Perizzites, Hivites, and the

Jebusites, along with numerous other people throughout the history of the Old Testament.

Most of God's killing is in the Old Testament although the book of Revelation also has God killing his children in retribution for the harm they did to their fellow man. Apologists defend God by saying that killing is not murder as murder is unlawful and unjust. God is just in these killings because most of these people were either enemies of the Jews or wicked to the core. God is God and can do what He wants, although if He is loving would He kill His own children? Again, we have the contradiction that if God wills that no one shall perish, then He did not give any of those people a chance to repent and change their ways. The answer from Apologists might be that God knew they would not repent and so His actions were justified.

In effect, God created a world where we are punished for doing what humans were created to do. We think we have free will but if He knows our future, then we are destined to do what we do since He knows what we will do. Scripture is very clear that God knows everything and even knew us before we were formed. Would God kill His own children created in His image and likeness?

The Bible says God is long-suffering, which means He is patient. He was not patient even for one lifetime in all these cases. If He knows we won't change, He created a flawed human and punishes us for it. He does not show mercy, love, compassion, patience, or forgiveness to the ones He killed. Either God is not all-knowing or all-loving, or the Bible is wrong about His actions. If God is a just God, would He let some people lose while others gain, either on earth or in Heaven? The Bible must be wrong about its depiction of God's activities in the world because the one true God is perfect love. The passages about God being love are true and He is only love, therefore, He cannot be anything else. If you believe the Bible is inerrant about God's actions and He is an unchanging being, why wouldn't He have the same laws and punishments in Heaven? Why would we think the cycle of suffering, sin, and punishment will not continue forever in Heaven?

The other way to look at God's nature is how His word plays out in the world. In Romans 8:28, Paul says, "And we know that all things work together for good to those who love God, to those who are the called according to *His* purpose." The Bible and our experiences also say the sun rises on the evil and the good and it rains on the just and the unjust. Belief in and following God does not give any follower an advantage in this life nor take away our troubles. There is comfort in God's word, but everyone will suffer in the world.

What are the advantages of being one of God's elect in our lifetimes if we are to suffer like everyone else? Jesus said God will take care of your needs even better than the sparrow, but again in this lifetime there is disease, natural disasters, starvation, depression, suicide, and a host of other problems. Even those who try to love God with all their heart and love their fellow man will suffer. The huge miracles of the Old Testament are hard to find in modern times, and the personal miracles that come sporadically do not live up to what God and Jesus promised in the Bible. The point is that the lofty things the Bible says about God and His love and care for His children, are at odds with how the world actually is. We can get some comfort from the New Testament saying we would suffer now, although it will be perfect in the Second Coming.

A final rationalization to problems in the Bible is that we don't know the mind of God. If we don't know the mind of God, how did the writers of the Bible know the mind of God? Why do we establish new dogma, laws and specific sins not found in the Bible when we don't know the mind of God? We are doing exactly what the Pharisees did thousands of years ago, filling a need demanded by the people to know exactly what God wants from us in our lives. There must be a better explanation of God's nature than what the Bible says it is.

ACIM's Explanation of God's Nature

Another way we know God is by the way we internalize Him personally. Aside from knowing what the prophets say about how God works in our lives, we know God by quieting our mind and asking Him to reveal Himself. God's substance is Spirit and His nature is love. He is everything, therefore, what is not of God does not exist. This means anything that is not loving is not true and not true about God. God and Spirit are outside of time and space; therefore, they are not form and do not specifically act in the world. God and the Holy Spirit are thought and their love may materialize into forms when the conditions are right, but they commune with us through our thoughts.

When we get in touch with our inner guide, we should be at peace knowing that any guidance given by the Holy Spirit will be good for everyone and include the proviso, no one will lose. God only gives and gives to everyone equally in our earthbound minds with the comfort and guidance of the Holy Spirit and in Heaven with love to all of His children. God did not create the world, kill his own children or give those Commandments to Moses.

Remember, perfection needs nothing, therefore God just loves. God does not demand sacrifices. He only wills us peace, joy, and happiness. Do we think we can thwart the will of God? No, we cannot, therefore we must be in those states in our real life in Heaven. There is great peace and happiness in knowing that the God of the Bible is not the true God. It's comforting to know that God did not create this world of suffering and did not put tremendous demands on us that we cannot possibly live up to. A huge burden has been lifted from our shoulders knowing there is nothing we need do to gain our Father's love. We need only awaken to Him in Heaven where all our dreams are forgiven and forgotten, except His love.

How happy can it make you to know that God is truly our Father or Abba in Heaven and we are safe and happy in His loving grasp dreaming that we are here? Jesus knew about the true God when he said your Father in Heaven is perfect. I sometimes think of this life and body as a fake wallet I carry when traveling. If the wallet gets stolen, I'm okay because I know my money is safe in my real wallet. This body is a fake or an illusion and I know my real self is in Heaven, no matter what happens in this life. God's nature is giving; love in Heaven and the Holy Spirit in the dream, regardless of how long it will take for us to decide to listen to Him.

7. God's Will

What is God's will for us? In order to determine that, we must first define divine will and differentiate it from human will. In the normal lexicon, what is willed is looked at as a wish, a want, or a desire. When we speak of God's divine will, we would say His will is something that is guaranteed since He is all-powerful and sovereign. As the creator of everything, whatever God wills must be accomplished. The problem is that His will as described in the Bible does not always come to fruition in this world. Scouring the Bible to find God's will leads us to several verses such as, God wills us to be saved and sanctified, come to the knowledge of the truth, be filled with the Holy Spirit, rejoice always, pray without ceasing, none shall perish, give thanks in everything, do good, know God, fear God and keep His Commandments, love mercy, walk with humility with God, and take up our cross and follow Jesus.

These cannot be the will of God using the strict definition that God's will is guaranteed to happen, or even the human definition of a desire, because in looking at the list, none of these is a reality for everyone at all times. If you agree that God is perfect, then by definition He is lacking nothing as perfection demands, and anything He wills must already be. If there is something that has yet to happen or happens occasionally, then it cannot be the will of God because that would mean God is lacking something and as such, He could not be perfect. All of the above wills of God are someone's opinion of what they think God wants.

If God wills us to be saved, then we would all be saved. If God wills that we be filled with the Holy Spirit, then we would all be filled with the Holy Spirit. If God wills that we all walk with God, then we would all be walking with God. If God wills us to rejoice always, then we would be rejoicing always. What God wills cannot be thwarted by man. Something in man's understanding of what God wills is misunderstood.

Paul adds to the list in 1 Thessalonians 4:3, "For this is the will of God, your sanctification: that you should abstain from sexual immorality." Paul is against sexual immorality, but is that really the main focus of the Almighty? Which one of the above 'wills' is God's true will for us? If they are all God's will then do we need to prioritize them? The problem with sins of the flesh, as long as they don't hurt anyone, is they take your time and attention away from getting home.

Apologists say that since we have free will, God's will for us may not become manifest in the world because we get to choose what we do. We do have free will, although our free will cannot supersede or overcome God's will. In reality, our free will only applies to how long we wish to suffer in the dream before we return our sleeping minds to God. We do not have absolute free will to alter that outcome, which God has willed. We think we have free will with our decisions on earth, but since it is an illusion, the only free will we have is how long we want to believe in the illusion. God wills that none shall perish and that is accomplished because in reality we never left Heaven.

The debate about free will, predestination, predetermination and other similar thoughts will always be argued. Endless discussions about these matters only does one thing – it delays our spiritual journey by drawing our attention away from the Kingdom of God. With that said, I would like to point out some questions I have about our free will opposing God's will. The beginning of the free will issue started in the creation story when a perfect God created a perfect Adam and Eve, who then rejected their perfection. We know human civilization is far from perfect, so we had to account for the problem that we were created perfect but all of humanity has not been perfect.

Apologists answer that God gave us free will to sin against Him. Because Adam and Eve used their free will to disobey God, they became imperfect as a consequence of their actions. In essence, Adam and Eve's free will trumped God's will that they be perfect. In reality, God's will is being carried out as we are perfect in Heaven with Him. If you think that God made us perfect, and in that perfection, gave us free will to be imperfect, then those two ideas are at odds because perfection cannot be imperfect. If you think our free will is part of God's will, then could Adam and Eve have gone back into the Garden of Eden to live in the land of plenty if they willed that? Can we choose not to go to hell if that is our will? Did I have free will to choose not to be joined to the guilt and consequences of original sin since I didn't eat from the tree? Do we have free will if God already knows what we will do? Do we have free will if God can take it from us?

In Genesis 6:5, God killed everyone else in the flood because He, "[…] saw that the wickedness of man was great in the earth and *that* every intent of the thoughts of his heart was only evil continually." God either knew they would continue to sin or killed them before they had a chance to repent. Either way their free will was taken from them. Do we have free will if some of the choices are forbidden? Did we have free will to be born on to this planet? Did I have free will to decide what characteristics I would be born with such as a weak and sinful person resulting in everlasting punishment instead of a God-fearing righteous person rewarded with eternal life?

If I didn't have free will to choose who I would be, then how can I be held responsible if I were born a psychopath, a hateful person, or a militant atheist? Should I be punished if I am too weak and helpless to change because that's the way I was created by the creator? Where does the buck stop when dealing with a system designed by the all-powerful sovereign God? Who is ultimately responsible for my faults if it's baked into my DNA, the creation or the creator? God punishes us for how we are made even though everything we do is supposedly based on heredity and environment. Apologists say the sin is not the problem; it's not repenting and asking for forgiveness that is the problem. Again, I didn't choose to be born a proud, stubborn, arrogant SOB who can't change his ways or ask for help or forgiveness.

If Adam and Eve communed daily with the living God and could not follow one simple Commandment, what chance do we have? Later, God added 613 new Commandments for their offspring to follow after Adam and Eve couldn't follow the first. I can just imagine a little Jewish boy who looks like John McEnroe in the back of the crowd when Moses delivers all of the new laws. The kid gets up on his toes and yells, "You cannot be serious!"

It is clear from the writings of King David, that God knew who we would be before we were born, before we were formed in the womb. Psalm 139:16, "Your eyes saw my substance, being yet unformed. And in Your book they all were written, the days fashioned for me, when *as yet there were* none of them." Therefore, God knew the hearts of man, knew they wouldn't repent and change their ways even though they had free will to change. He punished them anyway. This is not the God of love that only wills happiness; it is man's creation of a confused God who is not sure of what He wants.

Back to the question: what is God's will for us? In the Lord's Prayer, Jesus says God's will for us on earth is the same as it is in Heaven. The prayer says thy Kingdom come, thy will be done on earth as it is in Heaven. There are no bodies in Heaven; therefore, God's will for us on earth could not have anything to do with the body. God's Kingdom is Spirit and His only will for us must be in thought. The thought of love, peace, and joy are the will of God. God's Kingdom in Heaven is perfect love and happiness and God's will is sovereign. That means there can be no world to distort His perfection. His will is that we be with Him in a state of love and happiness. How do we do that on earth?

Perfect love cannot be described, we can only remove the blocks to love's presence. The blocks are anything that is not love, like anger, fear, envy, judgment, superiority. We remove all those blocks to love through forgiveness just like Jesus did. Instead of trying to be love or trying to work on those negatives, we simply forgive everyone and every situation for everything. After that, all that is left is love, which is our natural state and once we get to that state we will be saved or ready to awaken to our home in Heaven.

If it's God's will that we know and commune with God, then this world He created gets in the way. Our focus is on the needs of the body and the problems in the world, which get in the way of our spiritual journey. If you think about it, the system God designed, focusing on the world and the body, keeps most of our attention on survival and dealing with our physical, mental, emotional, relational, and societal problems, and not on all the things the Bible says are God's will for us. In John, Jesus basically said to be in the world but not of the world. While you think you are in the world and have bodily concerns, take care of them while making the Kingdom of God your main concern as Jesus did.

ACIM's Understanding of God's Will

God wills that we be happy and share His love in Heaven. Since God is perfect, He cannot be lacking anything, therefore we are in Heaven with Him and our apparent separation was not a loss of heavenly perfection, but a lessening of communication. Part of us is still communing with God fully, although another part, our ego mind, thinks it's separate. God sent the Holy Spirit to help us awaken to fully commune with God. God is God and His will cannot be broken, challenged or changed. Therefore, we will all eventually wake up or be saved and remember our lives with Him and each other in Heaven.

God's will for us on earth is not through Him but through the Holy Spirit because God does not recognize our sleeping dream. If He did, then it would make it real and there would be Heaven and something else; the oneness of God in Heaven would be split. The Holy Spirit's will for us on earth is that we use our time to transform our minds from thinking we are separate from God to thinking with the Holy Spirit about our oneness. To do the will of God on earth is to serve the Holy Spirit's purpose in the world as He sees fit, which would always involve love. Giving and receiving love is how we can be happy in our earthly incarnation no matter what seems to happen here.

God's will is ultimately that His children have everything. If we break down the meaning of God's will, it is that God is love and because He is Spirit, His will is thought. Therefore, God's will is actually extending loving thoughts. God's will for us is giving and receiving love. Jesus validated this in his two great Commandments to love God and love our neighbor.

8. Why Should We Love God?

Why do you love God? This is a provocative question that many of us have probably never thought to ask. We as Christians have been raised to believe that we should love God; it is ingrained in our psyche. Why do you love God? The Bible says God created us, created the world, loves us, sent his only begotten Son to die for us, and takes care of us. If you had to answer the question of why we should love God and could not use the Bible, then what would your answer be? I find it hard to come up with any reasons to love God with all our hearts if I take the biblical inducement and stories out of the mix. If I couldn't use the Bible that says He made us, made the world, and loves us, I'm drawing a blank.

If you didn't use the Bible, then you could assume God made the world. Given that less than a third of the world has probably ever read or heard of the Bible, most people have to decide about God without the Bible. You still might think some divine power or super intelligence created humans and the universe, but you have to admit, much of human existence has been less than pleasurable. We live better and more comfortably now than any time in history, yet we still suffer from disease, starvation, violence, accidents, natural disasters, and death. As a species throughout history, we seem to want or need a divine creator to explain how and why we are here. Is that explanation enough to compel us to love God?

An example of how the world is replete with suffering is the case of the United States. America is undoubtedly the most prosperous country of all time, yet according to the Center for Disease Control, we have about 130 people commit suicide per day. Almost 48,000 people per year take their life, and possibly one million more attempts that do not result in death. Globally the number of suicides is about 800,000 per year. Global record keeping might not be accurate; even so the United States might have a higher rate of suicide than the rest of the world. For this world to be created by a divine, all-powerful, all-loving being, there are a lot of sad people trying to end their lives, not to mention the drugs we take for depression.

If we should love God because He made the world, He has made a world of suffering. There are wonderful things in the world, but for every good there is bad and for every happiness, there is sorrow. Using His works of nature to reveal God would also depict a being that would let us suffer, including all the animals.

You could be thankful to God for what you have and for living a peaceful and joyous life. You must then consider all the people who are not living with peace and joy or basic necessities because of no fault of their own. If God is sovereign, did He decide to shine His favor on you and let someone else languish in agony? Can that be the kind of world a God who cares for everyone would create? You could also say that you feel God in your daily life and it comforts you. No matter the hardships in life, you are hopeful for your future life in Heaven with God.

It is true that the Holy Spirit is there to comfort us, but why does our earthly existence have to be painful as we strive for Heaven? A look back into history reveals that most ancients didn't think about or even believe in Heaven, they just thought that when you died you went somewhere else, came back as someone else, or were just gone. The Old Testament does not say much about Heaven or eternal life, focusing on getting right with God here on earth.

A related question is, do we believe in God or Jesus out of love or fear? The Bible uses the word fear over three hundred times, most in reference to God and His punishment. There is no way you can read the Bible and not fear God because of the retribution He hands out to the Israelites, their enemies, those who are wicked and others who go astray. When Jesus rightly says, by their fruits you will recognize them, the actions of God in the Bible reveal Him as very fearful.

A whole segment of Christianity preaches following God and Jesus as fire insurance against hell. The theory is that following God in this short life is a small price to pay in case there is an eternal reward. Belief is mainly to insure against missing out on Heaven. This is opposite of how the process should work. Instead of trying to not sin, the true searcher should open up to the love of God and Jesus and as your actions always follow your thoughts, you will leave sin behind as you seek to love. When considering an eternal penalty as justification for disobeying an eternal God, it creates even more fear.

Contrarily, some Christians believe hell is not a real place, yet there are over one hundred references to something like hell in the New Testament alone. 1 John said that perfect love casts out fear, but the God of the Old Testament and at times, Jesus as described, advance the concept of hell and its accompanying fear.

Sacrifice is another biblical practice that produces fear. Would someone practice religious induced sacrifice unless he fears rather than loves? Love demands nothing, including sacrifices. Love only gives and never takes. If you believe God demands sacrifices, you have made a God who you fear. Remember, love casts out fear and God is love.

How can God be all-loving and the cause of tremendous fear at the same time? How can we love God having so much fear of Him? Apologists negate this contradiction by saying that if you are right with God, you will not fear his eternal punishment. However, Paul says no one is righteous. As an example, the Jews had so much fear of God that they neither spoke nor wrote His name. He was not, as Jesus said, their Abba, but their overlord. This distanced them from a relationship with God and they relied on prophets to commune with Him. If you believe in the devil's power and sway on earth, you could ask yourself, what would be one of the devil's main tools to keep us from God?

The answer is FEAR! It is the fear of God and the fear of God's eternal punishment in hell, with the accompanying fear of eternal separation. If the devil could sow the fear of God in us, then we would be afraid to get close to Him, to seek His comfort, to express total unconditional love toward Him. If the devil could convince us we are sinners and are missing out on God's blessings, then we may become withdrawn from God, dismiss His reality, or become an enemy of His judgmental and fearful nature. The Old Testament advances a God who is to be obeyed and feared rather than loved and worshipped.

A story in the Bible that illustrates how hard it is to be righteous whether it is our own weakness or the devil's influence is the story of Aaron in the book of Exodus. Aaron was a prophet, priest, the elder brother of Moses, and his right-hand man when Moses confronted Pharaoh. When the Jews were traveling in the desert after fleeing from Egypt and Moses was on the mountain with God receiving the Ten Commandments, Aaron told the Jews to fashion a calf from gold and worship it. Yes, that Aaron, who saw the miracles that God performed to free His people. As Moses came down from the mountain carrying the Ten Commandments, which had Commandments saying, thou shalt not murder, Moses had all of the Jews who worshipped the idol killed. Was this what God wanted Moses to do with His first Commandment, "You shall have no other gods before me?" Coincidentally, these slain Chosen People did not have a chance to repent when God even gave Pharaoh at least ten chances to un-harden his heart.

What does the Bible say will send us to hell and not to Heaven? The answer is sin. The Bible, Christianity, and our religious leaders are obsessed with sin. The early literal translation of sin was to 'miss the mark'. This thought goes well with repentance, which is to look back, know and feel you need a change and commit to the change. How did we turn missing the mark and something that can be corrected, into such a grievous act that it can cause us to be unwelcome in our Father's house forever? This distortion started in the Old Testament story of creation and was perpetuated with the demanding Mosaic Laws.

Adam and Eve disobeyed God and ate the fruit from the tree, but they probably still loved God and each other. They just made a mistake, and on top of that, they were tricked by the supernatural serpent. The act of kicking Adam and Eve out of the Garden for eternity by an unforgiving God seems to set the stage for making all sins worthy of eternal expulsion. Paul confirms this in Romans 6:23, "For the wages of sin *is* death, but the gift of God *is* eternal life in Christ Jesus our Lord."

From the Course, the notion of sin should be understood as a lack of love or absence of love. If God is love and we have done anything to fall short of His love, then that is a deficiency of love on our part that can be corrected. Isaiah 59:2 says, "But your iniquities have separated you from your God; And your sins have hidden *His* face from you, So that He will not hear." As with most verses in the Bible, Isaiah would be true if it read, *But your decision to seek other than God has seemingly separated you from your God; and you do not see His face or hear His voice because of your attachment to the illusory world.* Our sins or iniquities are not the reason we are not in Heaven with God, it is our decision to entertain the mad idea of what it would be like without God. That idea is impossible and created in our minds the dream world we think we live in. Because we think this world is real, we have trouble hearing the voice for God, the Holy Spirit, although He is always gently calling us home. The answer with God is always love. We can correct the error by giving and receiving love to repent for our lack of love. Nature abhors a vacuum and we let fear and punishment fill the hole where love should be.

The fear of God and His everlasting punishment causes another impediment to loving God. Jesus said that one Commandment was the greatest Commandment. In Matthew 22:37–38, Jesus declared, "You shall love the Lord your God with all your heart, with all your soul, and with all your mind. This is the first and great Commandment." Here is a thought experiment to explain love and fear. If you draw a circle, call it everything, and fill it with love for the Lord God, you are accomplishing Jesus' Commandment perfectly. You are loving God with everything you have, with your all. But when you fear God, even a little bit, which is really the opposite of love, the fear has to go into the circle because it takes time and effort and thought to do. It takes up some of the space that was meant for love. Therefore, you do not love the Lord God with all your heart until you release the fear and replace it with love.

As 1 John 4:18 says, "There is no fear in love: but perfect love casts out fear, because fear involves torment." Believing in sin and God's Commandments not to sin along with the accompanying punishment is the root of our fear of God. With that belief, comes our belief, however unconsciously, that God is not totally loving and the resulting consequence is our inability to love Him fully. Building on what John said, if there is fear, then there is not total love.

Another problem with a punishing God is how He will be in Heaven. According to James, there is no variation in God, which means He is unchanging. If God punished Adam and Eve and as a result all of mankind, why do we expect Him to be different in Heaven and not punish us for our heavenly transgressions? Coincidently, if God is unchanging and has Commandments on earth, wouldn't He have Commandments in Heaven? Belief in Jesus does not totally change us; therefore, we could still be in danger of having transgressions and being punished or maybe being kicked out of Heaven.

If we don't change our minds to think with the Holy Spirit while in the body, then we really haven't changed. We are forgiven our sins by Jesus, but what would make us not sin anymore? Does faith in Jesus and/or good works make us righteous if we are still the same sinful people? We have to change to become purified and to become perfect love. God will always accept us because He only knows us as perfect in Heaven.

ACIM on Why We Should Love God

The answer from *A Course in Miracles* is that we are an expression and extension of God in Heaven and God is perfect love, therefore we are also perfect love. Extending and receiving love is what God does and that is what we do in Heaven. We love God in our earthly incarnation because He is our loving Father and showed His love by sending the Holy Spirit into the dream to stay with us until we wake up. God does not judge or command, He only loves. Everything in the Bible that has Him commanding, judging, condemning and punishing is not God. We usually don't personally realize God's love because revelation can only come to us where it is welcomed without fear. That is why fearful stories about God are counterproductive.

We should strive to know God instead of knowing about God. We know God not by someone telling us about Him, but by going into the classroom of silence and communing with Him. Fear breaks the communication with God because God does not know of fear and cannot relate to a fearful request or relationship. The thought of sin is detrimental because anyone who sees himself as guilty cannot avoid the fear of God.

Our behavior in the dream will never be absolutely perfect, but because God is thought, we need only change our thoughts to the Holy Spirit's thoughts of love and oneness. To accomplish this in a practical sense, we do this by practicing forgiveness. Forgiveness removes the negative emotions or blocks to the awareness of love. When we forgive, we will not judge or condemn and thus we will think like the Holy Spirit and remember our home in Heaven. Love is what Jesus became, and he did it by forgiveness and then his knowing and oneness with God became his reality. The answer is not trying to be perfect or worrying about sin. Sin is only a lack of love so the answer is to replace the lack of love (sin), with love. You don't have to become perfect, as you are already perfect as Spirit. You only need to release ego thoughts and let your perfect Spirit shine through.

Remember, all behavior follows thought, even if it doesn't seem like it does. Sometimes we appear to automatically respond to situations; however there is always a thought that precedes the action. Therefore, if we switch our thoughts to love, our behavior and actions convert to ones of love. This is the same as Jesus saying to seek first the Kingdom. Think of God and His love first, do not fear Him, and all else will fall into place. We should love God not because we think He created this suspect world and destructible body, because He didn't. We should love God because He created us perfect in Heaven and loves us as His children there. We should love God because He did not abandon us or separate us from Him. We originated our dream of separation and God so loved the world that He gave the Holy Spirit to us.

The introduction to the Course says, "The opposite of love is fear, but what is all-encompassing can have no opposite. This course can be summed up very simply in this way:

Nothing real can be threatened.

Nothing unreal exists.

Herein lies the peace of God." (T-in.1, 2)

The reason fear is the opposite of love is because fear is the driver of all other negative emotions, even hate. The simplicity of this statement is that God is love and God is all there is, so there can only be love. Fear is a made-up emotion from the dream world. Jesus was totally peaceful because he knew that only what is real exists, which is love. Nothing unreal exists, which is everything else including fear. Therefore, we can have the same peace as Jesus when we realize that only love exists and all else is part of the dream.

9. The Prophets and the Law

Since the Old Testament is a Jewish text, recounting the history of the Jewish people, the Jewish God, and the Jewish Messiah, why is it included in the Christian Bible? The main reasons seem to be that Jesus was a Jew, his disciples were Jews, Paul was Jewish, their religion was monotheistic, and the Jewish prophets predicted a Jewish Messiah. The problem is that the Jews believed and still believe that the Messiah is not Jesus and the Messianic predictions by the prophets are not about Jesus. A reason the Old Testament prophets are important is because their writings inform our understanding of God. They gave God lofty descriptions, while also characterizing Him as a fearful taskmaster, quick to anger, and unforgiving in his dealings with struggling people. If the prophets are right about God's nature, can you truly love what you fear since love and fear are mutually exclusive?

The prophetic prediction of the coming of Jesus and his death and resurrection superimposed the God of wrath and sacrifice onto the Jesus of love and peace. The main predictions of the coming Messiah came from Zechariah, Isaiah, and Psalms. The Gospel writers tried to make sense of Jesus' death and resurrection and went back into the Old Testament and used those prophecies to justify his existence. They made Jesus out to be God's sacrificial lamb based on the Jewish religion of sin, sacrifice, and punishment. The early Christian writers, who were Jewish, concluded that Jesus had to die for our sins based on the fulfillment of prophecy, because what other purpose could his death have? But what if they projected their religious fear and guilt on Jesus and there was another explanation? There is one, and Jesus declares it when he says, "I have overcome the world."

Some of the prophecies about the coming of Jesus are true and accurate. Some are vague and could mean several different people. There is no doubt that Jesus' appearance was a singular and extraordinary event so that someone with a sixth sense would know a shift was approaching. Someone open to inspiration sensed a being of light was coming, even though the Gospel writers retroactively used the prophecies to explain Jesus' birth, life, death, and resurrection, because they didn't understand. Were all the prophecies actually about Jesus? Most if not all of these prophecies are predicting the Messiah which means anointed one. This person was the promised deliverer of the Jewish people. Jesus did not fulfill the requirements of the Messiah based on the Jewish expectation of an earthly king who would free them from bondage and bring God's Kingdom to earth. Most early Jews could not fathom the idea of a little-known Rabbi who was crucified as a common criminal being their Messiah. Jews today are still waiting for the promised Messiah.

Isaiah's prophecies were used by early Christians to frame Jesus as the divine sacrifice. One widely used is Isaiah 53:5, "But He was wounded for our transgressions, He was bruised for our iniquities; The chastisement for our peace was upon Him, And by His stripes we are healed." This passage is highly debated because it was written about seven hundred years before Jesus, and there is no mention of the Messiah in the text. You can also see the verse is written in the past tense, prompting many biblical scholars to deduce that Isaiah's passages are referring to the suffering servant as the people of Israel. It was believed that the Jews suffered for the transgressions of their forefathers. Most Jewish scholars agree that it was written about the captivity and oppression of Israel because the Messiah had not yet come for them. Could the early Christians, not knowing how and why this could have happened to their leader, have looked back at the Hebrew Scriptures and found an answer there? Paul preached the doctrine of sacrificial salvation advancing the belief that Jesus, through his sacrifice for our iniquity, will save us.

The prophets of the Old Testament are accepted as God's messengers called to speak to God's people on God's behalf. Their message shows how much God wants to be close to His people and wants them to flourish and experience peace and joy. When the people are wicked, God sends prophets to help them repent of their sins and when the people listen, they're granted God's mercy. The main way to tell if prophets are speaking for God is if their prophecies come true. A difficulty is when they predict destruction, and it does not happen if the people repent. Another problem is that sometimes predictions don't happen for hundreds of years. Proving prophecies correct is a tricky proposition. I don't doubt that some prophets were inspired with messages from the Holy Spirit as we are today, even so, the God of love did not declare suffering and destruction by His own hand through any prophet.

There is a story in 1st Kings about the prophet Elijah who waged war against 850 false prophets. The seventh King of Israel and his wife Jezebel were killing prophets but there were still 850 false prophets Elijah had to denounce. Assuming they were considered prophets because of their predictive power, what made them false prophets? Did Elijah not like their message, or were they enemies of his camp? Again, there were and are people with the capability to predict the future, but what makes them prophets of God and their word Scripture? Doubtless it is that their observations and actions line up with God's law. Yet the Mosaic Laws are not loving so they could not be from God.

There are approximately 2500 prophecies in the Bible and some estimate that 2100 have come to pass with complete accuracy. Included in that number are about three hundred prophecies about Jesus that he fulfilled. The problem with this is that someone has to interpret the prophecy and the resulting predicted activity. In the secular world, there are many psychics who are correct in their predictions, still they also have incorrect ones. There is undoubtedly more to this world than the visible, and many call it ESP or Extrasensory Perception – the ability to receive information not gained through the recognized physical senses. Nostradamus is the most famous prognosticator and many have aligned current events with his vague predictions.

Apologists say that after Jesus, John was the last prophet and the canon is closed, meaning there are no more prophets to speak for God. Why has God decided not to communicate with us after John? There are many new issues and discoveries we need direction with. One answer is that the Catholic Church believes the Pope is infallible when he speaks on doctrine and he gets his guidance from the Holy Spirit.

Some of the predictions by prophets were correct, some were good guesses and some didn't come to pass. The Bible says God's way of designating prophets was through visions and dreams. Numbers 12:6 says, "Hear now my words: If there is a prophet among you, I, the Lord, make Myself known to him in a vision; I speak to him in a dream." Interestingly, this applies to prophets but not to Moses who God personally spoke to. Getting God's word through dreams and visions sounds like the inspiration the Gospel writers and

Paul used, and that we get today when we ask the Holy Spirit for help or guidance.

Was Moses even more special than Jesus in his interfacing with God? This is implausible because many of the Mosaic Laws are polar opposites of what Jesus taught. Jesus never commanded anyone to stone children, foreigners, Sabbath workers, blasphemers, false prophets, cursers, or adulterers, although he did forgive everyone. This must be why Paul discounted the Law when Peter and James wanted to include it in the new Christianity. Paul could not imagine reconciling God's laws to kill your neighbor with Jesus' law to love your neighbor. Moses must have created these laws out of his own mind and told everyone they were from God. Even the serpent was a prophet when in Genesis he told Eve she would not die if she ate the fruit even though God said that they would die.

An example of prophecy is the Oracle of Apollo at Delphi. This was an ancient Greek religious site where the temples to Apollo were erected. A priestess would answer questions about the future for those requesting, usually people making important decisions like kings going into battle. The priestess would enter a trance by breathing mind altering fumes coming from fissures underneath the temple. The predictions had to be somewhat accurate as the Oracle lasted well over one thousand years. It was reported that the Oracle would sometimes give out false information. Even in ancient times, God's prophets were not the only ones who could make accurate prophecies. An interesting parallel is the method used for the Oracle to get the predictions, the fumes from the caves. Moses first encountered God in front of a burning bush. There was a bush in that time and place called the acacia bush, and when it burns, it gives off a hallucinogen. Could this be the reason Moses was not delivering God's true message of love? Even if you believe the Mosaic Laws were for a specific people at a specific time, God knows not of suffering, death, or attack.

Another reason why Christianity shares its Bible with Judaism is the early Christians, who were Jewish, had a hard time letting go of their Jewish heritage. Peter and James wanted Gentile converts to Christianity to obey the dietary, cleanliness, and circumcision laws of the Jews. They all knew the long Jewish tradition was respected by the Gentiles and it was more valued to be a long-established religion than a new one with no history and relevance.

Paul disagreed, saying you could not be saved by the Law. He knew that the new Gentile converts would find it hard to incorporate the Old Testament laws of punishment with the Gospel message of love and forgiveness. To that point, many early Christians who were not Jewish thought the God of the Old Testament and the God Jesus spoke about were two different gods. One such ancient growing sect of Christianity that was forming around this understanding was called Marcionism.

ACIM on the Prophets and The Law

God did not create the world and so He did not communicate directly with any people, even Moses. The Holy Spirit being one with God is who Jesus and all the prophet's received inspiration from. The Holy Spirit does not see us as sinning or bad, He sees us as needing gentle correction and respects our free will to decide when to listen to His correction. It's oftentimes difficult to hear and understand the Holy Spirit's inspiration because we are wrapped up in being a body with all of its accompanying problems and needs. Some people, depending on their state of purification, readiness, willingness, and incarnation, seem to hear better than others. Jesus was advanced and heard the Holy Spirit clearly. He preached about God instead of the Holy Spirit because of his Jewish culture.

Since we are all one, there is no favoritism; everyone has the same gifts albeit at different times in their journey. This is why some people do seem to have a better spiritual or psychic connection. Helen Schuman scribed the Course and we didn't because she was in the position to be of help to Jesus in her lifetime. The Holy Spirit always calls, and Jesus grew in wisdom to be able to hear only the Holy Spirit's voice. The Holy Spirit, like God, would never punish, attack, or threaten. The Bible has some truth in it that the prophets were inspired to deliver, although Jesus corrected some of their ideas.

In this dream, it is very hard to discern between the voice of the Holy Spirit which is our right mind and the voice of the ego, which is our wrong mind. Jesus preached forgiveness because we need it to get back home, although we don't need it in Heaven because God has never condemned us. Jesus forgave on earth because he was attacked, but he never condemned, he only loved.

10. The Paradox of Scripture

A definition of a paradox is a statement or theme that contradicts itself. The way it's used in this section is when the Bible has contradictory statements or is used by religious leaders in contradictory ways. No one wants to consider that the word of God can have conflicting theological statements, but since it was written by man and is interpreted by man, there seems to be many contradictions.

Norman Geisler and Thomas Howe wrote a book to explain contradictions in the Bible titled, *The Big Book of Bible Difficulties*. They were emphatic that the Bible cannot err because it is the word of God although they admit there are many Bible difficulties. They present over eight hundred instances where it appears the Bible is wrong or contradictory and they make great efforts to show why it is not in error. Sometimes the contradictions and their explanations are straightforward and understandable. Sometimes they say Apologists disagree on the meaning and resolution, and sometimes they do mental gymnastics to devise somewhat plausible solutions. In the end, they give an explanation for all of the difficulties, but it is *an* explanation not necessarily *the* explanation. It is one of many possible explanations.

I am not concerned with variances such as dates, places, names, numbers, and genealogies. I am mainly interested in the theological problems and contradictions, specifically, religious and spiritual truths expressed in the Bible and whether we can trust what the Bible says. When I look at what I believe are some of the major theological contradictions, I have to conclude that the Bible is too conflicted to always give helpful and accurate answers on what it takes to get to Heaven and what God wants from us on earth. If there are contradictions and problems with some of the passages, then can we trust all of the passages? Could the Holy Spirit really have inspired a book with so many contradictions?

I begin by looking at the biblical claim that God is love and loves us. These Old and New Testament verses may be defended by Apologists as spoken and written in another time and place, taken out of context, having a different meaning, or misunderstood. If Apologists and lay people cannot agree on the meaning, understand the Scripture, relate to it today, or if everyone has a different interpretation, then God's plan for salvation will leave many outside Heaven. If it is ultimately up to each individual to understand and accept the message, we must trust and be able to comprehend the lesson.

The Bible implies and states God's love in several places including:

- 1 John 4:16, "God is love, and he who abides in love abides in God, and God in him."
- 1 John 4:8, "He who does not love does not know God, for God is love."
- Jeremiah 31:3, "Yes, I have loved you with an everlasting love."
- 1 Chronicles 16:34, "Give thanks to the LORD, for he is good; his love endures forever." (NIV).
- John 3:16, "For God so loved the world that He gave His only begotten Son, that whoever believes in Him should not perish but have everlasting life."

These, along with other verses, speak of God as love, and a perfect God would have perfect love. The problem is the Bible stories demonstrate God as non-loving in many situations. One of the more explicit examples mentioned is when God directly or indirectly kills His own children, including His Chosen People, people of iniquity, enemies of His Chosen People, and even innocent children. Would a God of love kill His own children? Would a being with perfect love also have conditional love for His children? Unconditional love means that regardless of what they do, you love them anyway. We don't know the mind of God; therefore, we can't say He is not loving for killing His own creations. Although our understanding of love from Jesus is contradictory to the actions of God in the Bible.

Jesus said in Matthew 7:18, "A good tree cannot bear bad fruit, nor *can* a bad tree bear good fruit." Jesus used this gauge for himself as the divine representative of God on earth when he said in John 10:38, "[…] though you do not believe Me, believe the works, that you may know and believe that the

Father is in Me, and I in Him." God is the tree and the fruits are His actions. Were God's actions loving?

If, according to the Bible, we only have one life to live, then the taking of someone's life before they have had a chance to repent or believe in God or Jesus means that not only is their earthly life over, but they could be destined for eternal suffering at the hand of God Himself. Does the Bible deem that loving? Perfect love casts out anything that is not perfect love, and justice is not perfect love. Contrary to perfect love, there are also verses that label God as other than love. In Exodus, Numbers and Isaiah, it says God is a God of war and has fierce anger.

In many Bible verses, it says God will never leave or forsake you. Yes, love does not leave or forsake, except the first-born male Egyptians were forsaken, along with all the inhabitants of cities that God either destroyed or commanded to be destroyed. People crying out to God for help, mercy, comfort, forgiveness, and love might feel forsaken and not loved by an inactive and punishing God. Psalm 5:5 says about God, "You hate all workers of iniquity." If God hates, can He be all-loving? If God can hate, could there be hate in Heaven? If we are all sinners, has God hated us at one time or another?

Christianity has adopted the saying, "Hate the sin not the sinner." Even so, the Bible has God casting the sinner into hell and not the sin. Contrary to Psalm 5:5, Jesus forgave the sin and the sinner. It is said about Jesus: the only one qualified to throw a stone, didn't. Jesus, in effect, proved that God's laws to kill your neighbor were not his teachings and likewise not from God.

The early Jews thought God was a punishing God, no doubt based on the myriad of stories about God threatening and instituting suffering along with their actual daily suffering. Even Jesus' disciples thought that is how God operated. In John 9:2, they asked Jesus about the blind man saying, "Rabbi, who sinned, this man or his parents, that he was born blind?" The Jews thought that their loving God punished you and/or your family with blindness for sins. The creation story also has God punishing others for someone else's transgressions. Adam and Eve did one wrong action resulting in humanity suffering for all of our existence. The Bible contradicts itself with some verses saying sin will not be visited on future generations and some verses say sin will be visited on future generations. Would a loving God punish all His children for the actions of some?

Another paradox is how people who lived before Jesus or in cultures that worship another deity would be saved. Christianity is clear that only through

Jesus can you be saved, but what about ancient peoples, especially the Jews; God's Chosen People who followed God's laws. Paul clearly says that salvation is not through the Law. Apologists might say the people living before Jesus could be saved by grace through faith in God and/or the belief in the future Messiah. The first problem with this argument is that almost all the people of the ancient world were Gentiles not Jews. These Gentiles worshipped all kinds of gods and none were the same as the Jewish God. Some were Pagans or heathens who worshipped no God at all. Given that most Jews did not believe Jesus was the Messiah, how are all of these outsiders going to be with God in Heaven? The Bible does say that Abraham and David were saved by faith in God, nevertheless that is not what Christianity says. Did a loving God change the rules with Jesus? How are people born before Jesus or not exposed to Christianity to be saved given God wills that none shall perish?

Another paradox concerns circumcision. In Genesis 17, God made an everlasting covenant with Abraham for him and all of his descendants to be circumcised. Those who are not circumcised shall be cut off from God's people. The Jews were a small percentage of the ancient population and very exclusive because of circumcision. Why did God identify His Chosen People through bodily mutilation? Did He not communicate with or care about uncircumcised men? This sounds like a traditionally paternal story as it leaves out all of the females from the boy's club. Paul again changes the rules by saying that you do not need to be circumcised because Christ will profit nothing from it. And if you do, you will become estranged from Christ as you attempt to be justified by the Law.

So not only does Paul do an end around the everlasting Abrahamic covenant, he basically dismisses most of the Mosaic Laws. Paul himself honors the Law but says you don't have to follow it anymore. Apologists say the old covenant with Abraham was replaced by the new covenant made by Jesus through his death and resurrection. If this is the case that everlasting covenants can be broken or replaced, then they're not everlasting covenants.

ACIM's View of Biblical Contradictions

There are many Bible difficulties and although the Course references the Bible over eight hundred times, it often does it to correct the text or explain the meaning of a verse that we misunderstood. The Course is very clear that God is love and even boils down everything that is real and true to two words, 'God Is'. In Heaven, God is love and all the attributes that come from love. Therefore, if anyone receives inspiration in the form of messages from the voice of the Holy Spirit, it will always be for the good of everyone and will exude a feeling of peace, joy, and love. The Bible could not be inspired by the Holy Spirit unless it only described and showed God as perfect love, because God could not do anything but love perfectly.

The Holy Spirit as the voice for God on earth never commands, He reminds you of the love of the Father. There are no special or Chosen People, God loves all His creations equally and without condition. The Holy Spirit is equal in all minds, quietly and softly calling everyone home. All are called by Spirit, but few choose to listen. Nor does God make things happen in the world to coax our obedience or to punish us. Anything that happens in the world coming from the Holy Spirit is from the love of God which is the power behind miracles. The love is the Holy Spirit's, but the form is from us. God only wants us to be happy and be with Him in Heaven. All stories about God as loving all for eternity are true. Any stories about God being other than love are from the fearful imaginations of men and their egos.

11. Interpretation of the Bible

The Bible is a collection of sixty-six books and letters written over 1,500 years by more than forty authors. With that much diversity, can we accurately interpret and trust its meaning? The Bible itself claims to be the inspired word of God or God-breathed. It purports to be the love story between God the creator, and the object of his love, humankind. It is the main document where God reveals himself and we discover His nature. It is the story of the creator God rescuing His creation from the rebellion, brokenness, corruption, and sin of this world through the death and resurrection of His Son. And it is the fulfillment of God's promises by putting the whole creation to rights through His laws and Son.

The Bible can also be a guide for living a good life, standards for right and wrong, morality and ethics, and a refuge for the sick, troubled, and suffering. The Bible has some beautiful and uplifting passages that give hope in a hopeless world, although you can live a great life if you have never read the Bible. In the Old Testament, God favors the Jews but Jesus makes it clear that no person or group is favored. The Bible says the sun rises and falls on the good and evil, and if God doesn't intervene on a consistent basis, then it doesn't matter in this life if you are religious or not. Aside from peace of mind and as a moral guide, there are not many earthly advantages to studying the Bible. The Jews were devoted to the Law, even so as a group throughout their history, they were no better or worse off than the general population. It may even be argued that the Jews were emotionally worse off because they had an expectation that God would take care of them. Regarding the afterlife, God's plan for salvation in the Bible is imperative for our immortal souls.

The obvious problem is that everything in the Bible, and I mean everything, needs to be interpreted. Other than some geographical and historical information, every verse and almost every word must be interpreted. A more recent problem is that most everyone can read the Bible for themselves and they may have their own interpretation of Scripture. This is in addition to the translation obstacles because of the different historical languages. To validate that statement, a practical test would be to try to find one verse in the Bible that everyone agrees on its meaning. Multiple interpretations are borne out by the fact that there are over ten thousand Christian denominations around the world. They may not all have different names, but if they preach different theologies, they're different.

Out of the approximately 2.5 billion Christians, about half belong to the Catholic faith. Although some do not like the rigidity of the Catholic Church, all Catholics must follow Catholic doctrine and are led by the authority of one Pope so you get the same message and theology no matter what Catholic Church you go to throughout the world. Catholics have the magisterium which gives a unified interpretation of Scripture, although not all Catholics believe all Church doctrine equally. Among some Catholics, there is the term *cafeteria Catholics*, which means they pick and choose what doctrine and rituals are important for their Christian practice.

There are also conservative and liberal sects in Catholicism, similar to the degrees of sin (mortal and venial) taught in Catholic doctrine. Specific mortal sins that might prevent you from entering Heaven could be adultery, fornication, idolatry, hatred, envying, drunkenness, thievery, covetous, abortion, and sacrilege. It's difficult for all Catholics to follow the Church teachings on abstaining from sex before marriage, the use of contraception during marriage, divorce, excessive drinking, attending mass every Sunday, etc. The significance of all of these transgressions must be interpreted. Incidentally, Moses and Paul gave us most of the direction on biblical theology so we are already getting their interpretation of what God and Jesus might have told them to tell the people.

The Protestant, Orthodox and other denominations make up the rest of Christians and go by many names and theologies. If the head of each congregation preaches different beliefs, then you have a lot of diverse teachings. All of these differences stem from different interpretations. If the word of God was that important, it should be clear enough for most rational people to understand and agree on its meaning. St. Peter gives God's will in a nutshell as God is not willing that any should perish but that all should come to repentance. If God wills it and gave the biblical instructions, it's problematic if most people don't understand the message, or get conflicting messages from their religious leaders.

St. Augustine famously wrote, "If we are perplexed by any apparent contradiction in Scripture, it is not allowable to say, the author of this book is mistaken, but either the manuscript is faulty, or the translation is wrong or you have not understood." There is a fiery debate about the accuracy of our current copies of Scripture given that all of the originals are probably lost forever and all we have is copies of copies of copies. Some biblical scholars estimate that there are tens of thousands of errors in the current copies based on the oldest versions that we do have.

Apologists say that even with those errors, we can still figure out what the originals would have said. They may be right about general understanding but what about specifics? Do errors in wording, spelling, and translation affect theology? Since the Bible is not a verbatim transcript, is it an accurate representation of the words and deeds of its characters and if it is, how was that accomplished? Was the Bible totally inspired by the Holy Spirit and every jot and tittle the word of God? Is the Bible entirely retold by eyewitnesses and secondhand accounts resulting in stories told by fallible humans? Was the Bible partially inspired because it has some truth, and partially orated by eyewitnesses and secondhand stories?

Even if the Bible was divinely inspired and perfectly written down, you still need to interpret it. If you don't do it yourself, then you must rely on someone else like a pastor, Apologist, or preacher. I believe the Bible was partially inspired and partially written through eyewitness and secondhand accounts influenced by the writer's bias and need for control.

There are many things that go into the interpretation of the Bible including issues of context regarding who said what to whom, what time period they said it or what time period they meant it for. There is also the type of literature such as historical, poetry, prophecy, wisdom, law, parable, metaphor, imagery, along with descriptive and prescriptive passages. There are also categories of interpretation such as literal interpretation, moral interpretation (divine lessons that God wants us to know), allegorical interpretation (what's behind the literal meaning), and anagogical interpretation (understanding meaning based on the life to come).

There is actually a science of biblical interpretation called Hermeneutics, which gives scientific guidelines to determine what the passage means. With all of these different tools to determine meaning, we still can't all agree on what important verses in the Bible mean and how to apply them to our lives. If God breathed these words into life through the authors, wouldn't He know there would be so many different interpretations? If someone believes that the Bible is the inspired and inerrant word of God, I would ask which interpretation is the right or true one. Their answer would obviously be their interpretation. You can google the meaning of any passage and you will get several different takes. You can even watch hundreds of sermons on the internet to hear the most notable preachers give their different individual interpretations.

Clouding interpretation is perception. Our perception of who we are, who God is and how the world works can influence our interpretation of the Bible. As an example, if we perceive God as a God of Justice and retribution, we will probably read the verses and see God as punishing. If we believe God to be perfect love, we will focus on all the loving and forgiving messages of Jesus and gloss over the God who killed so many of His children. If we perceive ourselves to be guilty and unworthy, then we will probably read fear and shame into the messages. We also have the problem that if the Bible is our roadmap to moral decisions, it does not address every life topic, and certainly not new areas such as stem cells, cloning, in vitro fertilization, germs and viruses, alien life, and advanced weaponry. These will be hotly debated by Apologists and interpreted differently.

The diversity of Christian denominations drives some religious leaders to accuse other religious leaders of being false teachers, watered down teachers, hell fire teachers, feel-good teachers, scammers, and the worst …prosperity Gospel teachers! Most Christian denominations relate their interpretation and mission back to the same Bible; they just interpret it differently than the others. An example is that many Protestants have a disdain for some Catholic teachings and say they are not Bible based. The Catholics will defend their tradition by saying they have the correct magisterium through the succession of Popes back to St. Peter. The Catholics might say the Protestants have splintered off from the true Church and are making up their own version of Christianity. Catholics and Protestants have had issues throughout history.

Here are a few of the problems with interpretation, mainly from the Old Testament. I will address New Testament problems in the next chapters. The shortest and what would seem the clearest Commandment in the Ten Commandments is number six, Thou Shalt not Kill. The first complication with this Commandment is how it is written in almost all literature and taught as thou shalt not kill. However in the Bible it is thou shall not murder. Killing and murdering are two different things. Murder is usually the unlawful and/or premeditated taking of a life. Killing is defined as taking someone's life and at times is acceptable. Are you biblically permitted to take a life?

Many of God's Mosaic Laws demanded death. Are you biblically permitted to take a life in self-defense? Can you take a life if you fight in a war? Can you support capital punishment? Can you take a life to save a life or lives? Can you abort a fetus or baby, even to save a life? Could you have killed Hitler and be in right standing? Which is it, thou shalt not kill or thou shalt not murder? Genesis 9:6 says, "Whoever sheds man's blood, By man his blood shall be shed." The early Jews had to interpret the Commandment and also answer these questions. Here is an example of a standard interpretation of the sixth Commandment as part of the original Mosaic Law. It is written that you can kill a man breaking into your house at night but you may not kill him if he breaks into your house during the daylight. You can see, this Commandment, though sounding straight forward, leaves many questions open to interpretation.

Another debatable Commandment is the fourth Commandment, remember the Sabbath Day. The first issue is the Jews named Saturday as the Sabbath and Christians worship on Sunday. Let's not split hairs, it is summed up as work for six days and rest on the seventh. Still, what does it mean to not do any work on the Sabbath? The question Rabbis had to answer is, if your mule falls down a well on the Sabbath, can you get it out? What exactly constitutes work? Several times, Jesus was condemned for healing on the Sabbath, which he thought was a good work and should be permitted. Interestingly, Jesus taught in the synagogue on the Sabbath on several occasions but was not admonished even though that was his profession as a teacher.

Similarly, all priests, ministers, and support staff work each Sunday. Most Christians will work on Sunday if they have to. They routinely perform work around the house, catch up on shopping, or prepare for their weekday jobs on Sunday without much thought about the specificity of the Commandment. Present-day orthodox Jews take this Commandment seriously and are very careful about everything they do to not violate the Commandment as they interpret it.

Another interpretative problem is the different writing styles in the Bible. There are descriptive passages telling what happened and how God and the people responded. It describes the event and we may or may not have to follow the laws because they were given to a historical people to follow. An example is the hundreds of Mosaic Laws. There are prescriptive laws that we do need to follow, like anything that Jesus said or affirmed from the Old Testament including the Ten Commandments. There are also biographies, letters, historical narrative, parables, poetry, prophecy, proverbs, and apocalyptic literature; each understood differently. Being aware of which type of literature you are reading helps, though it doesn't take away the need for interpretation. Who then decides which type of literature it is? Is it comforting and uplifting, or do we need to follow it to be saved? To muddy the water even more, Jesus spoke in parables which by their very nature need to be interpreted. His stories were meant to be timeless and impart a specific message, but even his disciples didn't understand the meaning.

An almost comical interpretation debate in conservative Christian circles is about the age of the earth. There are many Bible literalists who believe the world is about six thousand years old based on their interpretation of Genesis. This camp is called young earth proponents. The other camp is the old earth proponents who side with current science that maintains the earth is over four billion years old. You would think that in this advanced scientific age this wouldn't be an issue, but it is. The young earthers should party with the flat earthers.

ACIM's Interpretation Issues

I have often wondered why Jesus didn't write down or have his disciples write, in his presence, any of his teachings. That might lessen the debate on inspiration vs. eyewitness testimony vs. secondhand accounts years later, although we would still have interpretation problems. The reason might be because although he was the model of love and forgiveness, and the teacher of truth, he knew there would always be theological differences and no one would agree on everything. Jesus, in *A Course in Miracles* says, "All terms are potentially controversial, and those that seek controversy will find it. Yet those who seek clarification will find it as well. They must, however, be willing to overlook controversy, recognizing that it is a defense against truth in the form of a delaying maneuver." (C-in.2:1-3)

Jesus is saying that if you spend your time and energy picking apart any theology, you would not be spending your time practicing the theology to see what the benefits are. You are just delaying the practice by focusing on the letter of the law rather than the Spirit of the law. Human nature is such that all those who seek controversy will find it and all those who seek truth will also find it. Jesus used what he learned to point us in the right direction and then turned it over to the Holy Spirit.

The interpretation problem is complex although it can be cleared up by remembering that the truth of God is simple: He is perfect love, peace, and joy. Anything that is written that does not reflect this about Him is not true. The truth of Jesus on earth is that he was perfect love, peace, and forgiveness. Anything written that does not reflect this is not true. The Holy Spirit, who is part of the Trinity, would inspire everyone with only love, peace, and forgiveness. Anything contrary to this comes from the ego part of the mind and is an invention of man.

If you read and interpret the Bible using that foundation, then you can enjoy the beautiful passages, learn the truth and disregard the passages antithetical to love, peace and forgiveness. I've heard numerous sermons about how to tell if the voice in your head is from the Holy Spirit or the devil. It's difficult to discern between the two until we have forgiven our brother to remove the blocks to love so we can hear the Holy Spirit. If you still can't interpret the message, then forgive more and keep asking!

12. Is the Bible Inspired and Inerrant?

Is the Bible the Word of God? Was the Bible given entirely by God, accurately written down, and preserved with no substantive errors that would change its meaning? Apologists use the following logical deduction to validate the claim that the Bible is the inerrant word of God:

- God cannot make an error
- The Bible is God's word
- Therefore, the Bible cannot have any errors

I somewhat agree with both of the premises with conditions; however the conclusion is not totally correct. Yes, God in Heaven cannot make an error, but the God of the Bible that is made in man's image has man's errors. The Bible as the word of God is partially true because the Bible is partially inspired by the Holy Spirit. Inspiration can come from the Holy Spirit or our own minds inspired by the ego. After men wrote it and decided which books to include, they then called it the word of God. God did not decide which writings would be in the Bible. If you think about it, there was no Bible the whole time the Bible was being written, just many diverse writings that different groups thought were Scripture.

What exactly is inspiration? A point of clarification about inspiration is that the Holy Spirit is the voice for God so when the writers of the Bible say God said or my Lord said, we must realize they think they're talking about God, except they're really talking about the Holy Spirit. How does the Holy Spirit communicate with us? The Holy Spirit does not speak to us in words as in a normal conversation, but only in thoughts. Although God can communicate to us in revelation, which is pretty rare, it will also be in the form of thoughts. The Holy Spirit can inspire someone else to speak to us in words.

The Bible says inspiration comes to us in a dream which, along with thoughts, is the usual way we receive inspiration, although there are other promptings. The Holy Spirit, like God is invisible and non-material, although the love of the Spirit can at times create miracles. Therefore, when the Holy Spirit speaks in His still small voice as Elijah described, the message can be received as vague, fuzzy, and unclear. We are never hit over the head with answers and what decisions we should make. It is a gentle message of love that will benefit everyone involved. The Holy Spirit only speaks for eternity but all temporal answers are contained in His message. Anything that is not loving is not from the Holy Spirit. Any verse in the Bible that promotes attack, anger, hate, or loss is not from the Holy Spirit.

If this same Holy Spirit who communicates to us inspired the Bible writers, how likely is it that it was perfectly clear, concise, and memorable when it was written down? Was it exactly what the Holy Spirit intended? The communicator is perfect, but the receiver, mankind, is not because of our guilt, fear, judgments, and preconceptions. Are dreams, visions, thoughts, coincidences, and interactions always clear to you when you pray for guidance? The Holy Spirit gives us advice and counsel, yet we are so preoccupied with our earthly needs that the messages are not always intelligible. Some of the prophets of old transcended their physical needs by becoming ascetic and were more open to the still small voice. Jesus took care of his bodily needs but used almost all of his mental faculties to listen only to the Holy Spirit.

It makes sense to believe that the Bible is inspired because Moses, who wrote Genesis, lived over two thousand years after Adam and Eve. He either had the stories passed down to him through the generations or was inspired to write the account. There are also narratives in the Bible where only the actors were present and only they knew what happened. Jesus was interrogated by Pilot, prayed alone in the garden, and encountered the devil in the desert when no one else was present. Given there were no eyewitnesses, you must assume the stories were inspired. If Jesus later told his disciples what transpired, you would think the writers would mention it in the retelling as it would add significant credibility to the narration.

Some Bibles red letter Jesus' words, but if no one was there to hear, how do we know what Jesus actually said? One way you can tell that the Holy Spirit's inspiration is not heard precisely, is when two or more accounts of the same story are told differently. The Holy Spirit's narration would be the same, although the receiver (writer) would have a different circumstance, background or emotional quotient, and write it differently. Examples of this are the different narrations of the same accounts in the Gospels.

If the Bible is the inspired word of God and the only definitive communication from God about salvation, wouldn't the Holy Spirit supernaturally protect it from loss? We don't have any originals of the Bible, only copies of copies. Apologists believe that even with the copying errors, purposeful changes, translation errors from one language to another, we can still feel confident we know what the originals said. With so many contradictions, I have to ask if both the originals and the copies have errors.

An example is in Genesis when it said God made everything in the world and it was good, and then later it said that He grieved and was sorry He made man on earth. He then flooded the earth killing everyone. A perfect unchanging God changed his mind from it is good, to He was sorry, to promising not to do it again? This narrative is not God or inspired by the Holy Spirit.

God says He will not leave nor forsake us. It would seem that He certainly left all the people who died in the flood. Which passage was inspired by the Holy Spirit, God not forsaking anyone or God drowning everyone? The flood reveals the wrath of God but there is no real archaeological evidence of a worldwide flood. Moses may have mistaken a regional flood for a worldwide flood. He could have known about recorded flood stories from different cultures throughout history, like the story of Gilgamesh. Recently, many biblical scholars have begun to theorize that Moses did not, in fact, write the first five books of the Bible. Using their tools of textual criticism, they believe that different individuals or groups of people wrote the books. They have named these groups the Elohist, Jahwist, Priestly, and Deuteronomist. Regardless of who wrote it, in the case of God causing a worldwide flood to punish his children, the source was not the Holy Spirit.

Whether you believe the Bible was completely inspired by the Holy Spirit, based on eyewitness testimony, or secondhand accounts from oral tradition, there are many questions and discrepancies related to salvation that need to be addressed. I believe the Bible is a combination of partly inspired writings and stories from the mind of man that they thought were from God although were not. There are absolute and universal truths in the Bible, along with historical and genealogical facts. There are beautiful passages and true sayings of Jesus, but there are also descriptions of God and Jesus as judgmental and non-loving which are complete opposites of their true loving nature.

One indication the Bible is not wholly inspired by the Holy Spirit is the portrayal of the extreme differences between God and Jesus given that Jesus is God incarnate. This will be a major focus in the next several chapters.

Why do Apologists work so hard to declare that the books of the Bible, especially the Gospels, were written by eyewitnesses? If the Gospels were inspired then you don't need eyewitnesses to write what Jesus said and did. The criminal justice system knows that eyewitnesses tend to be wrong or contradictory in their testimony. You might get a general picture about what happened, yet the specifics often vary with each eyewitness. To summarize the three main camps on the subject of inspiration: the first are the people who believe the Bible is totally inspired by God and is without error. This means the Bible is a divine book written by God. Another camp believes that the Bible was written by eyewitnesses and secondhand accounts based on oral tradition. This makes the Bible a more human book that may not be exact in detail but is consistent in subject and meaning.

The third camp comprises those who believe the Bible is inspired in the parts that speak truth, but also written by some eyewitnesses, yet contains mostly stories handed down by secondhand oral tradition. This last camp is the one that I am in. There are too many problems and contradictions in the Bible for it to be accurate. I know inspiration is real because the Holy Spirit is eternal and is still inspiring us today. We get ideas, nudges, and serendipitous moments that point us in the right direction. Sometimes we feel the love of God when we are down or need help. The Bible cannot be the complete and final word of God because the Holy Spirit will communicate with us until the end of time, contrary to the belief that the canon of the Bible is closed. Why wouldn't the Holy Spirit continually talk to us? There is a joke that says, "We need Jesus to get to Heaven, but nowadays we even need Jesus to go to Walmart." There is peace knowing that the Holy Spirit forever calls us home, no matter what we do or think.

The question of inerrancy is crucial because if it's the plan for salvation, then just one error in the Bible calls into question all biblical claims. Then someone, namely you, must decide which passages are true and which are not. That my friend, is a huge responsibility, not to mention being frightening. Most of the theological claims, by nature cannot be proved, and so must be taken on faith. The Bible talks about having faith and we understand it as faith in the words, doctrine, and message that the Bible expresses. However, the faith we should have is in the Holy Spirit to guide us to the truth, whether it is in the Bible or through personal revelation.

Apologists say the original manuscript of the Bible is inerrant but the copies we have may not be. This is a convenient argument since we don't have the original manuscript of the Bible. Some fragments of the Old Testament dated a couple hundred years before Jesus do exist. The oldest complete copy of the New Testament is the Codex Sinaiticus dated around 350 years after Jesus. The way to tell if the theological writings in the Bible are inerrant is to first ask the Holy Spirit for guidance. Second is to run all Scripture through the filter of *does it promote love, peace, and forgiveness?* If it does, then it may be specifically or generally true. Jesus says by their fruits you will know them. The fruits of God and Jesus are love. In the Bible, God is not only harsh to His Chosen People, He basically neglects every other person throughout history. Do we know why other ancient civilizations like China or Egypt were left out of God's plan?

Every Bible believing Christian should answer these questions regarding the Bible as the inspired and inerrant word of God. If you believe that the Bible is the inspired and inerrant word of God, would you become Jewish if there wasn't a New Testament? If you never heard of Jesus, looking at the range of religious options or no religion at all, would you believe everything the Old Testament says about history and God? If Jesus had not fulfilled the Old Testament or softened God's image, would you follow all of the Mosaic Laws?

ACIM's View of Biblical Inspiration and Inerrancy

The Holy Spirit inspired some of the Bible and will continually guide us until we return to Heaven where His help will not be needed. The reason we don't hear His thoughts clearly is because we are fixated on our physical world. Because of our worldly needs, we do not seek first the Kingdom of Heaven. Could we go a whole day without thinking about the body? During his ministry, Jesus taught us to overcome the world of bodily needs as he did. The Old Testament writers were inspired in that they had the still small voice of the Holy Spirit available to them as we all do, but they were also extremely attached to the physical world, and the inspiration was not always clear.

An example of partial inspiration in the Bible is the story of the flood and the ark. It's an allegory invented by the writer, yet has some relation to salvation. The story says the animals were brought into the ark two by two. Moses sensed that to be saved you need your brother, therefore, the ark of peace or the Ark of the Covenant is entered two by two, with your brother. In order to get to Heaven, you need the guidance of the Holy Spirit or Jesus, but you also need to forgive your brother. Through joining with your brother, the awareness of the reality of our oneness in Heaven will be known. No one enters Heaven alone, for that reason we must enter Heaven together.

This is what Jesus meant when he said in Matthew 18:20, "For where two or three are gathered together in My name, I am there in the midst of them." Why wouldn't Jesus be in our midst when we pray alone? He didn't mean that two people had to be physically present for him to be in their midst. In typical Jesus-speak, he meant we need the realization of our brother as one with us in love for him to be heard more clearly. That is the same reason Jesus commanded us to love our brothers. The whole Course is teaching that forgiveness is the fastest way to become one. Moses had a faint understanding that we would all be lost without our brothers, but the story he used of God causing a flood was not true.

13. Jesus Misunderstood

Could Jesus' death and resurrection be God's plan for salvation of the world, but God's Chosen People didn't know it? Could Jesus' teachings and mission be so unclear that even the Apostles misunderstood them?

If Jesus' life and death was the plan, then most of the Jews, who were looking for the Messiah, clearly did not recognize him or understand the plan. Actually, the leaders of Judaism all thought Jesus was a fraud and had him killed rather than admit he was the fulfillment of thousands of years of prophecy. Obviously, God was not very clear to His own Chosen People about His plan to have His Son die to save everyone. The plan didn't convince most Jews to join a new religion. It is also evident from the Gospels that Jesus' own Apostles didn't understand the plan, even after Jesus made reference to his death and resurrection several times. There must be a better explanation of salvation.

An example of this misunderstanding is when Jesus asked the twelve who others thought Jesus was and they answered with John the Baptist or past prophets. Peter answered, The Christ. However, it is unclear if the Apostles thought he was the anointed King who came to overthrow the enemies of the Jews and rule them on earth, if he was a holy man from God, or the savior of the world. Not only did the Apostles misinterpret the grand plan, but they did not understand his teachings about the Kingdom of God or even some of the parables. Jesus is outwardly frustrated by their misunderstanding. If Jesus' main role on earth was as a teacher, why didn't his closest friends understand his teachings about his destiny?

A well-known story about Jesus is when he fed the multitudes that had followed him out of the towns to the surrounding countryside. Recounted in Matthew and Mark, Jesus feeds about five thousand with five loaves and two fish and collects twelve baskets of leftovers after all the people had their fill. Not long after feeding the first multitude, Jesus is again faced with a crowd of about four thousand in the countryside and feeds them with seven loaves and a few fish.

In both Matthew and Mark, the second time they do not have the food or means to feed the crowds, the disciples ask Jesus where they could get enough bread in the wilderness to fill such a great multitude. Either the disciples don't remember Jesus feeding five thousand, or the disciples still didn't understand who Jesus was and what he could do. Apologists say the stories might be out of order. However, in two distinct stories in the Gospels, the disciples fail to understand that Jesus can feed the multitudes by creating food out of thin air. Any rational person, after seeing this materialization of sustenance, would know that this person is more than a priest or prophet.

Jesus himself did not give clear reasons for his mission that the disciples and the Jewish intellectuals would understand. For one thing, he taught in parables, which are timeless stories but whose interpretation is sometimes confusing and debatable. Jesus himself said in all four Gospels that those who are outside, all things come in parables, seeing they may see and not perceive, hearing they may hear and not understand. Why would the messenger and main actor in God's salvation plan teach in such a way that kept people in the dark? Part of the reason is he knew the Jews were so steeped in their religion that they would not accept or understand his new and radical teachings.

He even said in Mark 2:22, "And no one puts new wine into old wineskins; or else the new wine bursts the wineskins." What he meant by this is that people who are so set in their ways, so attached to their traditions and religion, could not possibly accept or understand a new way of looking at the world. They are like the prisoners in Plato's Cave. Like an iceberg, Jesus only revealed the tip of what this world is all about. It's estimated that Jesus fulfilled over three hundred Old Testament prophecies and yet most of the Jews who knew the Scriptures, completely misunderstood who he was.

One of the reasons that Jesus could not be more direct and specific is that if he said anything against the Jewish law, he would be killed, along with those who passed along the message. In the Course, Jesus gives a more comprehensive understanding of the world, God, and why we are here.

Along with teaching in parables, Jesus asked a lot of questions. It's estimated that Jesus asked over 300 questions and answered about 180 questions. Why would the knower of everything and the teacher of truth ask so many questions instead of conveying knowledge given his limited time on earth? One explanation for this is that asking questions is a form of teaching where the teacher gets the student to absorb the information better if they come to it themselves. This is true and lines up with a Confucius saying, "I hear and I forget, I see and I remember, I do and I understand."

The problem is that Jesus' teaching method of asking questions on deep subjects gives the student the opportunity to misunderstand the lesson and any follow-up questions. Without specific explanation, Jesus left many significant theological points unanswered and up to interpretation. Even when Jesus did explain a parable, the explanation is still open for interpretation and is still being debated two thousand years later. Jesus did not make it easy on us to have confidence that the writers understood his words or interpreted the meaning he intended.

In Luke 4:17, when Jesus read from the book of Isaiah and declared that today the Scripture is fulfilled in your hearing, the townspeople could not envision Jesus as the Messiah because they knew him as the carpenter's son. If the birth narrative of Jesus is true, wouldn't the Jews have anticipated someone special coming after the wise men from the East followed the star to Jesus' birth? Wouldn't the people have been alerted by the shepherds who were told by angels and who made the birth widely known? Surely all the people of Israel would have remembered that King Herod had all of the two-year-old males in Bethlehem and surrounding districts put to death because a future Jewish king was recently born. Were there no faithful Jews expecting the Messiah to show up and after all these signs thought that it could be Jesus?

Coincidently, the story of Herod killing the male children happened to fulfill a prophecy by Jeremiah. In the birth narrative from the Gospels, Matthew is the only Gospel to say Herod had all the babies killed and there is no other record, either biblical or ancient sources, to record the Massacre of the Innocents. Josephus, a Jewish historian, who wrote a twenty-volume work called *Antiquities of the Jews*, which contains accounts about Herod the Great, never mentioned the slaughter of babies around the time of Jesus' birth. This massacre story resembles the Old Testament story of how Pharaoh had all the Jewish boys killed when his astrologers told him a deliverer of the Jews (Moses) would be born on a certain day.

Additionally, there is no record other than in Luke of an empire wide Roman census that required Joseph and Mary to go from Nazareth in Galilee, into Judea to the city of David which is Bethlehem. As the Gospel writers repeatedly say, this was done to fulfill prophecy and the prophecy of Jesus being born in Bethlehem was from the Old Testament prophet Micah. Another incredible part of the story is that the Roman Emperor Caesar Augustus would require everyone to go to his own city for a census. Joseph was a descendant of King David who lived about one thousand years before Joseph. It's hard to believe that everyone in the Roman Empire had to trace their lineage back one thousand years and travel to that city. Or was this also to have Jesus' birth ancestry come from King David, even though Mary was impregnated by the Holy Spirit and not Joseph?

Another incident of people close to Jesus not understanding who he was involved his parents. Mary and Joseph had been visited by angels concerning Jesus along with other signs. Yet, according to Mark 3:21, after Jesus performed miracles and healed many, his family came to get him out of the public eye because they thought he was out of his mind.

One of the most glaring misunderstandings of who Jesus was is by the Gospel legend John the Baptist. Even with his prominent title of prophet, he did not understand who Jesus was and his role in salvation. As told by Luke, when John's father Zacharias was promised a son, the angel who made the promise said John will be great in the sight of the Lord and will also be filled with the Holy Spirit, even from his mother's womb. When Mary, the pregnant mother of Jesus went to visit Elizabeth, the pregnant mother of John, Luke says in 1:43, "But why is this *granted* to me, that the mother of my Lord should come to me?"

Elizabeth, John's mother, knew Jesus as her Lord and John grew up filled with the Holy Spirit. John went on to be the preacher prophesied by Isaiah as the voice of one crying in the wilderness: prepare the way of the Lord. John was probably more famous than Jesus and is represented in John's Gospel as a man sent from God. He even baptized Jesus in the Jordan River, and when Jesus came up out of the water, a voice came from the heavens saying, "This is My beloved Son, in whom I am well pleased."

There was four hundred years of silence after the last Old Testament prophet Malachi, where the Chosen People had not heard from God. Then the Spirit of God alighted on Jesus and God's voice spoke about Jesus. In John's Gospel, John the Baptist said in 1:34, "And I have seen and testified that this is the Son of God." And in 1:36, "Behold the Lamb of God." John clearly testified about who Jesus was as someone he was not worthy to loosen his sandal straps. Yet, with all of this, John the Baptist still did not understand who Jesus really was and what role Jesus was to play. John's ignorance was borne out when he was in prison and he sent his disciples to ask Jesus, "Are you the coming one or do we look for another?"

If John the Baptist didn't know who Jesus was or understand God's plan for Jesus, why do we think that we do? Interestingly, when Jesus answered John's disciples, he didn't say he was God, he was divine, he was the Son of God, or that he was the way, the truth, and the life. He just told them about all the miracles he performed. Jesus was again being vague about who he was and his mission on earth.

Who was Jesus? There have been many books written and many lives dedicated to answering that question. Aside from being the central figure of Christianity, most Christians believe that Jesus is God incarnate who came to earth in human form, and in his humanity was resurrected by God for the salvation of humankind. He was a great moral teacher and went by many titles including preacher, good shepherd, King of Kings, lamb of God, light of the world, prince of peace, prophet, teacher, rabbi, Son of man, lord, the word, among others.

Given all we think we know about Jesus, there is more we don't know. Did he have biological brothers? What was he doing before his ministry began? What was he really preaching? Why was he so calm and dismissive about current events and the suffering of his people? Was he married? Why didn't he stay longer after his resurrection? Why didn't he give specific instructions for his new religion like God did? Why did he teach in parables and not directly? As a great teacher, why didn't he have his teachings written down as he taught? In what way was he divine? Did he personally have the power to heal or was it from God? What was his will for us? Was he an apocalyptic teacher who believed the world would end soon? Why didn't he fix the world that God made perfect and man corrupted?

Let's look at one of these questions regarding Jesus' apocalyptic teachings. An apocalyptic teacher thought that the end of the world would come soon. Jesus is recorded as saying in both Matthew and Mark that there will be a great tribulation; and from the heavens, the Son of Man will come in the clouds with great power and glory. Then in Mark 13:30 Jesus says, "Assuredly, I say to you, this generation will by no means pass away till all these things take place." The book of Revelation, also called the Apocalypse, is filled with prophetic events about Jesus judging the earth, remaking it, and ruling it with righteousness.

Apocalyptic thinking was prevalent in Jesus' time because of the great suffering in the world. If evil was so widespread, the end of time was near or at least those suffering hoped it was. Obviously, if it is written that Jesus said the end is near, he got it wrong or the writers of the Gospels got it wrong. Jesus must have meant something else when he said in Mark 9:1, "Assuredly, I say to you that there are some standing here who will not taste death till they see the kingdom of God present with power."

The leading Christian missionary Paul, also thought the Second Coming of Jesus would happen in his lifetime. In 1st Thessalonians 4:17, Paul says, "Then we who are alive and remain shall be caught up together with them in the clouds to meet the Lord in the air." Paul misunderstood because the end of the world has not happened regardless of how many present-day prognosticators say they know the date. Did Jesus also get it wrong or was his message mischaracterized?

To summarize, if the Apostles, the Gospel writers, St. Paul, John the Baptist, and the Jewish elect didn't understand Jesus' message, is the message of the biblical and historical Jesus a true representation of his actual life, teaching, and purpose?

Jesus of ACIM

Jesus was once a man on earth who saw the face of Christ in all of his brothers and remembered God. While on earth he was the first to identify with everyone as his brother and sister and became one with God. He knew the world was an illusion or a projection of our mind, and only God was real. That is why he didn't try to fix the world or worry about suffering. When you try to fix the world, you identify with the world or rather you must admit that there is a world that needs fixing. Jesus knew the seeming world was not good or bad, it's neutral. It's fine if you feel called to try to make it better, but when you become attached to the world of form, you will not see the real world of the Kingdom.

The Godhead doesn't have anything against taking care of yourself, participating in all activities, even getting ahead in the world, as long as your mind is returned to God where it belongs. Jesus made this point when he said, give to Caesar what is Caesar's and give to God what is God's. Jesus says in the Course, seek not to change the world, but choose to change your mind about the world. Jesus is saying the world of form is meaningless and if you change your mind to realize this, you will find peace and happiness regardless of what is happening in the world. This does not mean you should not care about the world, but when we all become enlightened, the world will disappear. Help where you can, be a good person, but do not become attached to the outcome because it is illusory. Be an ordinary human in behavior, and in your mind and heart seek the Kingdom of God.

Jesus taught in parables because they are timeless lessons, and he knew everyone was not ready for his extraordinary truths. He also knew everyone would eventually know the truth of Heaven. He did not teach everything because he understood that you need to teach to the level of understanding of your student. You cannot teach calculus to a five-year-old. He was the savior of the world because he taught through his death and resurrection that death is not real and life as Spirit goes on forever. He remains the savior of the world and continues to help the Holy Spirit remind everyone of the illusion that they think they are in and their true identity as one with God.

Jesus is divine in his heavenly existence just like we are. He learned he was an illusion and turned to the Holy Spirit for help. He eventually thought only with the Holy Spirit even though he was an illusory being. In the Course, Jesus says, "There is nothing about me that you cannot attain. I have nothing that does not come from God. The difference between us now is that I have nothing else. This leaves me in a state which is only potential in you." (T-1.II.3:10–13)

As a man, Jesus had unconditional love for everyone. Unconditional love is defined as a total love for someone with no conditions, meaning you love them no matter what. This type of love is usually displayed by a mother for her children. She is willing to do anything for her children including dying for them. Admirable, although that is not true unconditional love because she does it for *her* children, the condition being they are her children. True unconditional love would have to apply to all children at all times, not just your loved ones. We sometimes have unconditional love, but we also love with judgment, pride, or sacrifice. Jesus only had love and knew that forgiveness is the practice that helps us remove those negative traits.

One of the most inspiring verses in the Course is when Jesus says, "If you want to be like me I will help you, knowing that we are alike. If you want to be different, I will wait until you change your mind." (T-8.IV.6:3–4) We are alike because Jesus was a man and had to learn his lessons. Because we have free will, he will not force us to awaken; he will wait patiently until we want to change our minds to the truth. God's will is that we be happy with Him, and so it must be done. Therefore, we will eventually wake up to our happy home.

The first statement that Jesus made to begin his ministry in Matthew 4:17 was, "Repent, for the kingdom of heaven is at hand." Jesus is saying that we need to change our minds to think with the Holy Spirit, not repent from our evil ways. The Kingdom of Heaven is at hand means it is now, it is available to us, and is not something in the future. If you do what he did and seek with all your heart, soul, and mind, you will remember the Kingdom of Heaven. None of us will live a life exactly as Jesus, however we can all have his peace and be love.

Jesus did not say or do everything that is attributed to him in the Gospels and everything he said and did was not recorded. Jesus' overall message was the love of God and brother and anything that is contradictory to that was not part of Jesus' life or message. Gospel means good news and the Gospels per se were not as much the good news themselves as they pointed to the good news, which is the love God has for us. In the end, Jesus didn't want to be personally worshipped; he wanted to be the example to lead us to the worship of God.

14. Jesus, Paul, and the Old Testament

There has been much to ponder about Jesus' saying in Matthew 5:17, that he did not come to destroy the Law or the Prophets but to fulfill it. In the next verse, Jesus said, "[...] till heaven and earth pass away, one jot or one tittle will by no means pass from the law till all is fulfilled." This has been interpreted by Apologists as Jesus affirming the entire Old Testament. With this affirmation, Jesus would be giving validity to the historical events, prophetic predictions, God's interactions with the Jewish people, and, of course, the nature and laws of God. By declaring Jesus' nature as love, peace, and forgiveness, Jesus would have to be duplicitous to agree with some of the Mosaic Laws. Would Jesus have approved of God directly or indirectly killing people?

Jesus specifically mentions some of the Ten Commandments in the Gospels which make them part of the new covenant, while also correcting some. Here is a comparison of the Old Testament understanding of the Law and what Jesus says.

Old Testament	Jesus
Exodus 35:2: "[…] the seventh day shall be a holy day for you, a Sabbath of rest to the Lord. Whoever does any work on it shall be put to death."	Matthew 12:12: "Therefore it is lawful to do good on the Sabbath." Mark 2:27: "The Sabbath was made for man, and not man for the Sabbath."
Deuteronomy: 19:21 "[…] life *shall* be for life, eye for eye, tooth for tooth, hand for hand, foot for foot."	Matthew 5:39: "But I tell you not to resist an evil person…turn the other cheek to him." Matthew 5:43: "You have heard that it was said, You shall love your neighbor and hate your enemy, but I say to you, love your enemies, bless those who curse you…"

Deuteronomy 24:1: Men can write a certificate of divorce for their wives.	Matthew 19:9: "Whoever divorces his wife, except for sexual immorality, and marries another commits adultery."
Exodus 20:24: You shall make for me an altar and sacrifice on it your burnt offerings.	Matthew 12:7: "I desire mercy and not sacrifice."
Deuteronomy 13:15: "[…] you shall surely strike the inhabitants of that city with the edge of your sword, utterly destroying it."	Matthew 26:52: "[…] for all who take the sword will perish by the sword."
Leviticus 20:10: "[…] the adulterer and the adulteress, shall surely be put to death."	John 8:11: to the woman accused of adultery, "[…] neither do I condemn you, go and sin no more."
Deuteronomy 11:13: If you obey my Commandments I will give you the rain.	Matthew 5:45: "God sends rain on the just and on the unjust."

Jesus did not institute any of the animal sacrifices, dietary or cleanliness requirements in the new Christianity that were demanded in the Mosaic Laws. In Acts 10:15, God tells Peter to eat all animals negating the Old Testament laws. What else might the divine change? Jesus reserved his harshest criticism for the Pharisees, condemning their legalism, except he failed to mention that they were only trying to follow the laws that God gave in the Old Testament. Jesus reinterprets some of the Old Testament laws but how can anyone blame the Jews for following them the best they can. In reality, Jesus did not sanction any law that was not based on love and peace, and he would not attack someone else's beliefs.

Jesus commanded the two great Laws – love God and love your neighbor. Matthew 22:40 recorded Jesus as saying, "On these two Commandments hang all the Law and the Prophets." Jesus meant that all of the Law should hang on the Commandment to love. Some of the laws are opposed to love, with the prophets communicating the laws of death; therefore, Jesus would not have affirmed all of the Law. Apologists also use this verse to assert that Jesus affirmed the entire Old Testament as Scripture or God's word to His people. No rational person could look at those mortal laws and see any resemblance to love.

Jesus used the verb love and the Mosaic Law used the verb kill. The two laws that Jesus commanded are changeless and eternal. If the Mosaic Laws are from God for the Jewish people, why didn't Jesus follow them? He clearly did not kill anyone or command anyone to be killed. St. Paul said love is patient, love is kind, it does not boast and is not proud, and it is not rude or self-seeking. It is not easily angered; it keeps no account of wrongs. This does not describe the God of the Old Testament or His Laws.

After Jesus, Paul is considered the most significant person in the expansion of Christianity regarding growth of its churches and the development of its theology. Paul was a tireless preacher and traveled extensively, starting and shepherding new Christian churches. Paul's writings were letters or epistles that dealt with problems that the new churches were having, while giving guidance and encouragement to the followers. Paul had a difficult job because he mainly preached to Gentiles and had to introduce them to the Jewish God, enunciate the theology as he understood it, and help them build their newly organized churches.

After his conversion, Paul realized that if you could be saved or justified by the Law, then the death and resurrection of Jesus was for nothing. In his vision, Paul believed that Jesus was the new covenant. Paul himself had to move past the Old Testament laws. Paul felt the Law was for the Jews of that time only. How could Christianity's main evangelist move away from the Law if Jesus affirmed it? In Romans 10:4, Paul said, "For Christ is the end of the law for righteousness to everyone who believes." Being Jewish himself, Paul decided to marry the two and let those who wanted to, keep the Law. It's hard to believe the Gentiles would have converted to Christianity if they were commanded to kill their brothers to be righteous.

Interestingly, Paul says very little about Jesus' life and teachings in his letters and mainly focuses on the sacrificial salvation of God sending his Son to die for our sins. Paul never met Jesus although his vision of him on the road to Damascus changed his life from a persecutor of Christians to the main evangelist for Jesus and the new Christianity. As a Pharisaic Jew himself, Paul was steeped in the Jewish Law and proclaimed himself as blameless. He followed the Law to the letter, the same way the Pharisees approached the Law.

One of his greatest contributions to Christianity is his understanding of salvation as justified by faith in the death and resurrection of Jesus rather than the Jewish adherence to the Mosaic Laws. The Old Testament is about the Chosen People trying to gain God's favor and His promises to them for following the Law. Now Paul is preaching that Jesus is the sacrifice that fulfilled the Law and thus the laws did not have to be followed to be saved. His interpretation of divine salvation differs from some of Jesus' own Apostles who still believed one had to obey the laws to be justified.

The Jerusalem Apostles, mainly James and Peter, believed that the new Christians were justified by works; therefore, they still needed to follow the Jewish laws including circumcision and dietary and cleanliness rituals. Christianity may have become a sect of Judaism if it wasn't for Paul starting so many churches and converting so many Gentiles. Paul's passion and rate of conversion soon won out and the Church moved away from their Jewish roots.

The fourteen letters attributed to Paul were written in the early fifties through the late 60sCE, and the book of Acts written about Paul by Luke was probably sometime after that. Paul is really the only early writer to emphatically spell out the new Christian theology. Paul did not reference the stories and teachings of Jesus in his letters or in Acts, possibly because the Gospels were not written yet, although the oral stories that populate the Gospels were being passed around. Paul interacted with the Apostles Peter and James to resolve theological issues, but curiously didn't take away any stories about Jesus that he might have heard from the confidants of Jesus. Some believe Paul modified the religion OF Jesus into a religion ABOUT Jesus. Paul's letters were all about who Jesus was as the only begotten Son of God sent to die and rise for our sins, rather than focusing on Jesus' teachings.

We don't know if Saul was personally involved in the punishment or killing of Jews converting to Christianity, though we do know he was on his way to Damascus to seek out followers of Jesus to bring back to Jerusalem for questioning and possible punishment or execution. It's recorded that Paul is believed to have been involved in the first Christian Martyr's death, St. Stephen, around 36CE. What does this say about God, the Jewish religion and the Mosaic Law if the practitioners were supposed to kill all those who disagreed with them or left the faith?

It's ironic that when Paul had his vision, Jesus said to him, Saul, why do you persecute me? Paul's answer should have been because God commanded the Chosen People to kill all blasphemers, non-Jews, and those who serve other gods. Paul later wrote in Galatians and Romans 13:10, "Love does no harm to a neighbor; therefore love is the fulfillment of the law." Did Paul forget that it was God's Law that commanded the Jews to stone Stephen with Paul's approval? To resolve this conundrum, Paul had to move Christianity away from the Old Testament laws. Paul had to see that the two differing sets of Commandments, one from God about killing and one from Jesus about love could not be reconciled. He couldn't move Christianity totally away from Judaism, so he portrayed Jesus as the fulfillment of the Jewish religion and God's plan for salvation.

Paul's theology of salvation by grace through faith in Jesus was at odds with one of the main Jerusalem Apostles, James. About the same time Paul was converting Gentiles, James was trying to keep Jesus in Judaism when he wrote in James 2:10, "For whoever shall keep the whole law, and yet stumble in one *point*, he is guilty of all." James also tries to tie the Law into Christianity when he questioned faith without works. He said in James 2:14, "What *does* it profit, my brethren, if someone says he has faith but does not have works? Can faith save him?" And again in 2:17, "Thus also faith by itself, if it does not have works, is dead." Jesus even muddies the water about faith vs. works when Matthew 16:27 has him say, "For the Son of Man will come in the glory of His Father with His angels, and then he will reward each according to his works." Faith vs works continues to be a contentious issue for the faithful.

How did Paul discern that God's plan was salvation by faith in Jesus' death and resurrection and not by following the Old Testament laws? It may have been that since Paul heard the stories and saw that Jesus was alive after the resurrection in his vision, he understood that God raised Jesus from the dead. If God sent his only begotten Son to die, and he was resurrected, it could not have been for Jesus' sins but for ours. God substituted Jesus for us as the sacrificial lamb, just like the Jewish temple sacrifices that Paul participated in. Now Jesus was the main sacrifice that washed away all sin. Therefore, it is believing in the death and resurrection of Jesus and not good works and following the Law that saved you.

The Jews have a long biblical tradition of bestowing a blessing from one person to another and this is how Jesus could save us with his sacrifice. Paul still believed that good works came from faith and encouraged the Jews and Gentiles to continue that practice.

Paul was passionate about what he thought the theology of Christianity should be. He thought we needed Jesus because he believed in sin and was steeped in Judaism. Should we base our salvation on one man's interpretation and hope he got it right? Regarding our salvation, each and every one of us needs to ask the same question that Paul had to ask himself when he had his vision. Could I have been wrong in what I believed? Paul changed his belief and was eventually martyred in Rome for his new faith. He was also ostracized from the Jews and lived his life committed to Jesus as the fulfillment of the Law. Change is hard and we know from history and personal experience that just because everyone believes in something doesn't make it true. *A Course in Miracles* is a new way to understand Jesus and salvation.

ACIM's Insight into Jesus, Paul, and the Old Testament

When Jesus said he did not come to abolish the Law, he meant he did not come to look into the past or attack anyone's views. In order to make progress in our spiritual journey, it only matters what you do now because that is the only time you have and the only time that is relevant. Jesus said in Luke 9:62, "No one, having put his hand to the plow, and looking back, is fit for the kingdom of God." Jesus is saying you cannot focus on the Kingdom by continually bringing up your past thoughts of fear, guilt, regret, and sin. The past is gone and you cannot change it, rather it becomes an impediment to practicing forgiveness now. The past is a steppingstone to where you are now and Jesus never holds anything you did or thought in the past against you.

As Paul also said, love does not keep account of wrongs. God and Jesus, being perfect love, do not look back on our faults, they offer guidance through the Holy Spirit to help us change our mistakes now. According to the Holy Spirit, the only function of time is to learn from it. In the Course, Jesus' exhortation to all of us is always "choose again." The trials and lessons will present themselves over and over so that you can make a better choice, which should be love and forgiveness. The past does not matter. Jesus said the tax collectors and prostitutes enter the Kingdom before the Pharisees because what you do is not nearly as significant as what you think, and thinking is now. In John 6:63, Jesus said, "It is the Spirit who gives life; the flesh profits nothing." The Spirit consists of thought, so what you think matters and what you do will follow.

Jesus is also recorded as saying that all the Law and Prophets hang on the two great Commandments. It is obvious that all the laws and prophecies do not line up with the two great Commandments of love God and your neighbor. Jesus again is correcting the Old Testament by saying that all of God's real laws come from love and if they don't reflect love, they are not from God.

Jesus probably said that all of the Law and the Prophets SHOULD hang on these two Commandments. Because Jesus was perfect love, he used the Law to teach, but did not teach the Law. He had to relate to people where they were so he related to the Jewish people using the Jewish religion and Law. If someone believed in the Law, Jesus started from there, found the love in it and built on that. He knew that any of the Old Testament laws that promoted love were true.

Paul let his fervent belief in and history of Judaism dominate his Christian theological thinking, binding the two religions through God, Scripture, and Jesus. Paul took Christianity out of a Jewish sect and gave it its own platform but kept its roots firmly planted in Judaism by making Jesus the sacrificial lamb. Jesus' message was to overcome the world. Instead of tying Jesus to the world of religion, we must release religion to the truth of God in Heaven. Paul, like all biblical writers, lived and wrote from the ego mind of fear and guilt, as evidenced by his depiction of Jesus as a sacrifice for our sins. Paul did his part to spread the good news even though he didn't understand the whole picture.

15. Jesus Did Not Take Over the Family Business

In the New Testament, Jesus is described as the Son of God, which is true, nonetheless he does not act as the Son of the Old Testament God. There is absolutely no way that Jesus was teaching about the God of the Old Testament when he referenced his Abba or Father. If you read the Old Testament as it reveals God and then read the New Testament as Jesus reveals his Father in Heaven, they are not the same being. Jesus corrects the Old Testament on other matters and he does it again in referencing God. The reason the God of the Old Testament and the God who Jesus reveals cannot be the same being is that Jesus describes a God of love who is good and the Old Testament depicts Him differently. Since the biblical Jesus himself is God incarnate, wouldn't he be exactly like his Father in Heaven?

Jesus did not say a lot about God's character, he more often taught about the Kingdom of God. But he did say things like, God is good, and the Father is greater than I. Jesus said love your enemies, bless those who curse you, do good to those who hate you. Yet time and again, the God of the Old Testament punished and killed people for those reasons. In Matthew 5:48, Jesus says, "Therefore you shall be perfect just as your Father in heaven is perfect." If Jesus is saying that the God of the Old Testament is perfect, then why didn't Jesus' teachings include killing your brother and enemies? In Matthew 5:44, Jesus said to bless those who curse you, but God's Commandment in Exodus 21:17 was to kill a child who curses his parents. Jesus' answer was always to forgive. His admonition to forgive them Father for they know not what they do, couldn't be any farther from *stone them*.

Interestingly, Jesus says in Matthew 5:43, "You have heard that it was said, *You shall love your neighbor* and hate your enemy." Jesus said you have heard and not that it was written because the Jews must have believed that the Old

Testament promoted hating your enemy. Jesus had to correct the Jewish people who read the Old Testament Scriptures and believed it promoted hate based on the actions and directives of that God. Jesus also taught repentance, but when God killed people, He did not demonstrate mercy, or patience, or give them a chance to repent.

Jesus said in John 5:19, "Most assuredly, I say to you, the Son can do nothing of Himself, but what He sees the Father do; for whatever He does, the Son also does in like manner." Can any reasonable person say that Jesus did any of the destructive things that the God of the Old Testament did? In some Bibles, Hebrews 1:3 says the Son is the radiance of God's glory and the exact representation of His being. Again, not only did Jesus not do what the God of the Old Testament did, he often times did the opposite.

Jesus told the parable of the Good Samaritan as an example of how to interact with those who you consider your enemy or an unfriendly neighbor. However, God very specifically says to destroy the inhabitants of a city that will not make peace with you. Furthermore, God punished the people of Egypt unto death during the Jewish captivity. Jesus had a similar, if not so burdensome, existence as the Roman Empire occupied and enforced their will on the Jewish people. Jesus did not send plagues, kill any Romans, or even say anything against the occupying enemy, he just forgave them.

Another way Jesus did not take over the family business, was in not advocating the strict following of the 613 Mosaic Laws that God gave to Moses to give to the Jewish people. The Pharisees were in charge of directing the keeping of the Law in daily life. And yet, Jesus reserved his most vitriolic speech against the Pharisees, not the Romans, sinners, or Gentiles. Jesus admonished the Pharisees who were trying to follow the Law to the letter. What was the Spirit of the Law that said to kill your brothers for their transgressions? Jesus knew the letter and the Spirit of the Law was flawed but did not go against the Law because it was punishable by death to do so. Therefore, he corrected it by saying that his Commandment to love is what the Law should hang on. It's ironic that Jesus was killed for blasphemy based on God's Law against blasphemy. Blasphemy could be saying something against God, against God's Law, or elevating yourself to the level of God.

Many of the 613 Mosaic Laws were dietary and cleanliness laws, still Jesus said not to worry about your life or your body, showing the meaninglessness of the body. He let people suffer and consented to have his body killed. In

Matthew 15:11, Jesus said, "Not what goes into the mouth defiles a man; but what comes out of the mouth." Jesus knew we are Spirit and the body is not real on earth or in Heaven.

One of the main practices of the Jews in the temple was the animal sacrifices. God commanded that sacrifices be made at the temple. If you recall, Jesus had a problem with all of the commerce that took place in the temple area because it was supposed to be a house of worship. The buying and selling that Jesus railed against was necessitated by the command of God to sacrifice an unblemished animal. Travelers that went to the temple could not or did not have these animals with them, thus they had to purchase them to fulfill God's command. Jesus drove out the merchants and money changers from the system that was necessitated by God's command.

Jesus also seems to contradict God's sacrificial system when he quoted Hosea 6:6, "For I desire mercy and not sacrifice." The temple sacrifices eventually stopped, perhaps when the temple was destroyed around 70CE, but if they were a Commandment of God and God never changes, why did they stop? Why didn't Jesus tell his new Christian disciples to continue animal sacrifices to him or God? Even though Jesus said I desire mercy and not sacrifice, Christianity is based on the ultimate sacrifice of Jesus as atonement for our sins.

In Matthew, Jesus says we are more valuable than birds to the Father and then later in Matthew 7:11, he says, "If you then, being evil, know how to give good gifts to your children, how much more will your Father who is in Heaven give good things to those who ask Him!" Is this the same Father that in Numbers 21:6, sent fiery serpents that killed many of His people who were complaining and asking for a better situation? Additionally, Jesus said he came not to call the righteous but the sinners. He interacted with sinners as opposed to laws condemning sinners. If you disobeyed the Law, you were cut off, not only from your people, but also cut off from God. The Old Testament is based on God's promise that He will be their God and they will be His people…as long as they glorify Him and obey His Commandments. God basically said I will love you if you will do as I say or meet my conditions. God made it about approved actions and also birthright. If you weren't from the patriarchal line from Abraham, then you were excluded from God's favor.

Jesus also directly contradicts God's Law of an eye for an eye and tooth for tooth from Leviticus 24:20. In Matthew 5:38, Jesus says not to get even but to turn the other cheek when confronted with an evil person. He also teaches forgiveness instead of God's threat of punishment and retaliation. In Mark 11:25, Jesus says prayer won't work if you have not forgiven your brother. "And whenever you stand praying, if you have anything against anyone, forgive him, that your Father in Heaven may also forgive you your trespasses." Jesus teaches us to build our relationship with God through our forgiveness of our brother.

God was the Jewish God for the Jewish people, but the Bible leads us to believe that God used His Son to start a revolution against the religion that He started. Since Jesus was a Jew and the Jewish people were the chosen of God, why didn't Jesus make himself the King of the Jews, the Jewish Messiah, or the Chief Priest of the Sanhedrin? He could have done this before he was crucified as the crowds wanted to make him king when he arrived for Passover. He could have done it after the resurrection as he would have made a huge impact on all who saw him after he was raised. He didn't because he didn't take over the family business. Incidentally, Christianity was, for many centuries, actually hostile to God's Chosen for their treatment of His only begotten Son.

Jesus specifically enunciated and spelled out two Commandments: to love God and your neighbor. Neither of these is spelled out by God in the Ten Commandments. God's Ten Commandments are mostly thou shalt nots, from a God of control and punishment, but Jesus' two great Commandments are thou shalt love. In addition, Jesus did not say you would be killed or separated from God or society by not keeping these Commandments. Jesus did not fill his teachings with Commandments; he desired only to change the hearts and minds of everyone to unconditional love. An interesting observation is that if God made the world and grouped people into families, that structure makes it very hard, if not impossible, to love your neighbor if they're not part of your family.

ACIM's Understanding of God and Jesus

Jesus did not take over the family business if the family business was the vengeful, wrathful, judgmental, and punishing God of the Old Testament Inc. Jesus knew a totally different Father who was represented by the Holy Spirit on earth and who is only love, peace, and joy. Jesus knew the Jews projected their guilt from sin and fear onto God and he knew we would continue to do it until eventually, after many lifetimes, we would wake up to the truth. Christianity is a religion about Jesus, but Jesus' religion was love and his altar or temple on earth was a loving holy relationship with all of his brothers.

The Course says the holiest place on earth is where an ancient hatred has become a present love. Jesus knew there was no physically or materially holy place or object on earth. He played his part on earth as a human to teach us that it is okay for us to play our part as regular humans, while changing our minds. Jesus knew we could not and would not follow all of the Commandments of the Old Testament. He knew the important thing is to grow in love through forgiveness of our brothers. Jesus became aware of this first as Paul says he was the first fruits.

Jesus focused on his connection with the Holy Spirit and not on totally changing our understanding of God, the world, the Jewish religion, the Old Testament, the Roman occupation, or human suffering. Again, Jesus counsels us to seek not to change the world but seek to change our minds about the world. The world is an illusion and everything that is not love is also an illusion. If you think about it, the ego/devil would want us to try to change the world; better yet fight over our roles in the world to foster anything that takes our attention away from God.

The perfect plan by the ego/devil is to put us in bodies that need constant attention, in relationships that demand work, on a planet that always has an issue, so that we have little to no time and energy for God. Since we see what we believe, if we believe in the God of the Old Testament and His world, then we will not see the truth. We put all our attention on God's demands rather than Jesus' example of love. Our prayer should be for God to reveal himself to us the way Jesus knew Him and not the way that the Old Testament portrayed Him.

16. Reliability of the New Testament

How reliable is the New Testament if we don't know who wrote all of the books, when they were written, and how accurately the writers recorded events? Many biblical scholars disagree on who wrote the Gospels. How can we judge the credibility of the writers, and if they were close to Jesus or the Apostles, if we don't know who the writers were? We must trust the interpretation of the writers and decide if the stories about Jesus were fact or used to teach a lesson. We know that the parables Jesus told were made-up stories to teach a lesson and impart knowledge. If Jesus taught almost exclusively with made-up parables, why wouldn't the writers of the Gospels also make up stories about Jesus meant to instruct? An example is the story of the woman caught in adultery which was a later addition to John's Gospel.

Were the New Testament writings the inspired and inerrant word of God? A recent Gallup poll indicates that only about 24% of Americans believe that the Bible is the literal word of God and the percentage has been declining for decades. The other 76% of Americans probably believe that the Bible is a holy book written by man. The New Testament may be more believable as the word of God because it is more about love and forgiveness and has Jesus as the hero. Similar to the Old Testament, you can google hundreds of contradictions between and within the twenty-seven books of the New Testament. If the New Testament is inspired, it still needs to be interpreted and be inerrantly understood.

As I have said, the New Testament is inspired because inspiration is available to all; however the message was not perfectly received, and therefore is not an accurate representation of Jesus' true message. There is truth in the New Testament but many parts were influenced by the ego mind out of fear and guilt. The main tenet that Jesus was sent by God as a sacrifice for our sins, he is the only way to the Father, and if you don't believe you will suffer eternal punishment, are not Jesus' messages or his understanding on how to get to Heaven.

Again, I am not overly concerned with the minutiae of the contradictions in numbers, dates, chronology, geography, names, and the different telling of stories. My main focus is on theological questions. Here are some examples of reliability problems.

All of the writers of the twenty-seven books had a vested interest in what they wrote. Most New Testament writers were partial about the message because if they weren't extremely interested and passionate about the subject, then why would they write about it. Everyone has a worldview, or the unique way they look at the world based on their environment, upbringing, relationships, biology, and experiences. These worldviews cannot be unbiased because they're distinctive only to you. This doesn't preclude the storytellers from getting the story right, still they were all Jewish and you can see the import of their heritage in the writings. The margin notes of many Bibles indicate how often something Jesus said or did is the fulfillment of Old Testament prophecies.

You can look at this in two ways, one being Jesus fulfilled a lot of prophecies, or two, the writers who knew the prophecies in advance wrote the Gospels with Jesus as the hero fulfilling a statistically improbable number of prophecies.

Matthew wrote his Gospel stressing Jesus' Jewishness as the Jewish Messiah sent by the Jewish God to the Jewish people in fulfillment of Jewish prophecy while promoting the Jewish law. Matthew is the only Gospel to say that Jesus did not come to destroy the Mosaic Law. Matthew strains to insert Jesus into the Messianic tradition giving the genealogy of Jesus fourteen generations between each major figure, based on the writings of Daniel. Interestingly, the Old Testament's genealogy does not match Mathew's account. Even in the Gospels, Matthew and Luke give genealogies of Jesus with both saying Joseph was Jesus' father, but Luke has Heli as Joseph's father and Matthew has Jacob as Joseph's father, possibly to try to squeeze Jesus into the Jewish God's plan.

More evidence of a Jewish bias is that the Jews were looking for a Messiah throughout their storied history. Even though most Jews did not see Jesus as the Messiah, the early Christians who were previously Jews turned Jesus into the anointed one of God and the suffering servant, even though he did not have the characteristics of the Jewish kingly Messiah. As a new religion, Christianity proclaimed Jesus as the Jewish Messiah to give it deep roots. It's human nature to want people to believe what you believe and possibly write to subtly or plainly expose the readers to your point of view. Ultimately, all of the writers were biased and wrote to satisfy their particular leanings. Examining the meaning of what someone said or did, your bias can influence or alter the meaning.

Many biblical scholars have determined that the attribution of the names Matthew, Mark, Luke, and John were not in the original Gospels and therefore, were not the actual persons who wrote the Gospels. All the Gospels were written in the third person. Neither Matthew, Mark, Luke, nor John, used their names in the Gospels. They did not say we did this or I did this with Jesus. You would assume that one of the twelve Apostles or a close traveling disciple of Jesus would put themselves in the narrative of the most important story to ever be told, as Paul did in his letters and Luke did in Acts.

The Apostles were human and as such were prideful given they sometimes spoke to each other about who is more important or the greatest. Apologists say it doesn't matter what names were on the documents, just that the writer was in a position to know the facts they were reporting. How do we know if they are the facts if we don't know who the person is, their closeness to Jesus or to an eyewitness? We don't know if they have a position to advance, if they were trustworthy, or if their source was reliable, especially if the stories differ from each other.

The Gospels are essentially an unauthorized biography about Jesus since he did not authorize or review the content and accuracy. We hope the writers had so much love and respect for Jesus that they reliably cataloged his life and words, but all of the New Testament writings were done by human hands with human shortcomings. If you think the Bible is perfect, then you are making a statement of faith, not fact.

In the first three Gospels, Jesus conceals his divinity and preaches the coming of the Kingdom of God. In the last Gospel from John, Jesus continually talks about his divinity and eternal life after death, presumably because the Kingdom never came by the time John wrote his later Gospel. The similarity of the synoptic Gospels has led many biblical scholars to conclude that both Matthew and Luke used the Gospel of Mark as a source along with other sources. Biblical scholars give credibility to accounts with multiple sources, but if the original source is wrong, then the writings that borrow from it are also wrong and multiple attestations are invalid.

If Matthew and Luke used Mark, then they were probably not eyewitnesses to Jesus' life or they would have known what Mark knew. Biblical scholars use many variations of textual criticism to determine who borrowed from whom to make the claim against multiple attestations.

There are several questions about when the New Testament books were written. Most biblical scholars believe Mark was the first Gospel written about thirty or forty years after Jesus' death, and the other three Gospels sometime after that. Why did it take so long for the Gospels to be written after Jesus ascended into Heaven? Was it because the Apostles were uneducated, lower class, illiterate, Aramaic speaking Jews from Palestine, who couldn't write? Or because the Gospels were written later by well-educated Greek-speaking disciples, as some biblical scholars assert? If that's the reason, then the stories of Jesus had to be handed down orally through the subsequent decades before they were written down by distant parties.

It has been said that people in ancient times had great memories, nonetheless, could they pass down a long discourse verbatim? Was it because the early followers thought Jesus was coming back in their day and they didn't need a record of his teachings? In that scenario, everybody, including Jesus, misunderstood the timeline for the Kingdom to come. How did the writers know decades later what was said in situations where there were no eyewitnesses, like in the discourse with Pilot, Nicodemus, or the Garden of Gethsemane?

Another point about the timing of the New Testament is that we do not have any original New Testament manuscripts, called autographs, only copies of copies of copies of the original Gospels. Apologists concede that the copies we have may not be the exact word of God because of human intervention causing errors, but they claim the originals were the perfect inerrant word of God. It's hard to refute that argument seeing how we don't have the originals to compare. The earliest writing from the New Testament that exists is from the Gospel of John and is a credit card sized fragment dated to about 125CE.

The earliest complete copy of the New Testament is dated around 350CE, raising the question of how many times and how accurately it was copied. Depending on the researcher, there are thousands and up to a hundred thousand variations between all of the thousands of fragments and complete New Testament manuscripts that we have today. As a matter of fact, there are more variations than words in the entire New Testament. Most of these differences are spelling and word order discrepancies and do not have much impact on the meaning. Although, we really don't know about substantive differences if we don't have the originals to compare. Apologists say even though the copies we possess have errors, you can recreate the originals and have a high degree of confidence that the meaning is intact.

Since Jesus' message was so radical, I'm not sure that his extreme teachings were not changed because they were so different from any religion or teaching. To back up this claim you can see that we are still changing the Gospels today. In Luke 17:21 of the New King James Version, Jesus said, "For indeed, the kingdom of God is within you." In about half of the modern Bibles, the translation is the Kingdom of Heaven is among you or in your midst. The Kingdom of Heaven is within you is Jesus' teaching that we are truly Spirit. The new translations altered Jesus' message to say that Jesus is in your presence, which is fundamentally different and was altered based on what someone thought it should say.

Jesus was a Jew who spoke Aramaic, and his Apostles were Jews who spoke Aramaic. It's highly unlikely they could write given their professions and the fact that over 90% of the ancient world was illiterate. All four Gospels were written in Greek, and most likely by highly educated Greeks. If the Gospels were written by the Apostles or eyewitnesses of Jesus, then they would have been written in the tongue they knew. If they were written by close associates of the Apostles, then they too would be Aramaic speakers. The Jews stuck together and rarely spoke to foreigners, even Greeks. If the Apostles had highly educated Greeks write for them, you have the same problem of communicating different languages and insights. These circumstances present the problem of different stories being orally passed around in different languages until someone not personally connected to Jesus wrote the Gospels.

With the thousands of variations in the remaining manuscripts, it is highly debated whether the Gospels recorded exactly what Jesus said, partly based on the apparent contradictions between the Gospel writings themselves. Many scholars have tried to differentiate between the Jesus described in the New Testament and the actual man or historical Jesus. The Jesus Seminar was one such group in the 1990s. It was made up of fifty critical biblical scholars and one hundred laymen who voted on the likelihood of Jesus actually saying what the Gospels said. They used the normal methods biblical scholars use to determine the authenticity of ancient documents such as textual criticism, social anthropology, and historical analysis. They examined 1500 versions from approximately five hundred texts including parables, aphorisms, dialogues, and stories attributed to Jesus.

The Seminar determined that only about 20% of the words attributed to Jesus in the Gospels were definitely spoken by him. The other 80% were divided into: he probably said something like it, he probably did not say it but it contained Jesus' views, or he did not say it because it came from a later addition or a different tradition. They attributed the low percentage to the fact that the Gospels were hearsay evidence related from an intermediate party or secondhand sources. There was wide criticism of the Seminar, their methods, and their credentials. It was probably shocking to most people to hear scholars attribute such a low percentage given that we have built Christianity around the Gospel accounts of Jesus. Even if the percentage were reversed to say that Jesus actually said 80% of what is attributed to him in the Gospels, we would have to question if we are hanging our salvation hats onto things that he may not have said.

On the other side of the debate, another group of Evangelical leaders developed the Chicago Statement of Biblical Inerrancy in 1978. They also looked at the sayings and deeds of Jesus and defended the position that the Bible is without error and is the authoritative word of God.

There are countless people who have committed their lives to studying Jesus and his teachings, and they will probably make new discoveries. There are two discoveries that most biblical scholars have agreed upon for centuries which call into question the accuracy of the New Testament. Mark's Gospel ends with chapter 16, verse 20, but there is usually a footnote in most Bibles that verses 9 through 20 in chapter 16 were not found in the earlier texts. This is not an exact science although it indicates that the very end of Mark was added during one of the later copying's of the Gospel.

There is also John 8:1–11, which is the story of the woman caught in adultery and brought to Jesus. It demonstrates his cleverness, authority, and forgiveness when he declares, "He who is without sin among you, let him throw a stone at her first." Unfortunately, there is clear evidence that this passage was not originally part of John's Gospel. The earliest manuscripts do not have it and it is written in a different style than the rest of John. It appears to be a teaching story because if the woman was caught in the act of adultery, then there would have to be a man involved too, and according to Mosaic Law, both would be stoned.

In some Bibles, it is also footnoted that it may not be original. Whether this happened or not, it is a beautiful story (except for the potential stoning) and is truly indicative of Jesus' character. The addition in John does call into question the accuracy of the biblical chain of evidence.

In summary, we have to understand that what we have today may not be exactly what Jesus said and did, and there is no way to know for sure. It's common throughout history that students of great masters have written things and attributed them to their teacher. If it helps us learn and grow, then it might not matter if the master said it as it becomes a teaching lesson as long as it is in alignment with the master's curriculum. Average Christians are not biblical scholars, but we can do a rudimentary analysis of the Gospels ourselves.

If we believe that Jesus had a core set of characteristics, then anything that aligns with them he may have done or said and anything that doesn't, he probably didn't say or do. In John's story of the adulterer, Jesus may not have said those words, but if he were presented with that situation, that is what he probably would have said. The timeless lesson of this story is not if you are in this exact situation, do this. Rather, it is a general story of love and forgiveness to be applied to all situations.

This type of understanding works because the true Jesus was a teacher and wanted us to learn his lessons. In effect, this is how the New Testament and the Gospels came about anyway. The Church Fathers took certain writings from the hundreds available, along with what early Christians believed, made them orthodox and declared other writings to be heretical. An example of this comes from Paul declaring salvation by faith in the belief in Jesus, when Jesus seemed to teach salvation by works in the parable of the Sheep and Goats. Biblical scholars know there were many forgeries written in the name of influential leaders, also about Jesus. If stories were being invented and forgeries written in peoples' names, how can we be sure these stories did not make it into the Gospels if the Gospels were written after the stories circulated?

Apologists say that we cannot expect the level of historical accuracy in ancient documents because they were not intended to provide them. They contend that it is quite natural for ancient stories told by four dissimilar sources to be different by leaving out certain details, rephrasing, reordering chronological events, and interpreting the facts their own way. Which writing then is the closest to the true message if they're so different? If the writings were inspired by the Holy Spirit, can they be contradictory? If it is a cohesive message even though it is from different sources, why are there so many radically different Christian denominations? If there is a natural diversity of views in the twenty-seven books of the New Testament, what other views are in the hundreds of non-canonical writings that didn't make it in the Bible and were either lost or destroyed? Hopefully, there will be more discoveries and analysis in the future that may support or oppose the Gospels.

An interesting recent development is that Pope Francis declared the line, "And do not lead us into temptation," from the Lord's Prayer was a bad translation. He thought it should be "Do not let us fall into temptation." How long have we been saying this fundamental prayer incorrectly before someone with authority told us it was a bad translation and corrected it? Are there other verses in the Bible that are also bad translations?

Reliability of the New Testament from ACIM

The New Testament was written by men influenced by the ego and its purposeful misrepresentation of God, Jesus, and the world. The Course references the Bible to agree with it, correct it, or refute it. To believe that the New Testament was the inerrant word of God, you would have to believe that Jesus was judgmental, cruel, and unforgiving for his teachings about hell, and duplicitous if he agreed with the harsh Mosaic Laws. Some of the New Testament writings point to the truth. Some of what Jesus said and did in the Gospels are accurate, although some of it was put in to have Jesus conform to his Jewish roots.

Jesus did fulfill some of the prophecies because the Holy Spirit, who knows everything, inspired some of the Old Testament writings about Jesus. Jesus' purpose was not to fulfill Scriptures but to teach how to get out of the world and back home to God. Jesus' essence was beyond the world so you can expect his teachings to be out of this world and not represented accurately by mere mortal Gospel writers.

Jesus' core teachings were true, eternal, and for all people everywhere. Therefore, you can do your own textual criticism on what Jesus would have said by running it through this filter – was it loving and forgiving? If yes, then Jesus either said it or would have said it to teach you how to get home to God.

17. New Testament Orthodoxy

Orthodox is defined as conforming to what is generally or traditionally accepted as right and true. More specifically, what is established and approved. The twenty-seven books in the New Testament that we call Scripture are traditionally accepted as the true and the authoritative word of God. The decision by Church leaders on which books would be considered as orthodox came about over hundreds of years after Jesus. The orthodox canon was formally recognized by the Church in about 367CE as reported by the Church Father Athanasius of Alexandria.

Essentially, the twenty-seven books of the New Testament were formally authorized by the Church Fathers because they were approved and commonly used in worship services. Apologists may have you believe everybody agreed on these books because they were used for worship, but because most people couldn't read, the leaders had to present certain books at the services. In essence, the early Church leaders had to decide which books written about Jesus were true, accurate, and worthy of being called part of the new Christian Bible.

One problem is that there were many more than four Gospels to choose from in the first several hundred years of Christianity. There were dozens of Gospels we now know of that were not deemed orthodox, so not preserved. Along with the plethora of Gospels, there were probably hundreds of writings, again many of which were not deemed right and true that were destroyed because they were heretical. Admittedly, some of these writings were frauds although some were called heretical only because they had a different theology from that espoused by the leaders in power. Because the early Church Fathers had a lot to do with what became accepted as the canon, some biblical scholars say the writings that became orthodox won out against all the other writings.

In reading about early Church history, it is clear there were many diverse groups of Christians, and orthodoxy not being settled, resulted in struggles between the different factions. The Bible did not fall out of the sky with inspired texts predetermined by God. Therefore, orthodox Christianity took time to develop and someone had to decide. Some of the larger competing theologies of orthodox Christianity were quite large groups, like the Arians, Marcionites, and Gnostics. To substantiate this point, Irenaeus, a bishop in France, wrote a five-volume work called *Against Heresies* in about 180CE. He had strong opinions on what he believed to be the true Christian doctrine and wrote that about eighty different theologies or sects of Christianity existed and were heretical.

We only know about some of these theologies because of his writings against them. We do not have the opposing views themselves since they died out or were quashed. Irenaeus also said there can only be four Gospels, giving credence to the impression that there were more than four Gospels being used by worshippers.

To further solidify Scripture, the first council of Constantinople was convened by Roman Emperor Theodosius in 381CE. It solidified the doctrine of the Trinity and made Arianism heretical. Later in his reign, Theodosius forbade all Pagan worship and declared non-orthodox Christian sects heretical and illegal with punishment up to death. Some historians write that some of the cruelest tortures have been perpetrated against so-called Christians who were considered heretics because they believed a different Christian theology.

Today, we mainly study what was preserved and called orthodox, and as a result, we do not have the many different views of Jesus' teachings. Since we don't have the different accounts, we cannot make up our own minds about him based on this additional information. We are left with either accepting or rejecting what the canonical Gospels say. In early Christianity, the recognition of the books that were deemed orthodox was, in part, based on the proximity of the writers to Jesus and the Apostles. However, not all of the books that were authored by close followers of Jesus went into the New Testament. Gospels we know of and named after close followers of Jesus that did not make it into the canon are: The Gospel of Mary, Thomas, Peter, Nicodemus, Bartholomew, Judas, Philip, Paul, John, and James. These were either not in line with the established writings or were frauds or forgeries.

One Gospel that has recently come to light through the discoveries at Nag Hammadi in 1945 is the Gospel of Thomas. This Gospel was not included in the New Testament even though it has many of the same sayings as the synoptic Gospels. The Gospel was written by Jesus' Apostle Thomas who was known as the twin because he looked a lot like Jesus. He was portrayed as doubting Thomas in John's Gospel. The Gospel of Thomas was written as a 'sayings' Gospel, meaning Thomas only wrote what he heard Jesus say, and did not include accounts of Jesus' life or miracles. Thomas was killed in Asia during his ministry before he completed writing everything he heard Jesus say. The Gospel has 114 sayings and opens with, "These are the hidden sayings that the living Jesus spoke and Didymus Judas Thomas recorded."

I mentioned earlier that Irenaeus wrote about heretical groups and the Gnostics were high on his list as a group of religious who had a different understanding of Jesus. Because the Gospel of Thomas opens with the introduction of the sayings as secret or hidden, many have assumed that this is a Gnostic text. Gnosis is defined as knowledge and the various Gnostic groups emphasized personal spiritual knowledge rather than the authority of the Church. Irenaeus was vehemently against the so-called Christians claiming secret wisdom rather than following the Church's doctrine based on Scripture, tradition, and the Church Fathers' teachings.

It's estimated that about two-thirds of the sayings in the Gospel of Thomas are similar to the canonical Gospels, and yet it was not included with the four Gospels. The secret teachings that Thomas was referring to were simply things Jesus said in private to his disciples. Interestingly, in the synoptic Gospels, Jesus himself was clear that he taught certain things in private and another way in public, bolstering the claim of secret teachings. In Mark 4:11, Jesus said to his Apostles, "To you it has been given to know the mystery of the Kingdom of God; but to those who are outside, all things come in parables." Could we learn more about Jesus and his teachings from the remaining one-third of Thomas that were different from the four Gospels? If the sayings in the Gospel of Thomas are radical, then Jesus would probably tell them in private due to the Jewish leader's threat to kill all dissenters and their followers.

Several sayings in the Gospel of Thomas that point to Jesus' hidden message of oneness, forgiveness, miracles, and the unreality of form are:

Number 48, "If two make peace with each other in a single house, they will say to the mountain, 'Move from here!' and it will move."[i] Jesus taught that when you forgive and experience the unity of your brother, miracles happen.

Number 56, "Whoever has come to understand this world has found merely a corpse, and whoever has discovered the corpse, of that one the world is no longer worthy."[ii] Jesus was saying that the world is dead as in not real life which is only in Heaven. And when you discover this, you have overcome the world and know you are one with God who is waiting for you to awaken to your home in Heaven.

Number 61, "Therefore, I say that if one is whole, one will be filled with light, but if one is divided, one will be filled with darkness."[iii] To Jesus, wholeness is oneness with all, and light is understanding the truth. He is saying that when you realize and experience we are all one, you will understand all that the Holy Spirit is teaching. And if you are divided, meaning you believe that you are separate from your brother and God, you will be in the dark about God and His Kingdom.

Number 113, "Rather, the Kingdom of the Father is spread out upon the earth, and people do not see it."[iv] The Father's imperial rule is the Father's Kingdom of Heaven. It is spread out upon the earth because Heaven is not a place or a condition separate from us. It is all there is and it is available to us at any time but we choose not to see it because we think we are separate bodies. The world of the Spirit cannot be seen with the body's eyes. You either see the flesh or the Spirit but not both. This is what Jesus meant when he said no one can serve two masters. We must seek the Kingdom of Heaven and relinquish our attachment to form, and then we will see the Father's Kingdom.

Similar to the four Gospels, the Gospel of Thomas was changed and added to over the years. There are some sayings in the Gospel of Thomas that Jesus did not say. Using the model of Jesus as a being of love, peace, and forgiveness we can filter out some of the sayings that are not of Jesus. Two examples are: Number 55, Whoever doesn't hate their father and mother can't become my disciple. Jesus would not have promoted hate or other negative sentiments toward any of his brothers and sisters. Number 114, […] because every woman who makes herself manly will enter the Kingdom of Heaven. Jesus did not distinguish between the illusory forms of male and female, knowing that there is neither form in Heaven. Spirit has no form and differences between sexes are another ego device to separate us from each other.

As I read these sayings and others in the canonical Gospels, I am again struck about how vague and cryptic Jesus was in his teachings. I understand his need to be timeless and universal, but most of his teachings can have several interpretations. The only real explanation is that he was pointing to the truth and enticing us to go inside and ask the Holy Spirit what it means.

Another problem with orthodoxy is illustrated by St. Paul's letters. Paul is listed as the author of fourteen epistles or letters. However, through centuries of research using textual criticism, most biblical scholars are in agreement that Paul definitely wrote only seven of the Pauline letters attributed to him. There is no consensus among biblical scholars on who wrote the other seven letters, often called the Deutero-Pauline letters. This is important because letters possibly written by an unknown source are used in services, form theology, and are called Scripture because they're thought to be from Paul.

Some points in these letters differ from Paul's authentic letters, therefore pronouncing these writings as orthodox or Scripture must be questioned. This revelation has great impact because we believe that Paul was enlightened by Jesus on the road to Damascus and has more theological credibility than other writers who were neither Apostles, associates of Apostles, nor disciples.

The letters to Timothy are disputed; however, 2nd Timothy is used to validate all other Scripture. 2 Timothy 3:16 says, "All Scripture is given by inspiration of God, and *is* profitable for doctrine, for reproof, for correction, for instruction in righteousness." Timothy along with the other disputed letters may contain doctrine consistent with orthodox teachings, but there are some divisive teachings that Jesus may have disagreed with and no other writings support. 1 Timothy 2:12, says, "And I do not permit a woman to teach or have authority over a man, but to be in silence."

I have heard several prominent pastors say that they use this verse as a reason to not allow women to become pastors in their Church. Some churches are beginning to make women parts of the clergy, although many are not. Jesus was totally inclusive; therefore he would applaud the move to have loving, nurturing, compassionate women lead his flock. However, they are prohibited in many churches because of this letter and we are not sure who wrote it.

Hebrews is another contested letter and in 9:27, it says, "And as it is appointed for men to die once, but after this the judgment." Reincarnation is a historically contested issue, but it is believed the Pharisees of which St. Paul was one, believed in it. It's also clear in the Gospels that some thought Jesus was reincarnated from one of the prophets, and John the Baptist was asked if he was Elijah. Is the unknown author of Hebrews putting forth his own opinion that there is no reincarnation? Church leaders had to determine which writings were to be used by their congregations so they had to answer questions about theology, rituals, and right and wrong. Church councils were convened to solidify those decisions given the many theologies and interpretations. Since there are over 10,000 Christian denominations, each possibly following slightly different doctrine or theology, orthodoxy is really a myth. Everybody thinks they are personally orthodox; that their views are right or they wouldn't follow them…or at least admit to it in public.

Here is a hypothetical challenge to the development of early Christian orthodoxy based on it being true because most people believe and/or practice it. Using that model, we would have to say that since Roman Catholicism is the largest Christian denomination, everyone needs to become Catholic or they are heretics. To follow the methodology of the early Church, any other Christian belief that is not Catholic is heresy and should be illegal, and their books should be burned and the members cursed.

An example of how theology developed over a very long time and how it became orthodox because most people believed it, is the question of Jesus' divinity. Early Christians believed that Jesus was divine yet it wasn't until the council of Nicaea in 325CE that they agreed on how Jesus was divine. The Nicene Creed declared that Jesus was divine as true God and true man. At the time, there were many diverse beliefs about how Jesus was divine and it was a crucial question that needed to be definitively answered by the council. They answered it in an orthodox way but does that make it the right answer? It wasn't until the council of Constantinople in 381CE that agreement about the Trinity and the equality of the Father, Son, and Holy Spirit were answered. These and many other issues had to be explored as they were not directly answered by Scripture.

To summarize a complex issue, in early Christian formation, there were many diverse beliefs or theologies around Jesus. After the New Testament was put together, Christianity became more rigidly based and orthodox based on the main belief in the death and resurrection of Jesus. The Church tried to get everybody on the same page, but there were hundreds of sub beliefs that developed. The question remains: is the main Christian orthodox belief for the reason of Jesus' death and resurrection correct? Which one of the thousands of Christian denominations' different orthodox beliefs is true?

One of the intriguing theological evolutions that is orthodox in the Catholic Church is the existence of purgatory. During its first millennium, Catholics couldn't come to terms with a loving God sending people to hell if they died as sinners but were basically good people. Many realized that according to

Christian doctrine, many of their own family and friends were going to perish. The Catholic Church, through its interpretation of Scripture, developed an intermediate place of purification using some Old Testament passages to validate the concept of purgatory. They didn't officially define purgatory until the second council of Lyon in 1247. The understanding was that people who died in the grace of God but still needed purification for their temporal or venial sins could be purified before entering Heaven with prayers from loved ones and the clergy as intercession for those lost souls. This morphed into the historical abuses by the Church of selling indulgences to raise money and build ornate church buildings. Indulgences are the remission of the punishment for sins.

The practice of requesting money from people to keep their loved ones out of hell is one of the main factors that prompted Martin Luther, in 1517, to write his ninety-five theses against Church practices and theology. Today, most non-Catholic Christians do not believe in purgatory. The concept of purgatory seemed to develop because people were asking questions and seeking help. Answers were eventually given and became orthodox, even if they were not right.

ACIM on Christian Orthodoxy

There were many diverse Gospels, writings, and beliefs shortly after Jesus' death. Some were contradictory; hence they cannot all be true. There is some truth in most of the writings but usually not in the way that we understood. The orthodox Jesus is like a comparison between character and reputation. Character is how you carry yourself or how you behave and you can control that. You have little control over your reputation or what people think of you. Jesus taught and behaved a certain way, which was his character. Jesus' reputation is what people perceived about him and became orthodox Christianity. Jesus only taught love and what he said about the Kingdom of Heaven is inadequate and misunderstood. The early Church Fathers had to communicate Jesus' reputation and they understood it as a continuation of the sovereign Jewish God of punishment and sacrifice, which was not his character.

Jesus knew his life, death, resurrection, and teachings would be misunderstood by his followers, and incorrect views would become orthodox.

However, he wanted us to go inside and experience the wisdom of the Holy Spirit for all our questions. Jesus didn't worry about the world and taught us to not worry about the world but to seek first for the Kingdom of God. Switch over to the Holy Spirit's way of thinking and do not let differences in theology, Christian or otherwise, delay you. The Course says, "A universal theology is impossible but a universal experience is not only possible but necessary." (C-in.2:5) And the universal experience that the Course is aimed at is love.

18. Divinity of Jesus

The divinity of Jesus is confusing and had been debated throughout the early development of Christianity. Most Christians believe Jesus is divine, but how is he divine and when did he become divine? Jesus himself did not spend much time preaching that he was divine. Actually, most of the claims of divinity are in John's Gospel which was the last Gospel to be written in about 90CE. Some of the queries include: what the Jews think of Jesus, the different views of Jesus' divinity, what Jesus said about his divinity, what Paul said about Jesus' divinity, and the reasons why these matter.

The Jews had been looking for a Messiah for a long time and many of their writings in the Old Testament prophesied about the coming Messiah. Although Messiah or anointed one and divine are not exactly the same thing, the Jewish prophecies that predict the Messiah are used to verify Jesus as divine. A skeptic of the over three hundred prophecies that point to Jesus would say they either apply to thousands of people or are too vague to be specific to one person. Apologists say that even if Jesus fulfilled a handful of the prophecies, it would be an astronomical statistical improbability, indicating that it was a divine occurrence.

One of the problems with using these prophecies to point to the divinity of Jesus is that most Jews did not recognize Jesus as the Messiah. They knew the prophecies, heard the stories of his miracles, even heard him speak, even so, they rejected him as the Messiah. Moreover, the Gospel writers could have written Jesus into some of the prophecies since the Gospels were written decades after Jesus when it became harder to verify the accuracy of the reports. Having Jesus fulfill so many prophecies was a rational way to connect and legitimize the new religion of Christianity to the long-established and respected Jewish religion. In addition, the Jerusalem disciples thought Christianity would be a sect of Judaism, and the fulfiller of its prophecies should be the figurehead. The stories of Jesus' life were told orally before they were written down and that would give impassioned followers decades to make the story match the prophecies.

Jesus being born in Bethlehem is one prophecy from the Old Testament book of Micah 5:2, that some critics say is written to fulfill prophecy. Only Matthew and Luke said Jesus was born in Bethlehem and this helps to bolster the Messianic claim that Jesus was part of the Davidic line by being born in the city of David. Muddying the waters, Mark says Jesus is from Nazareth of Galilee and John says Jesus is from Galilee.

Some of the prophecies were accurate but some seem to be squeezed in to fit a narrative. Another prophecy is that Jesus is to be born from a virgin according to Isaiah 7:14, "Behold, the virgin shall conceive and bear a Son, and shall call His name Immanuel." Some scholars say the Old Testament written in Hebrew used the word Almah in this verse, which could mean a young woman, but the Greek translation uses Parthenos which does mean a virgin. The Gospel writers verified Jesus' divinity through his birth from a virgin to fulfill that prophecy. Joseph and probably Mary were dead when the first Gospel was written so there were no firsthand witnesses to verify if it was accurate.

A supernatural event like a virgin birth should have been widely known and foreshadowed something great. Everyone would have anticipated something wonderful from his birth until his ministry, yet no one knew about Jesus during that time. The first time that God acted to impregnate a human would be noteworthy at least for inclusion in the Old Testament. Virgin births are unusual although there are several ancient mythological exceptions. The translation of Isaiah from Hebrew to Greek is contested among scholars although several newer Bibles have replaced virgin with young woman.

Jesus' divinity is sometimes addressed by the term Christology. A low Christology views Jesus as starting out as a human and then becoming divine. A high Christology views Jesus as divine from a pre-existent realm and not human. The synoptic Gospels are categorized as low Christology because they do not promote the view of Jesus as God as much as John, who is regarded as high Christology. John specifically proclaims Jesus' divinity early and often. Why don't the three synoptic Gospels preach from the rooftops the divinity of Jesus when this might be the single biggest attribute about him?

The miracles throughout his life, along with the crown of divinity were a truly defining moniker. This is possibly because Jesus declaring that he is God or his followers repeating it was against Jewish law and could shorten his ministry since it was a death sentence. If Jesus was starting a Church, wouldn't the news that he is God be a great inducement for Jews and Gentiles to join his Church?

A corollary question that comes from the fact that the synoptic Gospels did not come out of the gate and announce Jesus as God from the beginning would be, when did he become God? John's Gospel says in the beginning was the word and the word was God, declaring Jesus as the word and divine from the beginning. Apologists say he was pre-existent as God, however some believe Jesus became divine at birth. Others think he was born as a man and became God either at his baptism, death, or resurrection. The thinking that he became God sometime when he was a man is called adoptionism. This might help us feel that we could relate to Jesus if he lived his life as only a man and suffered the same trials we go through, and then became divine.

Since Jesus' divinity was debated by the early Christians, the Church leaders had to come up with a doctrine that would be orthodox. At the Council of Nicaea in 325CE and Constantinople in 381CE, the Church defined Jesus' divinity as true God and true man. Further, the Godhead and their relationship with one another, as three persons in one, the Father, Son, and Holy Spirit. The Son, Jesus, was homoousios, defined as of the same being as the Father. Jesus was declared true God and true man, putting to rest the adoptionist's questions and splitting the Christology since he was both fully man and fully divine.

The Nicaean creed was written in part to head off the heretics who either professed low or high Christology. Even Paul seemed to be confused on when Jesus became divine. In Philippians 2:6, Paul said Jesus was equal with God but came in the likeness of man as a bondservant. In Romans 1:4, he said Jesus was declared to be the Son of God by the resurrection from the dead.

Diverse beliefs about Jesus' divinity in the early Church make sense because Jesus was vague about himself. The three main heretical factions of Christianity in the early days that caused great division and hostility were the Arians, Marcionites, and the Gnostics. Arius was a priest around 250CE who promoted the doctrine that Christ was subordinate to God the Father. He was opposed to the Nicene Creed that said God and Jesus were co-eternal. There was a wide following of Arianism which was deemed heretical by the orthodox Church and faded away.

Marcion was a Christian theologian who postulated, around 144CE, that the God of the Gospel who sent Jesus to save us was a good God and different from the God described in the Old Testament. It was estimated that the Marcionite Church was one of the largest sects of Christianity at that time. This doctrine was also deemed heretical and was stamped out by the Church.

Another sect was the Gnostics around the second century. Gnosticism was the belief in personal spiritual knowledge that was above and superior to the orthodox teachings and the authority of the Church. Gnostics separated existence into the material which was flawed or evil and the spiritual which was the good. This doctrine was also opposed by the Church and was suppressed. The reason this is important is because there were several competing views and only one became orthodox. But was it the right one, the most popular one, or the one influential leaders believed and promoted?

In the Gospels, Jesus did claim to be God, but most of the assumptions of divinity were from references to his divinity and the revelation of it from his actions and teaching. One of the clearest declarations of divinity is in John 10:30 when Jesus said, "I and My Father are one." Most of the other references were from the miracles he performed, showing unique wisdom, forgiving sins, being called by divine names, and saying he was the Christ to the High Priest. These references were not specific pronouncements of divinity, but pointed us in that direction. These works and declarations are interpreted differently by most people.

Jesus' Divinity Based on ACIM

Jesus is certainly divine according to *A Course in Miracles* because he is divine in his real form in Heaven. Coincidently, everyone is divine in our real life in Heaven with God, but we have forgotten it while we dream about the illusory world. Jesus was born a man and had to learn his lessons, just like us, and awaken to his divinity and home in Heaven as a part of God. We really don't understand what Heaven is, although the Course says it is the awareness of perfect oneness and we are all one with God in our reality as Spirit. Remember if God is perfect, He cannot create anything that is not perfect or not like Him. Therefore, we must be as divine as Jesus in Heaven.

Jesus' divinity did not make him special as the only begotten Son of God. He was only more advanced than us in understanding who we really are. Jesus' awareness of his divinity gave him a very strong connection to the Holy Spirit and allowed him to perform miracles and even reanimate his body after his death. Jesus said in John 14:12, "[...] the works that I do he will do also; and greater *works* than these he will do." Jesus is saying that if the miracles he did make him divine and we can also do miracles, then we can also remember our divinity.

Apologists who believe that Jesus and God are separate from us will say the works referenced in John are ordinary works such as righteous actions. But the Course is clear that miracles are natural and when they don't come through us, we are acting unnaturally.

Jesus was an advanced spiritual master and we will all get there someday. Most Christians believe miracles happen today even though Jesus is no longer walking the earth. Jesus figured it all out first and is in Spirit to help us to remember God, while directing miracles through us. Jesus was not sent to earth to be God as true God and true man in order to suffer and die for our sins and the salvation of the world. He, like the rest of us, had a thought different from God and he also found himself in the dream. He then listened exclusively to the Holy Spirit to wake up from the dream. As with almost everything in the Bible, the writers got some of it right and some they didn't understand. Jesus is divine, but not in time in his physical form as a man, rather in eternity, as Spirit. Jesus awakened to his divinity the same way we all will do, as part of God's will that no one shall perish, or rather no one will fail to wake up.

As mentioned, Jesus said, "I and My Father are one." This is a true statement regarding his life in Heaven as Spirit. Though Jesus also said in John 14:20, "At that day you will know that I *am* in My Father, and you in Me, and I in you." Jesus is saying that we don't recognize our own divinity now, but we will wake up to the fact that Jesus and all of us are one with God. That day is the one that is at hand although we are too attached to the world to see it.

The Course says that it is impossible to see two worlds. The two worlds are the real world of the Spirit, which includes your divinity, and the illusory world of form. You either see yourself as a mortal body or you relearn that you are a divine Spirit. However, you cannot see yourself as both.

19. Belief in Jesus Is Salvation

Christianity's salvation theology teaches that you are saved by grace through faith in Jesus. This belief comes mainly from Paul's letters and John's Gospels. The synoptic Gospels talk more about Jesus' life and teachings rather than how to get to Heaven. The Old Testament talks mainly about God's relationship with His Chosen People and their struggles to obey His Law. If salvation requires faith in Jesus, how are the Jews, other religions, agnostics, and even atheists getting into Heaven?

Not to leave the Jews out of salvation, Apologists say the Jews might be saved by their belief in the Messiah and devotion to God. However, the Jews did not and still do not recognize Jesus as the Messiah. If they did, they would be Christians. They're still waiting for their Messiah. It might also be said that their salvation is from devotion to God through righteousness by following the Mosaic Laws. Although Paul, a fervent Jew, said very forcefully that the Law will not save you. Additionally, the exclusivity of Christianity says that Jesus is the only way to salvation and any other belief will not work. This includes most everyone in ancient civilizations who may have believed in other gods. The exclusivity of most religions say that because we are right, everyone else must be wrong, therefore everyone believes that they are right. Some Apologists say your response to the light (God or goodness) is sufficient for salvation. Others say believing in God's general revelation of himself in nature could warrant passage into Heaven. What is the way to be saved and if there is only one way, is everyone else damned?

What does the New Testament say about salvation so that we can get a clear picture and specific instructions on how to get to Heaven? The New Testament uses different words that might mean salvation, such as Heaven, God's Kingdom, everlasting or eternal life, redemption, atonement, adoption, justification, righteousness, or remission of sins. Along with the orthodox version of grace through faith in Jesus Christ, below are several verses from

St. Paul that could be viewed as different from faith in Jesus. The Gospels also seem to have different criteria for salvation, and, of course, there can be multiple interpretations. I have only provided the verse or a part of the verse, so please read the entire passage to understand the context and meaning.

- Ephesians 1:4–5, "[...] just as He chose us in Him before the foundation of the world, that we should be holy and without blame before Him in love, having predestined us to adoption as sons by Jesus Christ to Himself, according to the good pleasure of His will." Does this mean that only those who are chosen by God before the world was formed can be saved or adopted into the family of Christ? Are we chosen based on predestination according to the pleasure of God's will?

- 2 Thessalonians 2:13, "[...] because God from the beginning chose you for salvation through sanctification by the Spirit and belief in the truth." Again, are the saved ones chosen by God before creation?

- Romans 2:6–7, "[...] who *will render to each one according to his deeds:* eternal life to those who by patient continuance in doing good seek for glory, honor, and immortality." And Romans 2:13, "[...] for not the hearers of the law are just in the sight of God, but the doers of the law will be justified." Is Paul saying that good deeds and doing the Law will save you?

- Romans 10:13, Paul quotes the Old Testament when he says, "For *whoever calls on the name of the Lord shall be saved.*" The Lord in the Old Testament was God. Is calling out to God the path to salvation?

- James diminishes salvation by faith alone, when he says in James 2:14, "What *does it* profit, my brethren, if someone says he has faith but does not have works? Can faith save him?" Does James question if faith is enough by saying you need faith and works? Apologists argue that James is saying that you need to prove your faith with works.

All four Gospels talk about salvation in different ways yet John's gave voice to Jesus' role in salvation. His is the traditional Christian theology that through the death and resurrection of Jesus, sinful humans can be reconciled with God and can therefore be offered eternal life. Here are some Gospel verses on salvation.

- John 3:3 and 3:5 says that unless you are born again and born of water and the Spirit, you cannot enter the Kingdom of Heaven. Being born again is another term that is subject to interpretation, but is being born again a requirement for entry into Heaven? Many people are born again by recommitting their lives to Jesus when they're of age. What Jesus actually means is that we must remember our spiritual selves and connect to the Holy Spirit even though we think we are bodies in the world.

- John 6:47, "Most assuredly, I say to you, he who believes in Me has everlasting life." This is similar to the famous John 3:16, and these verses are the foundation of orthodox Christianity.

- John 5:24, "[...] he who hears My word and believes in Him who sent Me has everlasting life." Does this mean that the Jews and all other religions who believe in God and honor Jesus can be saved?

- John 6:44, "No one can come to Me unless the Father who sent Me draws him." Does this support God's Chosen People and only God's new chosen will be saved?

- John 8:51, "Most assuredly, I say to you, if anyone keeps My word, he shall never see death." Is Jesus' word the two great Commandments of love God and love your neighbor? This is different from believing in Jesus, as most religions teach love. Can you follow these two Commandments and not believe in the death and resurrection of Jesus and still be saved?

- In Matthew 5:3–10, the Sermon on the Mount, Jesus teaches the famous beatitudes and describes some of the blessed and what their reward would be, which is salvation or a place in Heaven. The first group is the poor in Spirit, "Blessed are the poor in spirit, For theirs is the kingdom of heaven." You would think someone on their way to Heaven would be full of the Spirit. Would the poor in Spirit even believe in Jesus? Jesus is actually saying that those who recognize their own spiritual poverty will seek the Kingdom of Heaven and those who seek will find. Similar to little children who are poor in understanding but willing to ask, learn, and ultimately accept the truth.

- Matthew 5:8, "Blessed are the pure in heart, For they shall see God." If you are pure in heart, does that mean you are a good person, and will that get you to Heaven? Jesus used heart and mind interchangeably so pure in heart meant pure in thought as Jesus rarely said anything about behavior.

- Matthew 5:10, "Blessed are those who are persecuted for righteousness' sake, For theirs is the kingdom of heaven." Do you need to be righteous and be persecuted? These beatitudes seem to describe what you can do to get to Heaven but do not include belief in Jesus or belief in his death and resurrection.

- In Matthew 7:21, Jesus says, "Not everyone who says to Me, 'Lord, Lord,' shall enter the kingdom of heaven, but he who does the will of My Father in heaven." Is it doing the will of the Father that gets you to Heaven? What is the will of the Father? Is it the Ten Commandments, the 613 Mosaic Laws, worshipping God, loving our neighbor, believing in the sacrifice of His only begotten Son, or being righteous? In Romans 12:1–2, Paul says what he thinks is the will of the Father. "[…] that you present your bodies a living sacrifice, holy…And do not be conformed to this world, but be transformed by the renewing of your mind, that you may prove what is that good and acceptable and perfect will of God." By purifying both body and mind, will you be doing the will of God?

- Matthew 10:22 says that if you are hated and persecuted in Jesus' name and endure to the end, you will be saved.

- Matthew 13:43, Jesus explains the parable of the tares of the field and says the Son of Man will send out his angels and they will split the righteous and the unrighteous. The unrighteous are cast into hell, and the ones that are left are the righteous and will shine forth as the sun in the Kingdom of their Father. What do you need to do to be righteous? In Judaism, it was following the Old Testament laws. Does being a good person toward your fellow man make you righteous?

- In the parable of the Sheep and Goats, Jesus again splits humanity into the blessed which will inherit the Kingdom and the cursed who will go away into everlasting punishment. To inherit the Kingdom you must feed the hungry, give drink to the thirsty, take in the stranger, clothe the naked, visit the sick and prisoner. Conversely, not doing these things grants us everlasting punishment. Belief in Jesus is nowhere to be found in this parable of salvation's requirements.

- In Luke 10:25–28, Jesus is asked by a lawyer what shall I do to inherit eternal life. The lawyer's answer is the two great Commandments: love God with all your heart, soul, strength, and mind and love your neighbor as yourself. Jesus says, "You have answered rightly; do this and you will live." There is no mention by Jesus of believing in himself, only loving God and neighbor. Conversely, if belief in Jesus is salvation, what is the reason to love your neighbor?

Whether it is belief in Jesus or the other ways previously pointed out to get to Heaven, does it work? We don't know because no one other than Jesus has come back to tell us. I would like to do a mind experiment to see if the biblical claims of belief in Jesus are salvation. Let us imagine that we have died and are standing in front of the pearly gates with St. Peter. We are very excited to make the transition to Heaven and ask Peter what it's like. He says Heaven is the dwelling place of God and as such is absolute love, peace, and joy. In a word, it is perfect. Then Peter asks if we are worthy to enter Heaven. We tell him that we believe in and have faith in Jesus, that he was sent by God to suffer and die for our sins and that he rose on the third day.

We also tell him we tried to be a good Christian by going to Church, doing our best to keep the Ten Commandments, and by loving God and our neighbor the best we could. Peter asks if we are perfect love, perfect peace, and perfect joy because that is what Heaven is. We say we weren't exactly perfect on earth but that Jesus died for the forgiveness of our sins. Peter says, yes your sins are forgiven, but if you are not perfect and Heaven is perfect, how can you fit in? Peter then asks if we harbor any judgment, anger, envy, despair, or hate? Have you relinquished these and other negative attributes? If you are not perfect and I let you in, then Heaven would not be perfect because of you. In essence, you will taint Heaven.

We ask about purgatory and whether people can pray for us so that we become purified. No he says, you have to do your own work on earth as Jesus did and grow in perfection. We say that if we are forgiven and believe, we are supposed to become glorified bodies and purified souls to fit in. Peter counters that God gave you free will and cannot violate that and change you into something that you are not. We say that God's grace is sufficient and Peter would say yes, God sent the Holy Spirit into the dream to help and that is His grace. Since you decided to dream, you must decide to awaken.

We argue that the Bible says Jesus died so that we may have eternal life. Peter would respond lovingly that Jesus lived and died as an example of perfect love, peace, and forgiveness. Jesus said follow me, meaning his example. Jesus said I am the way, the truth, and the life, and wants you to become like him. Jesus died not to be worshipped but as an example to teach you the reality of your immoral Spirit and the unreality of the body and the world. When he said he overcame the world, he meant that you too need to overcome the world and become one with Spirit. You misunderstood because you are too attached to the world of form and the body. Peter sees your deflation and tells you not to worry because God wills that none should perish and God's will is almighty and cannot be thwarted. God's will is done in Heaven and on earth!

Now you are going back and you will carry on in the dream until you learn your lessons of love, peace, and forgiveness. We exclaim that Christians don't believe in reincarnation. Peter smiles and asks you who wrote Hebrews and how did he know that it was appointed for men to die once in the dream? Early Christians and many other religions believe in it, who decided it wasn't real? As we fade back into the world of form, we cry out, what do I need to do to become perfect? Peter tells you to ask the Holy Spirit for help to forgive everyone for everything and then only love and peace will be left in you. It will take many lifetimes and will not be easy, but I know you will do it because God's will is done.

With the many verses that try to describe the path to salvation, there are also several verses that try to describe how to avoid hell. There are several terms that might describe the opposite of Heaven such as hell, perish, everlasting fire, outer darkness, and weeping and gnashing of teeth.

Matthew 5:29–30 indicates that you can use your body parts to cause you to sin. Therefore, it's better to remove them so your whole body is not cast into hell. This sounds much more like the Old Testament laws against the body than grace through faith in Jesus.

Matthew 13:41, "The Son of Man will send out His angels, and they will gather out of His kingdom all the things that offend, and those who practice lawlessness, and will cast them into the furnace of fire. There will be wailing and gnashing of teeth." What offends who, and is it the Mosaic Laws that need to be followed? Later in Matthew 13:49, Jesus again is reported as saying, "So it will be at the end of the age. The angels will come forth, separate the wicked from among the just, and cast them into the furnace of fire." This passage is adding the wicked along with the offenders and the lawless as being at risk for the fires of hell. Is entrance into Heaven based on being just or to believe in Jesus?

Matthew 22:1–13, Jesus explains that the Kingdom of Heaven is like a king arranging a wedding. One of the guests did not wear a wedding garment and on the king's command was bound and cast into the outer darkness. There are many interpretations of the guest and his attire but it is clear that if you are not prepared, you will not be able to attend the feast. What Jesus was really conveying in this parable is similar to the Heaven mind experiment discussed earlier. You have to be compatible with Heaven to enter Heaven. The right standing cannot be belief in Jesus as the wedding guest truly believed in the marriage, the king, and the feast. It is in purifying yourself through your forgiveness work to be pure in heart (thought) so that you can fit into the circumstances of the feast (Heaven).

Matthew 25:14–30, a servant did not invest his master's money, and he was cast into the outer darkness. The servant who did not invest his master's talent is unprofitable, meaning he is not ready for Heaven because he did not do the work necessary to get to Heaven. You must practice forgiveness to become love and peace and then you will fit in as a perfect child of God.

Mark 10:23, Jesus remarks how hard it is for a rich man to enter the Kingdom of Heaven. This has nothing to do with material wealth, as God promised several Old Testament figures wealth. What this means is those who are rich are usually comfortable in the world and focus their attention on making and keeping their fortunes. They do not have the time or the need to seek the Kingdom of God. What you put your attention on, there your treasure lies. You are in the world so worldly possessions are okay, although your main concern should be purifying your mind through love and forgiveness to fit into Heaven.

Luke 13:5, "[…] but unless you repent you will all likewise perish." The typical Jewish and Christian understanding of repent is to feel sorry for your sins and turn away from them. Jesus is saying to change your mind about what and who you are. Your behavior will follow and is secondary.

Luke 13:27, "But He will say, I tell you I do not know you, where you are from. Depart from Me, all you workers of iniquity. There will be weeping and gnashing of teeth." The first prominent thing to note is that Jesus says you will not get into Heaven if he or God does not know you. This is partly true because if you don't seek first the Kingdom and think with the Holy Spirit, you will not know who you are. Secondly, does this passage say that a worker of iniquity will not get into Heaven even if you believe in Jesus? Is Jesus saying he is not there for us if we are sinners?

You might ask why is it that being good isn't enough to get you into Heaven. The answer lies with the example of St. Peter at the gates. Heaven is the awareness of perfect oneness. To be one with God, you need to be like God, who is perfect love, peace, and joy. We can only do this on earth by turning our minds over to the Holy Spirit. When we think like Him, we will become love and one with our brothers and God and then fit into Heaven once again. Being good is a byproduct of right thinking with the Holy Spirit, and then you can enter His dwelling place.

ACIM's Insight into Salvation

As you can see from the above examples, there are many verses about different ways to go and not go to Heaven. The ancients didn't think much about Heaven, they just wanted help in getting by day to day. Today we have more leisure time and freedom to consider our eternal destiny. This is one of the reasons *A Course in Miracles* was written recently. According to the Course, salvation is a promise made by God that you would find your way home. Salvation is the atonement or undoing of the thought of separation from God.

In essence, salvation is thinking you are not separate from God, rather one with Him. Salvation is simply remembering God and thinking with the Holy Spirit to become aware of our perfection in Heaven. Salvation does nothing, it just undoes the erroneous thought we had of what it would be like to be different from God. Salvation is only a recognition and not a change, except in our mistaken thoughts. Those mistaken thoughts created the universe of time and space. The Course says the thought of separation from God is the only lack we need to correct. There is no sin, guilt, or fear; there is only a thought we have that we can be different from our creator. The manifestations from that thought are not real because only God is real and we are part of God dreaming that we are not.

Salvation in Christianity is getting to Heaven. Salvation in the Course is remembering we are in Heaven. Accepting the thought that you are the way God created you as perfect Spirit, is Heaven. You are saved when you think the same thoughts as the Holy Spirit.

20. Jesus' Teachings and Message

Jesus was a teacher and his message is the most read story in history, but there are continuous debates over the meaning of his teachings and message. The first point to make is that many Apologists say you need to understand first-century Palestine to understand Jesus' message. I would say you need to understand first-century Palestine to understand Jesus' language and what the Apostles and early writers thought Jesus' teachings meant. Jesus' message, if from God, would be timeless and universal. God's plan for salvation of the world could not be relevant only to a certain time period and to a certain people. The message of salvation must be true for all people at all times and in all circumstances.

Over time, the understanding of language is lost. That is why Jesus taught in parables to give the simplest explanation of his teachings that would be timeless. The Old Testament laws are not followed by Christians because they are said to be for a specific people in a specific time. Therefore, they cannot be from an eternal God. The Jews strove to keep the Law for thousands of years just to have Paul say the Law is to no avail. If the laws of God are null and void for Christians, could that happen to Jesus' teachings? Could Jesus' teachings change at the Second Coming?

The interpretation of Jesus' message is what is important and confusing. The parables Jesus used are indeed timeless stories that will hold up for eternity. The problem is they're often misunderstood because they do not convey a direct and concise message that some of us need for understanding. The central and unifying theme of Jesus' ministry is the promise of the Kingdom of God or Heaven. Jesus taught several parables about the Kingdom; that it was like a man who cast seed, a treasure hidden in a field, a mustard seed, leaven, ten virgins, a king who gave a wedding, and a labor-hiring landowner.

All of these parables paint a picture of what Heaven might be like, but they don't tell us what Heaven is in a way we can understand. The parable leaves the specifics up to different interpretations. Jesus' parables seem to describe how valuable Heaven is, to be prepared for it, and focus on it, although they do not describe it. The parables point us to the truth with just enough information for us to be curious but not enough to be comprehensive. One of the reasons Jesus did this is he intended for us to go inside and seek the council of the Holy Spirit.

Jesus also referenced the Kingdom in vague and hard to understand terms, including the Kingdom of Heaven is within You, In my Father's house there are many mansions, Heaven and earth will pass away, and You must be born again. Jesus knew we would not understand and possibly reject his characterizations because we were so steeped in our understanding of our religion and fixated on the world of form. The biblical writers gave Heaven limited earthly characteristics because that's all they knew. This is similar to the way we think we know about God. The description we use to claim ownership of our God is not the described.

The Course describes Heaven this way: "Heaven is not a place nor a condition. It is merely an awareness of perfect oneness, and the knowledge that there is nothing else; nothing outside this oneness, and nothing else within." (T-18.VI.1:5–6) Jesus did not use this description while on earth; possibly because you need to teach at the level of the learner and the beginning student is not ready for a mystic answer.

In analyzing what timeless teachings Jesus would have certainly taught, we have to look at his two great Commandments. They are found in Matthew, Mark, and Luke and the first one is, You shall love the Lord your God with all your heart, with all your soul, and with all your mind. If this is the first and greatest Commandment, then we are asked by Jesus to love God above all else. If you remember the circle exercise in chapter eight, it showed that in the circle is everything and Jesus wants us to fill it with love. However, the Bible describes a God of fear which is opposite of love. I believe Jesus taught and believed his Commandment while teaching and experiencing the God of love and knew that God cannot be the author of fear. Jesus, through his growing relationship with the Holy Spirit, was subtly repudiating the Old Testament version of God. If we are to love God with our all, then God must be love and anything that is not loving said about God in the Bible cannot be true. The two ways of interacting and having a relationship with God, one out of love and one out of fear are contradictory.

The second great Commandment is to love your neighbor as yourself. Total love is again the singular requirement and it fits into the same circle with God. If the circle is full of love for God and your neighbor, there is no room for fear, hate, anger, envy or any other negative sentiment. That is what Jesus meant when he said to be perfect as your Father in Heaven is perfect. He didn't mean acting perfectly, he meant loving perfectly or the best you can. By practicing forgiveness, you remove all of the negative emotions that get in the way of perfect love. Although the Bible has numerous places that implore us to love one another, it also has verses about hating, judging, and destroying each other.

As mentioned, Jesus used the Scriptures to teach, but did not teach the whole of Scripture. How could he teach Old Testament laws that commanded you to stone your brother if his great Commandment was to love your brother? Jesus taught that you would know them by their fruits. Accordingly, all actions stem from our thoughts, either loving or not loving. Jesus practiced the two great Commandments showing his love through the fruits of his words and deeds.

Another compelling message that was a veiled teaching of Jesus was how many times he said that his Father was in Heaven. Christianity's most well-known prayer, the Lord's Prayer or Our Father, starts off with Our Father Who Art in Heaven. In Matthew, Jesus says his Father is in Heaven fourteen times, specifically saying, "My Father who is in Heaven." In John 20:17, Jesus says he has not ascended to his Father yet. If God is everywhere in the universe, why would Jesus say that his Father was in Heaven? Why would he say he was going somewhere else to be with the Father? This is significant because Jesus could not always come out and say what was true as it would put himself and his followers in danger. This is similar to Peter who denied knowing Jesus three times because he thought he would be crucified right along with Jesus.

Most Christians would say that God is everywhere, but we also want to go to Heaven when we die. Jesus was subtly confirming that God is in Heaven and not part of this world because it is a dream and not real. There are not two places, Heaven and earth, there is only Heaven and earth is a dream we are reviewing while in Heaven.

Another interesting thing is that in about half of the references by Jesus to God, he says our Father or your Father and the other half he says my Father.

He knew we are all children of God just as he is, no different except in understanding. Jesus reiterates this when he says the old Jewish prayer, O Israel, the Lord our God, the Lord is one. Furthermore, in John 14:20, Jesus says, "At that day you will know that I am in My Father, and you in Me, and I in you." Jesus was teaching that we are all one with the Father which was blasphemous and punishable by death. How can God be in Heaven and yet we are all one? The answer is only if we are Spirits in Heaven with God now.

Jesus' main teachings of love, peace, and forgiveness have had a huge impact on humanity. He is not the only one throughout history who has taught these moral teachings, but he is definitely the most famous one who lived them during his life, even unto death. Recently there was a movement to try to exemplify Jesus with the phrase, *What Would Jesus Do*. The movement to use Jesus' teachings in everyday life was so relatable that bracelets were made with WWJD emblazoned on them. This was a great image for people trying to get clear on their actions and reactions in all situations. The problem is we think we know what Jesus did and would do based on the Gospels.

Unfortunately, the Gospels sometimes portray Jesus as judging, condemning, preaching punishment, and performing acts out of sacrifice rather than love. These verses are contradictory to the passages about love, peace, and forgiveness and could not have been taught by the same teacher. Because we don't have a comprehensive list of Jesus' actions in all situations, a better phrase might be *Jesus What Should I Do,* or JHMD, *Jesus Help Me Decide*. Jesus said ask and we shall receive, and he would send the Holy Spirit to help us. He didn't mean we would receive physical gifts, he meant guidance from the Holy Spirit. Therefore, in any situation we should call on the Holy Spirit or Jesus, who knows everything from the beginning of time till the end of time, and He will have the answers that are best for everyone.

The next time you don't know what to do or have an important decision to make, employ JHMD. What would Jesus, the prince of peace, do? The answer is always to love and forgive. Instead of trying to do all the thinking and decision making on your own, ask Jesus. Follow Jesus' habit of relying on the Holy Spirit. Ask for divine guidance ahead of time, instead of praying that your own naïve decisions are fulfilled.

Jesus saw the face of Christ in all people. Every single human, without exception, was his brother in Christ. This is the message Jesus would have us learn to be like him, to overcome the world and return to our home with God.

Mother Teresa was a modern-day saint. She lived her life with the belief that when she encountered anyone, she simply saw them as Jesus in all of his distressing disguises. *A Course in Miracles* was not available to Mother Teresa, but she knew that forgiveness led to love. She said, "If we really want to love, we must learn to forgive." This would be the way we could all live if we, in fact, recognized everyone as brothers.

There is a story about Mother Teresa's theology when she came to the U.S. to raise money for her Calcutta mission. She was at a radio station and the host was imploring her to tell him what he could do to help her. She finally said that he should get up at four A.M., go out onto the city streets, find someone living there who thinks he is alone, and convince him that he is not! She understood the oneness of Heaven in an earthly way and that was her very practical way to live the message of Jesus.

ACIM's Teaching and Message by Jesus

Jesus, as a man, could completely detach from his ego mind and connect his mind to the Holy Spirit. He knew the world of form as dualistic and the real world of Heaven as non-dualistic. A dualistic concept of the world is where you have at least two of everything. You have Heaven and earth, right and wrong, good and bad, happy and sad, black and white, male and female, God and us, etc. This is the world we think we know and live in, and that thought keeps us separate from God who is pure oneness. The real world of Heaven is non-dualistic, meaning there is only one and that one is God.

Since the real world of Heaven is non-dualistic, or one, then we must be part of God because that is all there is. This is what Jesus meant when he said, I am in my Father, and you in Me, and I in you. Jesus meant there is only one, acting as many in the world. Jesus knew there was only God and that we were part of God in Heaven so there could not be anything else but God and His love. He realized that he had to awaken from the dream of duality to his home of non-duality.

In the Gospels, Jesus said the end is near although he did not mean his Second Coming to rule the world. The end is the disappearance of the dream world caused by everyone waking up. Jesus' role was to help speed up the process by teaching the truth with his ultimate example of crucifixion and resurrection. Teaching and displaying love and forgiveness, along with proving the unreality of the world, were his contributions to the salvation of mankind. The value of all teaching is in its usefulness. If it helps you to love now, then it is good. The end is near because we can all make the decision to love now and return home, it just takes willingness to be open to the truth. The Kingdom of Heaven is within you was a literal message, and Jesus' central teaching that we are all really Spirit. It's up to us, with the help of the Holy Spirit, to decide when we realize and accept our oneness.

21. Jesus' Life, Death, and Resurrection

Jesus was without doubt the most influential person to ever live and more books have probably been written about him than any other subject. It's agreed by most historians that Jesus was a real person and most of the historical facts about Jesus in the Bible are accurate. However there are many questions about the meaning and reason for his life, death, and resurrection. The problem is the historical facts about the man Jesus can be validated by historical analysis but why he came, died, and rose are not provable and are subject to faith and interpretation. How do we know if the Gospel stories about the reasons for Jesus' life, death, and resurrection are accurate and were not embellished during the oral tradition? The reason given by Christianity of why he had to die and rise generates many questions and has me asking if there is another explanation.

People started putting stories about Jesus on paper in the decades following his death with the first Gospel written about 70CE. The twenty-seven canonical books in the New Testament became official in about 363CE. Coincidentally, there are many more than twenty-seven books, letters, and writings that were candidates for the canon. Some of the early Gospels about Jesus that we know of but were not put in the Bible are: The Infancy Gospel of James, Infancy Gospel of Thomas, Gospel of Pseudo Matthew, Gospel of Thomas, Gospel of Peter, Gospel of Nicodemus, Gospel of Bartholomew, Gospel of Judas, Gospel of Mary, Gospel of Philip, Gospel of Marcion, Dialogue of the Savior, Coptic Apocalypse of Paul, Gospel of Truth, and Apocryphon of John.

There were numerous Acts of (name a famous disciple) and numerous letters or epistles of (name a famous disciple). Historians believe most of these writings were written late and do not add to the understanding of the historical Jesus. If they were written after the disciple's death and have the name of a close companion of Jesus, then someone may have forged the writings wanting them to be authoritative. Some of the writings had outlandish claims but were written about Jesus and named after a famous disciple.

Throughout history, some of these writings were lost and then found, and several were discovered in the Nag Hammadi Library in 1945. Given what we know about the competition to have the one true meaning of Jesus, you can bet that many more writings were destroyed than have survived. It was so pervasive to have writings that could not be verified and were thought to be forgeries that Church leaders wrote against these writings. Remember Bishop Irenaeus, dubbed the heresy hunter, who wrote the five-volume work entitled *Against Heresies*, which named about eighty different Christian sects he thought were heretical.

There were many reasons for someone to write something and falsely attribute it to someone famous, but the practice seemed to be tolerated or uncontrollable. There were not many ways to detect who wrote what, especially after they died. An example is the fourteen letters of St. Paul that most biblical scholars agree that only seven are from Paul and the rest were written in his name.

A Gospel that was recently discovered, written by an anonymous author but attributed to the Apostle Simon Peter is The Gospel of Peter. Biblical scholars have determined that it is pseudepigraphic, meaning it has the name of an author who did not write the work. It was written sometime in the second century, is mainly about the passion narrative, and has many of the same themes as the synoptic Gospels. It also sounds a lot like the letter to the Hebrews. Some of the early Church Fathers have referenced the Gospel of Peter although it is not considered canonical.

Peter gives a detailed account of the passion narrative including the unreality of Jesus' body and doubts about his physical suffering. It may not be viewed as Scripture because the writer describes Jesus' tomb scene with three men coming out of the tomb with the head of two reaching into Heaven and the third's head reaching beyond the heavens. If Peter wrote this, it totally changes or contradicts the way we see and understand Jesus. Without the story of the giant angels, this story may well have made it into the Bible.

Another interesting point about the relevance of this alleged Gospel is if Jesus was God and knew everything God knew, especially that he would be resurrected after three days to return to the Father in Heaven, he would not have suffered mentally as much as someone who had no hope in the afterlife and mentally and emotionally suffered from fear and abandonment. Many martyrs died with a smile on their face or at least in the contentment that they were dying for a cause. The Gospel of Peter seems to say that Jesus did not suffer physical pain, and if he was an advanced master who could perform miracles and knew the body was an illusion, maybe he didn't.

There are many interpretations as to why Jesus needed to die and rise. Commonly accepted reasons include: the resurrection means that Jesus was able to remove sin and its consequences that all will die, Jesus' sacrifice puts us in right standing with God and there is hope, and it proves Jesus was divine. Along with the meaning of the resurrection, the actual mechanics of it have to be interpreted. Some believe Jesus' Spirit was resurrected and lives in Heaven with God. Others believe Jesus' body and Spirit were resurrected similar to the assumption, or how it will be at the Second Coming.

If the death and resurrection of Jesus was part of the grand plan by God for salvation, then neither the Jews nor Romans could be held at fault because they had to play their part in the plan. Jesus did forgive both groups so whether they were part of the plan or not, he knew forgiveness was the way home. Why did Jesus have to die and rise to save us? Couldn't an Almighty God devise another way to redeem us, rather than have His Son tortured and killed? Jesus continually preached about the Kingdom of God which was clearly not here on earth as he preached, seek first the Kingdom of God. He also said he overcame the world. Could it be that Jesus' death and resurrection was our lesson on overcoming the world for our own salvation? Not to die to sin but to die to our attachment to the world of form or the separation from God.

It's written in the Bible that Jesus' death is a sacrifice for our sins because God needed a sacrifice to atone for our sins. Remember Jesus said I desire mercy and not sacrifice. The willful sacrifice of his life was to put us into right standing with God so we could be saved, as it indicates in the Scriptures that all salvation comes from Jesus. You can look at it as God was having mercy on us through the sacrifice of Jesus.

But, you can also say, as some skeptics do, that God sacrificed God to God to satisfy the requirements of God. God required sacrifices from the Jews throughout their relationship with Him and now Jesus is brought to earth as the sacrificial lamb. God, being Omnipotent and omnibenevolent, could have offered a non-sacrificial and loving way to get our attention instead of attack and death. This is displayed by Jesus when he said that with God, all things are possible. God can do what He wants, but a God of sacrifice and a God of mercy are two opposing beings.

Aside from the historical facts, there are many things about Jesus' life that do not make sense. In the Gospel stories, Jesus came into Jerusalem for the Passover and the people praised him by singing Hosanna, blessed is he who comes in the name of the Lord. Jesus was generally very popular with the common folk because they knew his miracles and thought he was a holy man. When the chief priests turned Jesus over to Pilate and he found no wrong and wanted to release Jesus, the crowds cheered for Pilate to release a common criminal, Barabbas.

First, there is no record of the governor granting the release of a prisoner for another prisoner. Pilate was an uncompromising tyrant who didn't really care about the Jews except that they feared him. He was so egregious toward his subjects that during his governorship, the people of Jerusalem lodged a formal complaint against him with the Roman Emperor. Historians have also said that up to 30,000 Jews were crucified by the Romans in the time around Jesus. Second, Barabbas was a murderer and under Jewish law should be killed.

Third, were the same people who were praising Jesus when he came into Jerusalem, cheering for him to be killed a few days later? The chief priests charged Jesus with blaspheming God, but the crowds did not hear Jesus blaspheme. Supposedly, every person knew about the worldwide census but everyone did not know about a man who John said did so many miraculous things that even the world itself could not contain the books that would be written.

Another interesting observation in the life of Jesus is how he spent his time on earth. The New Testament authors put their own understanding of Jesus into their writing, exemplified by John, Peter, and Paul saying that Jesus lived a sinless life. Since we only know about the last three years of Jesus' life, how did they know Jesus was sinless? How did they know he was sinless when some sin is not exhibited outwardly but are sins of the heart? Did turning over the money changers' tables with apparent anger not count as a sin even if it was for noble purposes? Did they only assume Jesus was sinless because they believed he was the only begotten Son of God and was divine?

Luke said that Jesus grew in wisdom, stature, and favor with God. Could this mean Jesus worked toward enlightenment or salvation by the power of his mind by seeking the Kingdom first over all other things including his family, friends, religion, and even the world? Jesus' sinlessness is only important because we think that we are sinners and could never be like Jesus. If Jesus was just a man and grew in knowledge and holiness, then there is hope for us. Ultimately we are all sinners in time, but not in eternity.

If God created the world and declared it good, then why didn't Jesus return the world back to the way God originally created it? If Jesus can forgive our sins to get us into Heaven, then why can't he make us perfect here? Why wasn't Jesus a social justice warrior; correcting wrongs, restoring the poor and outcasts to equality with others, making lives good for those who love God, elevating the lowly, and reducing the mighty? He said some of it would be done later, but why not now in God's good creation? God seemed to be active in the Old Testament, but Jesus was divine and living as flesh and blood among his people.

Jesus could be measured as a failure in helping the people he resided with. Jesus never criticized the Romans who were killing his fellow Jews, God's own Chosen People. He didn't open any schools, establish any orphanages, build any hospitals, start community projects, or become a philanthropist. The Church today does all of these things and is often focused on fixing the world and taking care of their fellow man, yet Jesus didn't do any of those things. Jesus didn't really start the Christian religion; it was started in his name after his death. The answer to why Jesus didn't try to fix the world is because the world is an illusion and needs to be overcome by awakening from the dream that contains the world. The world is only an effect of our thoughts and once we stop thinking that it is real, it will disappear. There is nothing wrong with doing good in the world but the real good is recognizing your guiltless brother and helping everyone to awaken together.

The writers of the New Testament had the difficult task of making sense of Jesus' life, death, and resurrection. Being steeped in Judaism, they worked it out that since Jesus was a holy man from God, killed by God's own Chosen People, he must have been sent by God in a plot twist to save all people. The early Church Fathers fervently worked to put Jesus in the grand plan as the Jewish anointed, then elevated him to the savior of the world. Stories about Jesus that fulfilled Scripture were one way they cemented his role. Their understanding was that Jesus was special and the only begotten Son of God.

They had never seen anyone who lived his life in complete love and forgiveness.

It's so hard for us to believe that we can be like Jesus in unconditional love, true forgiveness, and total peace; as a result, we think he is alien to normal humans. Looking at Jesus' attributes of love, peace, and forgiveness, it doesn't mean he wasn't kind, caring, patient, happy, empathetic, etc. It means that all positive attributes start with love and peace.

ACIM's Interpretation of Jesus' Life, Death, and Resurrection

Jesus was born a man, but through his many incarnations similar to ours, was the first to realize and internalize the fact that his life was an illusion and his real life was in Heaven with God. Did Jesus sin while on earth? The answer doesn't matter because sin is not real. If you kill someone on stage in a play, does that matter when the play is over? In the Gospels when Jesus said your sins are forgiven, he was not saying it because he was the only one who could forgive sins. He knew there was no sin and nothing could harm the children of God.

If Heaven is the only reality, then hurting someone and sinning in the dream doesn't matter because it's all an illusion. Even though Jesus did not believe in sin, he forgave them because the Jews believed in sin and you must teach at the level and understanding of the pupils. Jesus forgiving sins was just reminding the person's mind that they were innocent in the eyes of God. Forgiving sin and healing the body are the same because they're both illusions. Jesus being born as a Jew in first century Palestine is not significant; it's where he was and it allowed him to teach those particular lessons with that life and death.

I've often wondered why Jesus was not more specific and comprehensive with his teachings. I can only answer that question with what he says in the Course about why it took two thousand years for Jesus to give the Course. The answer is that we were not ready for it any sooner than when it came. We have a much more open culture and can handle new ideas better than in the past. The people at that time and up until the present day were not ready for his complete message. Many reading this are not ready, and that's okay because the exposure might be a step in your journey.

Since this is all an illusion and we are at home in God's loving grasp dreaming that we are here, the timing of the message doesn't really matter. If Jesus was too engaged in our earthly plight, then it would be as if he thought the world and our suffering were real, and he knew it wasn't. You teach by the way you act, therefore if you know the world and all the people in it are not real, you don't get upset about their situation.

The Holy Spirit guided Jesus on what to teach and guides us on what to learn. Using our free will, we decide when to listen. It takes willingness on our part and some time to hear His voice. We typically think that Jesus is special because he rose from the dead, but his lesson is that death is not real, and life is only in Heaven.

22. Jesus' Miracles

The subject of Jesus' miracles has fascinated people for thousands of years. Most of the faithful would agree that Jesus performed miracles during his ministry. There remain many questions about the execution of the miracles. Where did Jesus get the power to perform miracles? Why didn't Jesus perform more miracles? Why couldn't Jesus do mighty works in his hometown? Why did Jesus say that everyone could perform miracles although we can't perform them at will?

Where did Jesus get the power to perform miracles? Was it because he was true God even though he was true man while on earth? Was he just being used as an instrument of God? Was it because Jesus was connected to God even though he was a man? If we go with the supposition that Jesus could perform miracles because he was God, then how did the Apostles and people not related to the followers of Jesus perform miracles? People had been performing miracles in the Old Testament days. People believe that miracles happen today, so how do ordinary people perform them? Since Jesus said we can all do miracles, the answer cannot be that only Jesus could do them because he was God.

Jesus' declaration that everyone can perform miracles rules out him having a special gift for performing them. The Apostles eventually lost their ability to perform miracles. If you can only perform miracles from God, how could the Bible say the devil performed a miraculous event when he took Jesus to the top of a mountain?

Jesus had the power to perform miracles because he was so connected to God through the Holy Spirit, had such faith and understanding in his real life as Spirit, and was a being of pure love. If this accounts for Jesus being able to transform the laws of nature in a supernatural way, how could the Apostles or adversaries of God, or miracles happen today? In John 14:12, Jesus says, "Most assuredly, I say to you, he who believes in Me, the works that I do he will do also; and greater works than these he will do, because I go to My Father." Jesus performed some pretty amazing feats such as calming the storm, healing people, and raising several people from the dead. With all of that, is Jesus saying we can do these things and even greater works? How can that be?

To summarize a rather complex subject, here are the basics of healing miracles from *A Course in Miracles*. The miracle is an expression of love that supplies a lack in one person from another person that has more love. This exchange reverses the physical laws as it brings more love to both the giver and receiver. You must first accept the atonement for yourself because you cannot give what you don't already have. Prayer is the medium for miracles and starts as a universal blessing from God where love is received from Him, and through miracles, love is expressed through you to your brothers.

Miracles are the absence of the body and the realization that the Spirit or right mind is the altar of truth. The truth being that you are not a body only Spirit, and as such are not subject to the physical laws. Miracles are natural expressions of total forgiveness, where you affirm your acceptance of God's forgiveness by extending it to others. The miracle is a correction and can heal because it denies body identification and affirms that we are all truly Spirit. Miracles are everyone's right but purification of the mind is necessary first. Purification involves the relinquishment of fear and the acceptance of God's love and the extension of that love to all brothers as one with you. In essence, the miracle is a correction and does nothing, it undoes, which is atonement. It accepts what is true (God and Spirit) and rejects what is false (separation and form). When you love like Jesus, you become like him.

My understanding of miracles is that you do need to believe that miracles are possible and have faith that miracles can happen. You do need to be open to and connected with the spiritual because that is what miracles are, a correction of the material world by turning it over to the non-material or spiritual world. Ultimately, you need to be in a loving state, oftentimes through the practice of forgiveness which is the means to removing the blocks to the awareness of love's presence. There are no miracles that would be used to hurt or attack someone. Any supernatural event, especially in the Old Testament, that attacks others and is not based on love was not a miracle and probably didn't happen the way it was written. Faith is oftentimes needed for the reason that the fear of healing is the antithesis of expecting to be healed. This is also why being fearful of God is not conducive to healing and miracles.

In the three years of Jesus' ministry, it is recorded that Jesus performed thirty-seven miracles. In over one thousand days with all of the people in need that Jesus came across, why didn't Jesus help more people? If Jesus was really trying to start a new religion, wouldn't a multitude of miracles be a great way to attract people and verify that he was indeed from God? Almost all of the healings were people who came to him, meaning he didn't seek out people to heal. His healings were very individually impactful, but you could say Mother Teresa was much more involved in helping people physically than Jesus was. In thinking about miracles and his ministry, most of his energy was probably nurturing his connection with God, and after that, teaching. Wouldn't touching many more people with the gift of healing bring that many more closer to God?

At the end of his Gospel, John said there were many other things that Jesus did, that if recorded, even the world itself could not contain the books that would be written. If John is talking about miracles, surely he and the other Gospel writers would include them as a demonstration of Jesus' power and as an inducement for the Jews and Gentiles to convert to Christianity. It's curious that out of the thirty-seven documented miracles Jesus performed, sixteen of them are recounted in only one of the four Gospels.

In addition, Luke says Jesus healed many, although he gives no specifics. The resurrection of Jesus is the central point in Christianity and the miracles Jesus performed helped lead the disciples to conclude that Jesus did, in fact, rise from the dead. That makes Jesus' miracles extremely significant to not be recounted in all of the Gospels. It's perplexing that John would say Jesus performed an extraordinary number of wonders since there is not much written about Jesus in the first century up to the year 110CE by any Roman or Greek authors.

Paul used the greatest miracle, the resurrection of Jesus, as the main point to gain converts to this new Christianity. Although Paul never met Jesus or wrote about his miracles, the stories of Jesus' miracles had to be circulating among Jews even before the Gospels were written. Many more miracles would have put Jesus on the world map. A possible reason Jesus did not perform more miracles is he knew it was the Holy Spirit's job to save everyone, that the world of form was not real, and that he was not here to fix the world. He also did not intend to start a new religion so a public display of miracles was not necessary to entice new followers.

A question posed by non-believers is, if Jesus could heal the blind man, why didn't he heal blindness? Going back to Jesus' second great Commandment to love your brother, why wouldn't he heal all diseases? Apologists say that it is not part of the grand plan. It's unfortunate if the grand plan includes countless generations of suffering. Jesus did not heal all blindness because healing is a personal or individual occurrence. It is one person sharing his love and convincing the other that they are one with God. In the grand scheme, Jesus had his part to play in teaching that sickness is the result of the thought of separation from God. Being healed shows that we are not separate from God in the same way that healing and forgiveness are the same.

One example of how Jesus knew that this life was not the real life is how he did not express concern for the Jewish condition of suffering and subjugation to the Romans. Jesus never said anything against the oppressive Romans and their crucifixion of the Jews. Jesus was not the first or the last Jew to suffer crucifixion. The Jewish historian Josephus, who lived shortly after Jesus, wrote that after the destruction of Jerusalem, in about 70CE, the Romans crucified so many Jews that they ran out of crosses. Why didn't Jesus, who had compassion for his fellow man, say anything against the Romans, instead saving his most vitriolic rants for the Jewish leadership? Jesus even said give to Caesar what belongs to Caesar, because the real power is not of this world. We still don't understand Jesus' ministry. He didn't heal that many people, or wipe out any diseases, or lead his people out of Roman domination, but he did show us how to overcome the world.

Why wasn't Jesus revered or accepted in his hometown? Apologists reference the fact that a prophet is not without honor except in his hometown and even his own house, as to why Jesus could not or did not perform many miracles in his hometown. The people who grew up seeing you as an ordinary person cannot believe when you have extraordinary powers. They knew you as a snot-nosed brat from just an ordinary family down the block. The birth narrative of Jesus shows that everyone involved knew he was special. His mother and father were visited by angels and had other prophetic announcements. In an age when most everything was orally communicated between families and towns, Jesus should have been known as a special person throughout the land as he grew into adulthood. Doesn't it seem strange that the Son of God, announced at his birth through visions, through huge historical events, revered by the very popular prophet John the Baptist, could have been so invisible for about thirty years in a small town? Did he perform any miracles in that time? The answer is that Jesus had to purify himself like all of us in order to perform miracles. He didn't perform many mighty works in his hometown because his townsfolk did not have faith that he could.

The miracle of healing another person does take that person's agreement and/or faith. Under the guidance of the Holy Spirit, Jesus would go into the person's mind and convince them that they are perfect, whole, and loved. If the person wants to be whole, believes that they can be healed, and is in a frame of mind where the fear of a physical healing would not be too fearful for them, they were healed. You might ask, how could Jesus heal a dead person who did not ask to be raised and does not have the wherewithal to have faith? All healing is done at the level of the mind and not at the physical level. Actually, healing miracles have nothing to do with the body.

Being a great spiritual master, Jesus could connect with the person's Spirit which is separate from the body and goes on eternally after the body dies. The woman who touched Jesus' garment and was healed was the opposite, as Jesus didn't know who touched him. She was healed because the Holy Spirit is in all minds and her faith and desire were so great that the Holy Spirit basically took over for Jesus. Jesus said to her, daughter your faith has made you well. Jesus said if you have the faith of a mustard seed you can move mountains. That means we can heal ourselves if the conditions are right. We can heal as Jesus did when we turn our minds over to the Holy Spirit and He directs our healings with His love through us.

It appears that in most of Jesus' healings, he asked the healed to give glory to God rather than to him. It makes sense because Jesus said he could do nothing apart from his Father. Miracles are because of the love of God and happen because we are all connected in Spirit. If you believe that miracles happen today, how can that be if Jesus no longer walks the earth or God is not performing miracles through His Prophets? It is because we are all one in the immaterial realm of Spirit. Consequently, you must believe and connect to the spiritual realm, usually through prayer and silence. That is why Jesus said you can do all that I do and even greater things. Jesus' disciples were able to perform miracles early on because they were so filled with faith, love, and understanding. However, over time after Jesus was gone, the world pressed in and they digressed from overwhelming love to worldly concerns. That is why it seems miracles don't happen on a regular basis or on command. We are caught up in the world of form and have drifted farther from the belief that we can do miracles. Humans do not have a single-minded goal to the exclusion of everything else to purify themselves and become miracle minded. To purify yourself, you must make the decision to release all that is not true from the mind. And what is not true is all form and anything that is not of God.

The miracle of moving mountains by overriding the natural laws is similar to healing miracles but does not involve another person. You correct the mistaken thought that you are separate from the love of God and accept His love and forgiveness as your own. You then realize the unreality of the physical world similarly to the unreality of the body. Through faith and conviction, the love that is the miracle, transcends the physical laws when you exchange belief in the untrue (physical world) with the belief in the true (spiritual world). This is a simple process although not easy as we have been here for millennia and have not mastered miracles yet.

ACIM on Jesus' Miracles

A Course in Miracles says that the real miracle is the love that inspires miracles. The will of God is to love and be loved and we are happiest when our will and God's will are one. Miracles should be natural occurrences and are available to convince us of the reality of Spirit because they arise from conviction in it. We can all do miracles but we must be in the right frame of mind first. The purification necessary is thinking with the Holy Spirit's love and the fastest way to correct your mind to a miraculous state of mind is through the practice of forgiveness. Forgiveness, as Jesus practiced it, retrains the mind to know that we are all one and in that state it is possible to access someone's mind and shine your love on them and remind them that they are perfect children of God.

You basically heal your brother by accepting God for them. This is how Jesus raised the dead. Jesus was the light of the world, and the sick mind recognized the light, believed in Jesus as the light and trusted him because they wanted to be healed. Healing is the effect of minds that join. Jesus often said your sins are forgiven instead of you are healed because he did not give power to sickness by recognizing it.

The laws of physics are transcended when our mind believes the true laws of God and Spirit. If the world is an illusion made by the mind, then the mind can change the illusion once it has realization over it. God only knows us as whole and when you return your mind to God, you become whole. Interestingly, in several of the stories of Jesus' healings in the King James Bible, it uses the word *whole* instead of healing. The reason it is imperative to know we are one through forgiveness is if we are one then we are whole and being whole we cannot be sick.

Jesus did not perform miracles as a public spectacle to induce belief because miracles are to be used as an expression of love. Miracles should be directed by the Holy Spirit, and as such, using selective miracles for our purposes can be misguided. This is partly why we cannot perform miracles on demand. Only the Holy Spirit knows what is right and helpful to everyone, and we do not.

23. True Sayings of Jesus

We have no way to prove exactly what Jesus said, so believing the Gospel writers transcribed exactly what he said is a statement of belief or faith, not a statement of fact. There are many indications that the eyewitnesses to Jesus did not directly write the Gospels, and if they did, after over thirty years could it be word for word? Believing that the writers were inspired to record the words by the Holy Spirit is also a statement of faith. The Holy Spirit is perfect and there are too many inconsistencies for that to be the case. The truth lies somewhere in between where the eyewitnesses passed on the stories and someone decades later wrote the Gospels with inspiration from the Holy Spirit.

Therefore, the words attributed to Jesus are not his exact words, and at times, are not even close. I process what Jesus would have said through the filter that he only taught and acted with love, peace, and forgiveness. Jesus only taught what is true, and for an eternal spiritual being, truth must be eternal and unchanging. If something changes, then it wasn't true because it changed. Additionally, Jesus' teachings would be universal, meaning they would be for all people in all places at all times. That is one reason Jesus taught in parables because the lesson is not specific to a person or group and is valid forever.

To revisit truth, a textbook definition of truth is that which is consistent with fact or reality. Some so called truths are relative because what is true for some people may not be true for other people. And it might be true at one time but not another, and it might not be true in all circumstances. Reality is subjective because it has to be someone's reality, and it might not be yours. A universal truth or absolute truth must be absolute, unalterable, eternal, unambiguous, and all-encompassing. In short, a useful definition of truth is 'that which never changes.' I used the example of the plastic water bottle, displaying that it does change over time, so the definition of it as a plastic water bottle is only relatively true.

Jesus' true teachings have to be for all people, all circumstances, in all locations, and for all time to meet the definition of that which never changes. Truth by definition, also cannot contradict itself, meaning there can only be one truth and all other postulations, if different, must be untrue or false. Truth excludes, which is why Christians say that all other religions that do not believe in Jesus as the savior are not true. Examining various writings in the Bible, there are some contradictions; therefore, they cannot all be true. There are even things that Jesus said which seem to contradict each other, and for that reason cannot be exactly what Jesus said.

All of Jesus' teachings must confirm all others or be unified in some way. Jesus can't preach forgiveness and then say I will not forgive my brother for not feeding the hungry. Jesus cannot heal strangers with love and then condemn others with everlasting fire. Also, the truth of Jesus' words can exist independent of anyone's knowledge, belief, or experience of the truth, and must stand on the quality of the evidence. You are known by your fruits, which is the way Jesus espoused truth resulting in miracles to help and heal.

There are some places where what Jesus said or was written about him contradicts his character. There are some verses that the Jesus of peace, love, and forgiveness would not and could not have said. There are also many passages from Jesus that we just don't understand or have misinterpreted. When we look back at the development of Christianity, we need to ask ourselves why some writings and doctrines were accepted as orthodox and added to the Bible realizing that someone had to decide. Church leaders thought eyewitnesses or close associates were credible because they lined up with the theology of Judaism and the Old Testament God through to Jesus.

If the biblical teachings of Jesus are not about love, peace, and forgiveness, and are not eternal and universal, then they are not from Jesus. If Jesus and God are one and the same, the only difference being God created Jesus but Jesus did not create God, then God's essence must be love and peace. If you question my attributes of Jesus' essence and would include judgment, condemnation, punishment, and anger, you must ask yourself if they are the opposite of pure love. If you are honest, ask if those other qualities merit worship. Apologists may be able to make sense of some of the contradictions and misunderstandings, but you are responsible for your own salvation and need to work these out for yourself…with the Holy Spirit's help.

Thomas Jefferson developed what is called the Jefferson Bible which he termed, *The Life and Morals of Jesus of Nazareth*. He took out the supernatural stories from the Bible and focused on Jesus' teachings. He explained this to a friend as "extracting the pure principles which he taught, we should have to strip off the artificial vestments in which they have been muffled by priests, who have travestied them into various forms, as instruments of riches and power to them." Jefferson did a similar thing to what I am doing in the next three chapters which is to assume the Gospel writings were misinformed or biased and filter them through the lens of Jesus as love, peace, and forgiveness. Since I am *A Course in Miracles* student, and Jesus dictated the Course, these are the traits that he expounded in the Course.

Following are some examples of sayings that Jesus would have said based on love, peace, and forgiveness and my understanding of them based on *A Course in Miracles*.

Matthew 4:17, "Repent, for the kingdom of heaven is at hand." Jesus is saying to repent or change your mind about who you are. You will be able to enter the Kingdom of Heaven when you give up the things of this world, including the judgments of your brother. The Kingdom of Heaven is at hand because you can change your mind to love and make the decision for Heaven at any time by listening to the counsel of the Holy Spirit.

Matthew 5:14, "You are the light of the world." Light and truth are the same. In our real identities as perfect children of God, not here on earth in our meat suits, but in Heaven, our existence is light and truth. Jesus knew that all of us were his brothers and as such the light of the world. Jesus said we are the light of the world but we don't recognize or accept it because we think we are sinners and separated from God. In John 8:12, Jesus said he is the light of the world because he had the humility to recognize that God created him in truth and he accepted his role in salvation. We do not yet have the humility to know we are as God created us in Heaven and to know we are also the saviors of the world. All those who appear to be here and know the truth can truly be the light of the world for others.

Matthew 5:39, "But I tell you not to resist an evil person. But whoever slaps you on your right cheek, turn the other to him also." This does not mean you should let someone abuse or take advantage of you, or you should not protect yourself. Jesus himself fled and also instructed his disciples to avoid dangerous situations. Jesus' message is to show everyone that they cannot hurt you because you are true Spirit, not an illusory body. The body is not real and you can teach others this by going past the attachment to the physical form and display that you are Spirit. Someone can attack your body but that is not who you are in truth. The body is not as important as how you respond – by not attacking their body or condemning them for their attack. Jesus exemplified this as his final lesson when he let his body be killed in order to prove that they could not hurt the real Jesus.

Matthew 5:48, "Therefore you shall be perfect, just as your Father in heaven is perfect." Jesus is telling us both to be perfect, and that we are in fact perfect. Why does Jesus tell us to be perfect if belief in Jesus is enough for salvation? Because Jesus knew that to get into Heaven, as he said in the beatitudes, we must be pure in heart which is pure in thought. The Course's way to be pure in heart is not through perfect behaviors but by perfect forgiveness which leads to perfect love. Jesus also says our Father in Heaven is perfect, because he knows the Father as pure love experientially. Being perfect means to lack nothing and when you have perfect love, you are whole and need nothing else from this world.

Matthew 6:33, "But seek first the kingdom of God." This is one of the keys to salvation. When you truly want the Kingdom of God above anything that the world can offer, you will begin to find the answers for how to return to the Kingdom. *A Course in Miracles* says there are many paths to God, but listening to the Holy Spirit is mandatory because we cannot heal our unconscious guilt by ourselves. The first step is to want the Kingdom. The second step is to realize you don't know how to get it. The third step is to ask for help from the one who knows. The next step is to be willing to do your part to change your mind about who you are. The Course says the last and final step is taken by God as you will remember you are one with God.

Matthew 8:20–22, "Foxes have holes and birds of the air have nests, but the Son of Man has nowhere to lay His head. Follow Me, and let the dead bury their own dead." Jesus is saying that this is not his home and he is not of this world because he is Spirit. The only difference is we don't know it yet so we have not become totally dependent on God the way he was. Next, Jesus is saying that those who do not follow his example are dead in Spirit. While you think you are a body and separate from God, you do not have real life and are dead in the spiritual sense, for God is life. You must do the work to change your mind or you will continue to seem to live and die until you eventually wake up to your real eternal life.

Matthew 10:39, "He who finds his life will lose it, and he who loses his life for My sake will find it." When you realize your real life is in Heaven, you will lose your earthly attachments. Similarly, if you relinquish your earthly attachment to life or lose it, you will recognize your life is with God in Heaven. Jesus is not asking us to be martyrs by losing our physical lives for his sake. He is asking us to take up our cross of discipline to his teachings by losing our attachment to the world, which takes work, dedication, and practice.

Matthew 18:3, "[…] unless you are converted and become as little children, you will by no means enter the kingdom of heaven." Little children are totally dependent on their parents and know they don't know and understand everything, so they ask what it means. Jesus is saying that unless you convert or change your mind about who you really are, you cannot get to Heaven. Jesus also said he could do nothing apart from the Father. How often do we ask the Holy Spirit what to do before we make a decision? The Course says, "Those who remember always that they know nothing, and who have become willing to learn everything, will learn it." (T-14.XI.12:1) This is what Jesus meant when he said the Holy Spirit would reveal everything. In our lives we say we need God, yet we are not totally dependent on Him or the Holy Spirit for all of our decisions and needs. Jesus was.

Mark 8:36, "For what will it profit a man if he gains the whole world, and loses his own soul?" Wouldn't Jesus be happy if you gained this whole world that God created? No, in this saying Jesus knew that God did not create the world and that it is the domain of the ego's thought system. Your soul/Spirit remains hidden by focusing on conquering the world because that is where your treasure is. Jesus has nothing against wealth or accomplishment, but you cannot be attached to it as who you are. Even during the grind you still need to focus first on the Kingdom to be saved. This is similar to Mark 10:23, "How hard is it for those who have riches to enter the kingdom of God."

Luke 9:62, "No one, having put his hand to the plow, and looking back, is fit for the kingdom of God." In Jesus' message about forgiveness, he says you cannot look back at the past sins of your brother and fit into the Kingdom. In the Course, Jesus makes it clear that you must look past your brothers' supposed sins to see that he is a perfect child of God. The sins you think he committed, although seemingly real in the world, he did not commit if the world is an illusion. There is no time in eternity; therefore, all the alleged sins have happened in the past, and the past can only be in time which is temporal and not eternal. Look at what you are plowing now and see the innocence in every brother and you will fit into the Kingdom of God.

Luke 17:21, "For indeed, the kingdom of God is within you." This is the quintessential line from Jesus that can only mean one thing; we are the Kingdom of God. We are God's creations, not this frail dying body, but pure Spirit or soul or divine essence. God is our Father and we are His children. God created a Kingdom and who else but us, his precious children, would he love and care for and include in His Kingdom? The Course sums it up as: we are at home in God's loving grasp dreaming we are here. This verse needs a minor correction to make it perfectly true. It should read, "For indeed the Kingdom of God *IS* you." What else would God's Kingdom be except you? This is why all of the Scriptures about eternal punishment in hell and separation from God are from the writer's imagination. In God's world, you can't lose or be exiled from what you are.

John 7:6, "My time has not yet come, but your time is always ready." Jesus was teaching that his lessons of forgiveness and the unreality of the body through his death and resurrection had not yet occurred. He told his disciples that their time is always ready because they were not teaching and experiencing the same lessons that he was. We all have a different path to learn our lessons to wake up to the truth of life in Heaven. The awakening in the Course is called the Holy Instant and it only takes a truly sincere instant to turn your mind over to the Holy Spirit at any instant.

John 10:30, "I and My Father are one." Jesus is declaring his divinity, and as a result the Jews tried to stone him. Jesus also says in John 14:20, "At that day you will know that I am in My Father, and you in Me, and I in you." Jesus is saying that he is one with the Father and that we are one with him, and hence one with the Father also. The difference between us and Jesus is that he knew he was one with the Father and had awakened to that fact, and we have not yet acknowledged it. In Jesus' day, this kind of thinking was blasphemy, and in our day it is sacrilege. We are the current day Jews and have been indoctrinated to believe that we are not and never will be divine. We have difficulty believing that Jesus would teach that we are one with God. Our senses, the world, the Scriptures, and the ego, all tell us that we are in no way, shape, or form, divine. In John 18:36, Jesus says, "My kingdom is not of this world." If Jesus is not of this world in Spirit, and Jesus is in us and we are in him, then we are not of this world. God loves you and creates only what is exactly like him and as such there must be another answer to our existence.

John 14:12, "[…] he who believes in Me, the works that I do he will do also; and greater works than these he will do." WOW, Jesus is clearly saying that we will do all the works that he did and even greater. He did some spectacular miracles and he is saying that we can do these also. It's not by believing in him as the special Son of God, but believing we are one with God and then purifying our hearts through forgiveness to be exactly like him. Jesus is saying that when we reach his level of enlightenment we will be able, under the direction of the Holy Spirit, to do similar miracles. The truth is we are limitless beings and we haven't figured it out yet.

John 14:19, "Because I live, you will live also." Jesus knows there is only life in Heaven and all of us are part of that life. He proved there is only life by proving there was no death. He is saying that we will also experience that there is only life. We reason you cannot have life without death, however, there is no death in the eternal Heaven.

John 17:22, "And the glory which You gave Me I have given them, that they may be one just as We are one." Jesus is saying we are all one in God even though we don't know it. The Course's definition of Heaven as the awareness of perfect oneness and the knowledge that there is nothing else, further confirms the oneness of God and all of His Sons.

24. Misunderstood Sayings

Following are some verses that Jesus probably said or a close approximation but are misunderstood. They include his teachings but what did Jesus really mean when he said them? What would Jesus have said based on his nature of love, peace, and forgiveness? My commentary based on *A Course in Miracles* is included.

Matthew 5:17, "Do not think that I came to destroy the Law or the Prophets. I did not come to destroy but to fulfill." Based on Jesus' essence, he could not have believed in the laws that promoted violence, killing, guilt, and oppression. If he said something like this, he meant that he does not attack or destroy what we value. He did not come to destroy but to correct, and all the laws and prophets should fulfill the Law and Spirit of God, which is love. He will not take away our free will and we can believe what we want until we decide to follow his teachings and example.

Matthew 7:1–2, "Judge not, that you be not judged. For with what judgment you judge, you will be judged." On the surface, this seems to confirm divine retribution where we will be treated or judged by God the way we treat or judge others. What Jesus meant was, since we are all one in reality, if you judge someone, you are really judging yourself. If you judge someone, you are saying their physical and sinful nature is real. Since your unconscious knows that there is only one of us, when you judge others, you are telling yourself that you are worthy of judgment. This keeps our guilt going, and then we project that guilt onto others and attack them. The word judge is misused in the saying as it is okay to make practical judgments about people. The verse is consistent with Jesus when written and understood: Condemn not, that you be not condemned. If you condemn anyone, you are condemning yourself.

Matthew 7:7–8, "Ask and it will be given to you…For everyone who asks receives." This verse is pretty clear although it does not work in reality. Jesus could not mean that if we ask for anything we will get it, or if we pray hard enough we will be healed. What Jesus means is ask and you will be given the Holy Spirit's guidance. Jesus clarifies this in Luke 11:13, when he says, "[…] how much more will your heavenly Father give the Holy Spirit to those who ask Him!" The function of the Holy Spirit is to be that still small voice who counsels us on how to be saved. The only way to get to Heaven is to think with the Holy Spirit, so we need to ask Him for guidance. We may be able to perform miracles after we turn our minds over to the Holy Spirit, but they should be directed by Him.

Matthew 11:30, "For My yoke is easy and My burden is light." This is typical Jesus-speak and needs clarification. Breaking it down, a yoke is the implement that brings together the animals and the burden is following Jesus' message. This saying restated is, it is easy to come together with your brothers as one following Jesus' message of love and forgiveness.

Matthew 16:19, "And I will give you the keys to the kingdom of heaven, and whatever you bind on earth will be bound in heaven, and whatever you loose on earth will be loosed in heaven." We often think this represents the authority of the Church to forgive or bind sins. It really means, if you bind your brother, condemn him, or don't forgive him, you will be bound to be separate from him for a while longer. You will not awaken while you condemn your brother because you think you are separate. If you loose or overlook the supposed sins of your brother, by forgiving him, you will see that we are all one and the love for all your brothers will get you to Heaven. The way you look at your brother is a cause because the way you look at him is the way you look at yourself. You bind yourself to the body when you judge your brother's body. An analogy of this saying is one of a jailer and a prisoner. The prisoner is bound by the jailer and the jailer thinks he is free, but he is not. The jailer is bound to the prisoner he is charged to guard. There are no instances in Jesus' life where he held or bound the sins of others against them.

Matthew 18:11, "For the Son of Man has come to save that which was lost." Jesus did not say *who* was lost, but that which was lost. What is temporarily lost is the remembrance of who we really are. If you think you are a lost soul, this verse should be read and understood as, *for the Son of Man has come to teach salvation to those who think they are lost.* You cannot be saved vicariously by anyone. Jesus only points you to the Holy Spirit, but you must do the work to change. You are not lost because you are at home with God, but what you think you are is lost indeed.

Matthew 19:21, "If you want to be perfect, go, sell what you have and give to the poor, and you will have treasure in heaven; and come, follow Me." This is not a command to help the poor or become poor yourself. It is a teaching that if you are attached to the seeming reality and riches of the physical world, then that is where your treasure is and you will focus on that. You don't have to sell everything and give to the poor to get to Heaven, however you need to let go of your attachment to the things of this world. What we have attached ourselves to is usually money, power, status, or the body. That is why Jesus also said it is hard for a rich man to enter the Kingdom. A rich man or self-made man is not totally dependent on God like a little child. Vows of poverty are sometimes taken to help focus only on God.

Matthew 24:35, "Heaven and earth will pass away, but My words will by no means pass away." Some view this verse as describing the New Jerusalem on earth from Revelation. What Jesus meant was the thought of a separate Heaven and a separate earth will pass away as everyone wakes up to their only life in Heaven. There is only Heaven in reality, being an awareness of perfect oneness. Jesus also said the Kingdom is near and the Kingdom is within you, meaning the Kingdom of Heaven is all there is. The idea of a separate Heaven and a separate earth will disappear.

Mark 4:30–31, The Kingdom of God is like a mustard seed which is the smallest seed then grows to become greater than all. One interpretation of this is about Jesus' ministry starting small and then taking over the world. Actually Jesus is likening the Kingdom of God within us now as a small voice of truth. A little willingness to listen to the small voice of the Holy Spirit will produce huge gains in our spiritual journey. When we listen to the Holy Spirit, the Kingdom will grow in us like the largest plant.

Luke 6:40, "A disciple is not above his teacher, but everyone who is perfectly trained will be like his teacher." Jesus is the teacher and is saying that when we attain the level of love and forgiveness that he had, we will be like him. We have mistakenly made Jesus special and different from us. The goal of any good teacher is to make the student equal in knowledge with the teacher. Jesus was in a state that is just potential for us. When we know the truth, we can do the miracles that Jesus did and even greater works.

Luke 8:18, "For whoever has, to him more will be given; and whoever does not have, even what he seems to have will be taken from him." This saying is not about physical things. Jesus is talking about the light in Luke's previous passage. When Jesus talks about light, he is talking about truth. Therefore, whoever seeks the truth or the light, he will be given more, or more will be revealed to him. He who seeks will find. But he who seeks truth and life in this world, that little bit of understanding of the real truth will not grow but die because he is looking in the wrong place, the world. The truth will not actually be taken from him because the Holy Spirit always gives and never takes. The truth will merely be crowded out by the world.

Luke 9:23, "If anyone desires to come after Me, let him deny himself, and take up his cross daily, and follow Me." When Jesus says deny himself, he means deny your attachment to the physical world and body. To get to Heaven, you must deny yourself as separate and realize that we are all one. Take up your cross means you have to work at changing your mind about who you think we all are. You don't have to suffer on the cross, rather everyday needs to be committed to the work of thinking with the Holy Spirit. When times get tough, your cross, like Jesus' is to love and forgive when the stuff hits the fan. When Jesus says follow me, he means follow his example like you would an elder brother who has figured it out and successfully made the journey.

Luke 18:29–30, "I say to you, there is no one who has left house or parents or brothers or wife or children, for the sake of the kingdom of God, who shall not receive many times more in this present time, and in the age to come eternal life." Jesus is not saying to physically leave, rather leave the complete attachment in your mind to the physical form of home and family because they are not real. The special relationships of family cause us to love those close to us but not everyone else equally. Jesus said to love your brother as yourself, but the way the world is set up, causes us to love and care for our families to the exclusion of those who are not family.

Luke 23:46, "Father, into Your hands I commit My spirit." Jesus was dying but did not say I commit my body. He did not believe in the reality of the body. The theology of glorified bodies going to Heaven is incorrect as there are no bodies in Heaven. The Trinity which includes us is formless. We are not humans having a spiritual experience; we are Spirits having a human experience.

John 2:19, "Destroy this temple, and in three days I will raise it up." Most Religious think this means Jesus is talking about the temple of his body and predicting his bodily resurrection. He does not believe in the reality of the body or any physical form. He is saying in three days he will prove the unreality of the body by defying all of the laws of the universe and re-animating his body. He then set it aside and returned his mind/Spirit/soul back to the Father.

John 3:3, "Unless one is born again, he cannot see the kingdom of God." Jesus means that one must be born to Spirit and not from the body. We must repent or change our minds to rethink or rebirth ourselves as Spirit. Turning our minds over to the Holy Spirit, we can recognize or hear the voice for God more clearly.

John 3:16, "For God so loved the world that He gave His only begotten Son, that whoever believes in Him should not perish but have everlasting life." This is one of the most famous lines in the Bible, promoted on street corners and at sporting events. This is where we get Jesus as the sacrificial lamb born to suffer and die for our sins. God did not send His Son to die for the remediation of our sins. Jesus used his death and resurrection as a lesson on the unreality of earthly life and death and the overcoming of the world, which he wants us to follow. We must believe in Jesus' teachings, and although it may take many lifetimes, we will all eventually be saved. Heaven is not complete without everyone and God is not perfect if He is lacking anyone. According to the Course, Jesus said, "For God so loved the world…that He gave it *TO* His only begotten Son." (T-2.VII.5:14) We are all God's begotten Son in Heaven and God loves us and gave us the real world of Heaven.

John 6:54, "Whoever eats My flesh and drinks My blood has eternal life, and I will raise him up at the last day." Jesus could not mean this literally for obvious reasons. Many Christians eat the consecrated host at mass as Jesus' real presence through the process of transubstantiation. Jesus knew that acts and forms will not get you to Heaven. What you think in your mind to reconnect to the divine mind grants the awareness of eternal life. If Jesus said something like this, then he meant that whoever takes in my teachings of becoming pure love through forgiveness has eternal life and will not die spiritually.

John 6:65, "[…] no one can come to Me unless it has been granted to him by My Father." Everyone is part of the sonship and will be saved or reunited in Heaven when their time has come. We all awaken at different times depending on our level of advancement. The plan of when everyone should return to Heaven is known only by the Father and the Holy Spirit. Jesus meant that no one could go where I go until he accepts that he is one with the Father. If Jesus said no one comes to me, he was not claiming any specialness or demanding to be worshipped. We cannot come to or hear Jesus until we open ourselves up to the oneness of perfect love which is the Father. Spirit will not force Himself where He is not welcome because we have free will.

John 10:34, "Is it not written in your law, 'I said, You are gods'?" Jesus is quoting the Old Testament to affirm this verse. He is referencing a verse from Psalms 82:6. He quotes this to the Jews right after he said that he and God are one in John 10:30. They want to stone him for his blasphemy but he says that if they believe Scripture, they cannot condemn him if King David calls the one who receives the word of God, a god himself. Apologists say that god in this verse is spelled with a small g, although Jesus knew that we are one with God which he again affirms in John 14:20.

John 11:25, "I am the resurrection and the life. He who believes in Me, though he may die, he shall live." Jesus is saying I have overcome the world of death. He who believes that fact and follows my example of unconditional love and forgiveness will also overcome the world of death and awaken to true life in Heaven. Belief in the man Jesus is not necessary for salvation, rather the realization that there is no death. Believing you are not of this world through the guidance of the Holy Spirit is required to be saved. Not everyone knows of Jesus but the Holy Spirit continually calls out to everyone without exception. Initial belief in God, Heaven or an afterlife is not necessary either. As you truly forgive and love unconditionally, the voice for God will become so clear that you will believe as the truth is revealed to you.

John 12:26, "If anyone serves Me, let him follow Me." Jesus said people should believe him and his message, but he never said anyone should worship him. When he said follow me, he meant follow my example of love, peace, and forgiveness.

John 14:6, "I am the way, the truth, and the life. No one comes to the Father except through Me." This is a divisive verse as it purports to exclude all other religions and beliefs from entering the Kingdom except those who recognize Jesus as the savior of the world. This would exclude over three-fourths of all of humanity from being with a loving God. This also bolsters John's claim that Jesus is the special, only begotten Son of God and we are not him. If Jesus said something like this, he meant that he is part of the oneness along with everyone else. Jesus was the first to complete his awakening and through his teachings we can all be saved. We do need Jesus to be saved just like we need everyone because we are all one. The second great Commandment makes it clear that you need to love your neighbor. Why do you need to love your neighbor if believing in Jesus is the way to salvation? Because we must be love to enter Heaven and Jesus was the first example of being perfect love here on earth, so his example is the truth and the way to life.

John 20:23, "If you forgive the sins of any, they are forgiven them; if you retain the sins of any, they are retained." In Matthew 12:31 and Mark 3:28, Jesus says that every sin and all sins will be forgiven. How can Jesus say all sins will be forgiven but also say that if the disciples retain sins or bind all sins, they will be retained and not forgiven? The answer is because you are doing it to yourself. If you hold someone's sins against them, you are telling the unconscious mind that you are a sinner and you become attached to the world of sin. There is no one else because we are all one in reality.

You cannot get to Heaven if you don't love your brother and if you think they're wretched sinners then you do not love them as they really are, perfect children of God. You must look past or forgive all your brother's supposed transgressions as if they didn't happen in order to realize we are all one and in this together.

25. Sayings Contradictory to
the True Jesus

The Gospel writers did not capture Jesus' words exactly as he said them. Jesus spoke cryptically and sometimes in mystical language that the writers didn't understand and we still don't. The Gospel writers also saw and interpreted things differently depending on their background and beliefs. Below are two examples of the differences in the four Gospels of what the sign or inscription on Jesus' cross said and what was recorded as the last spoken word of Jesus before he died. Coincidentally, John said that Pilot wrote the inscription for Jesus. With salvation as an end, words do matter as they become theology. Here is each Gospel's account.

Matthew's account of the sign: This is Jesus the King of the Jews. Last Words: My God, My God, why have you forsaken Me?

Mark's account of the sign: The King of the Jews. Last Words: My God, My God, why have you forsaken Me?

Luke's account of the sign: This is the King of the Jews. Last Words: Father into your hands I commit My Spirit.

John's account of the sign: Jesus of Nazareth The King of the Jews. Last Words: It is finished!

There are many examples in the New Testament when the writers wrote dissimilar accounts. Most of the contradictions about Jesus are what the Gospel writers thought he said versus what he actually would have said given his nature of only love, peace, and forgiveness. Here are some sayings that Jesus, based on his nature and taken at face value of the writings, would Not have said because they contradicted or were incongruent with his life and teachings. Included are my comments about why he wouldn't say this and what he might have said.

Matthew 6:15, "But if you do not forgive men their trespasses, neither will your Father forgive your trespasses." God has never condemned, therefore He has no reason to forgive. Forgiveness was one of Jesus' main teachings, and living in the dream would always forgive. Jesus might have said, if you don't forgive men their trespasses, then you will not see God until you do. You must be pure of heart to see God and enter Heaven. Until you transform your mind to learn and practice forgiveness, you will have trouble experiencing God.

Matthew 10:14–15, "And whoever will not receive you nor hear your words…it will be more tolerable for the land of Sodom and Gomorrah in the day of the judgment than for that city!" Jesus would not condemn someone or a whole city because they were not ready to hear his words. That would mean he basically condemned everyone who was not a Christian. He would forgive and turn it over to the Holy Spirit to remind them of their true home. Again in ACIM Jesus said, "If you want to be like me I will help you, knowing we are alike. If you want to be different, I will wait until you change your mind." (T-8.IV.6:3–4) Those who do not hear and receive the good news will suffer in this world with what seems like death and destruction, however not by God's plan.

Matthew 10:34, "Do not think that I came to bring peace on earth. I did not come to bring peace but a sword." Jesus was the prince of peace and lived and taught peace. He might have said, I did not come to bring peace on earth but to cleave you like a sword from your earthly attachments. There will never be complete peace on earth because Heaven is where peace resides. Although, with the practice of forgiveness, you can be at peace in your mind while on earth no matter what happens.

Matthew 10:37, "He who loves father or mother more than Me is not worthy of Me." Jesus might have said, He who loves the special relationships of father and mother more than all of your true brothers and sisters in Spirit, which I am one, is not ready for the Kingdom of Heaven.

Matthew 12:31, "[…] but the blasphemy *against* the Spirit will not be forgiven men." Everything is forgiven because it never happened. In John 20:23, Jesus says that if you forgive the sins of any, they will be forgiven. He does not mention the sin of blasphemy against the Holy Spirit as an unforgivable sin. We cannot get to Heaven without the Holy Spirit because of the unconscious guilt in us that we do not know about. Jesus might have said, the Holy Spirit is your guide and if you do not think like Him you will not be saved until you do.

Matthew 22:14, "For many are called, but few are chosen." This saying is in direct contrast to God's will that none shall perish and for all to be saved. The Holy Spirit continually calls all of us home but our attachments to the world prevent us from listening. From the Course, Jesus actually said, "All are called, but few choose to listen." Then he adds, "The chosen ones are merely those who chose right sooner." (T-3.IV.7:12, 14)

Matthew 26:24, "[…] but woe to that man by whom the Son of Man is betrayed!" Jesus did not believe in betrayal because he knew none of this is real and we are all equal brothers in Christ. He knew it was all a dream and that no one could be hurt in a dream. He preached turning the other cheek to show them that they cannot hurt you.

Matthew 26:28, "For this is My blood of the new covenant, which is shed for many for the remission of sins." Jesus did not die for our sins rather as a teaching lesson on the unreality of this world including sin. Jesus may have said, I bring a new teaching and shed my blood to show you that sin is not real.

Matthew 28:19, "Go therefore and make disciples of all nations." Some view this as Jesus starting a new religion. He only wanted us to learn from his life and teachings by following his example of love and forgiveness. Disciple comes from discipline and Jesus wanted all men to be disciplined in his example which is the good news. Jesus might have said, Go therefore and make all nations disciples of the good news.

Mark 9:43, "If your hand causes you to sin, cut it off. It is better for you to enter into life maimed rather than having two hands, to go to hell into the fire that shall never be quenched." First, Jesus did not believe in sin except in the context of mistakes that needed to be corrected. Second, Jesus knew that behaviors were less important than what you think. More significantly, Jesus did not believe in a literal hell except as a concept of anything separate from God. Jesus knew that it is not the goal to have no impure thoughts. The goal is to not hold onto impure thoughts. If the world is the domain of the ego/devil, then you will have impure thoughts, just work to shed them after they come. He might have said, if your body causes you to have impure thoughts (sin), shed them quickly so you will not continue to suffer in what seems like hell (a mental state of separation from God).

Mark 14:36, "Take this cup away from me; nevertheless, not what I will, but what You will." Jesus was not sent by God to die for our sins, but willingly used his final lifetime to teach everyone the lesson of love and forgiveness when you perceive yourself as persecuted. Jesus might have said, this is the cup that we have agreed upon and our wills are one, to share the lesson of love and forgiveness.

Luke 12:5, "Fear Him who, after He has killed, has power to cast into hell: yes, I say to you, fear Him!" Not believing in hell, Jesus knew that no one could cast you into hell. Since we seemingly left Heaven on our own accord, we cast ourselves into the dream world of suffering and separation known as hell. There is a Jewish thought that Heaven is closeness to God and hell is distance from God. Jesus would reinterpret that as he does most sayings as: Heaven is oneness with God and hell is anything else. Also, Jesus would never promote fear or strengthen it because it is the opposite of love.

Luke 12:49, "I came to send fire on the earth, and how I wish it were already kindled!" Jesus is not the threatening God of the Old Testament. He might have said, I came to light the fire of zeal for the Kingdom of Heaven and I wish it was already kindled.

Luke 13:3, "[…] but unless you repent, you will all likewise perish." Jesus did believe you need to repent; that is to change your mind and think with the Holy Spirit instead of the ego in the world. If you don't repent now, you will not perish, you will continue to reincarnate until you change your mind and learn your lessons. He might have said, but unless you repent, you will all likewise suffer. We will continue to suffer in this world until we awaken to Heaven.

Luke 17:3, "If your brother sins against you, rebuke him; and if he repents, forgive him." Jesus forgave everyone whether they repented or not. Because we are one, the forgiveness of others benefits us first. True forgiveness is knowing that your brother cannot sin against you if the world is untrue. Did Jesus wait until the Jews and Romans repented before he forgave them on the cross? Jesus said if you love those who love you, what reward have you. He also said turn the other cheek.

John 3:18, "He who believes in Him is not condemned; but he who does not believe is condemned already." Jesus does not condemn as John 3:17 says, "For God did not send His Son into the world to condemn the world." If Jesus' message is repent, then this verse says that you do not have a chance to repent if you are already condemned. Is Jesus condemning all non-believers? No, we all have many lifetimes to repent. Jesus might have said, he who does not believe the truth is condemned to suffer until he does believe.

John 5:14, "Sin no more, lest a worse thing come upon you." Jesus does not threaten or attack, he only loves and forgives. Jesus previously told his Apostles regarding a man born blind that no one sinned to make someone infirmed, as he knew that physical maladies are the script of the ego in the world. He also did not believe in sin except to agree that the term sin was missing the mark or not seeking the right thinking of the Holy Spirit. He might have said, repent or change your thinking so you do not have to suffer through a worse life next time around.

John 6:70, "Did I not choose you, the twelve, and one of you is a devil?" Jesus would not have called one of his brothers the devil. He loved everyone equally as his brother without exception. That is what unconditional love is, loving everyone equally without conditions. He might have said, and one of you is in his wrong mind or listening to the ego/devil.

John 8:23, "You are from beneath; I am from above. You are of this world; I am not of this world." Jesus knew we are all from and still in Heaven. The only difference is that Jesus knew he was from Heaven and we do not know it yet because we are attached to this world. Jesus might have said, You believe you are from this world, from beneath and I know we are from above in Heaven and not of this world. In the Course, Jesus said the only difference between him and us now, is that he was in a state which is only potential for us.

John 13:33, "Where I am going, you cannot come." This is viewed as Jesus being special and the only begotten Son of God and implies that you are not like him. In this saying, Jesus was returning his mind to Heaven or awakening to his home in Heaven. Heaven is perfect love, peace, and joy, and Jesus attained that, and no one else was in that state at that time. We must in our minds first be purified in our thoughts. We do this by practicing forgiveness of ourselves and others. Jesus would have said, where I am going, you cannot come yet.

26. Parable of the Sheep and Goats

There is a parable told by Jesus known as the Sheep and Goats, the Judgment of Nations, or the Final Judgment. This parable seems to contradict salvation by faith and Jesus' teachings of forgiveness. This is the last story told by Jesus and is only in Matthew's Gospel. I will summarize the story but please read it in Matthew 25:31–46. It begins when the Son of Man comes to sit on his throne in all his glory. All the Nations will be gathered before him, and he separates them as a shepherd divides his sheep from the goats. The sheep are on his right hand and the goats on the left. Then the King will say to those on his right hand, come, you blessed of my Father, inherit the Kingdom prepared for you from the foundation of the world; for I was hungry and you gave me food; I was thirsty and you gave me drink; I was a stranger and you took me in; I was naked and you clothed me; I was sick and you visited me; I was in prison and you came to me.

These righteous answer him saying, when did we do all of these things for you? The King answers, assuredly, inasmuch as you did it to one of the least of my brethren, you did it to me. Then he will say to those on the left, depart from me you cursed into the everlasting fire prepared for the devil and his angels; for I was hungry and you gave me no food; I was thirsty, I was a stranger, naked, sick, and in prison. And they will say Lord when did we see you this way and the King will answer you did not do it to the least of these, you did not do it to me. Matthew 25:46 says, "And these will go away into everlasting punishment, but the righteous into eternal life."

This parable looks like salvation by works, given that all of the works done to the least of us will result in salvation and not doing the works will result in everlasting punishment. The Christian doctrine is that we are saved by grace through faith in Jesus Christ. Because of passages like this, some Christians believe that good works are also needed to get to Heaven. It's confusing because the sheep that did good works earned eternal life, and the goats, everlasting punishment.

Apologists say this story does not specify that good works cause salvation rather they are the effects of salvation. They believe those who follow Jesus and are saved will do these kinds of works, except the text does not say that. Apologists may be using this to justify Christianity's salvation by faith theology.

Everything needs to be interpreted, however, this parable clearly contradicts salvation by faith with Jesus saying that specific works are the way to salvation. Paul taught that the works of the Law were dead. Why aren't these acts in the Ten Commandments, or the creeds, or even in the Old Testament laws? The confusion between faith and works is why Jesus would not have told this story as written. Jesus preached forgiveness and said in Matthew 6:14, if you forgive, my heavenly Father will forgive you. Jesus also said to forgive seventy times seven times, which was understood to mean always and continually. If Jesus taught us to forgive and he himself forgave, why would he then say that you are damned if you didn't visit someone in prison even though you might be a forgiving person?

Further, Jesus himself said in Luke 6:37 and Matthew 7:1, judge not and you will not be judged. If we don't judge and also don't visit the prisoner, will we be judged for not making the visit? Does Jesus teach that we should not judge, and then as the King, turn around and judge us? Jesus doesn't go against his proclamation in John 8:15, when he says, "I judge no one."

This story says the Son of Man is judging us for not physically taking care of our brother. Jesus did not judge when he was on earth nor teach judgment, so why would he judge when he was in Heaven? Not only did he not judge, he forgave everyone. If we will be judged for not feeding the hungry, visiting the sick and imprisoned, clothing the naked and taking in the stranger, then what are the expectations and basis for measurement?

Jesus' teaching to forgive is clear: forgive everyone for everything always. If our salvation is based on these works, then we need more information. How many times do I need to visit the prisoner? Do I give food from my surplus or give the little I have? This parable clearly says that works are needed for salvation, but who determines how much and how often? Can we make that determination ourselves on what seems right? Do we have to perform all of these stated works or just a couple? If this is the way to eternal life, why didn't Jesus teach that throughout the Gospels except in this one passage?

If these works are needed for salvation, and Jesus is the teacher and model, Jesus himself didn't seem to perform many of these kindnesses. We don't know all of Jesus' life and none from before he started his ministry, yet what we have indicates that he did not perform all of these works himself. A specific example is that his cousin John the Baptist, who prophesied about Jesus, passed his final days in prison before he was beheaded. In his last days, John asked his disciples to go to Jesus and ask if he was the one or if there was another. Jesus did not take the time to visit his own cousin, John, in prison.

Another example is when Lazarus was sick and Jesus said he purposely waited to go to Lazarus until he died, acting more like a goat than a sheep. Jesus did heal some sick people and fed the multitudes gathered for his sermons, but he did far less physically for the people of his time than Mother Teresa. The point being, Jesus roamed the countryside and had ample opportunity to do these things. As God incarnate, he had the power to perform miracles and only performed thirty-seven miracles in his ministry. Jesus didn't fully live up to his own parable of the talents, requiring that to whom much is given much is expected. As God incarnate, he could have been good to the least of his brother by wiping out starvation and disease, but he didn't.

Is the Gospel considered the good news for those who will suffer eternal punishment for not doing something while not understanding exactly what they are expected to do? At least the parable is more inclusive than orthodox Christianity as it gives everyone the reward for helping a brother.

Jesus could have been preaching his second great Commandment to love your neighbor in this parable and Matthew who was steeped in the Old Testament, transposed the reward and punishment of God on to a simple lesson to be kind to your brother. When Jesus said to love your neighbor, he didn't add that you would go to hell if you didn't. If you look at all the parables, Matthew by far has this Jewish judgmental slant, especially in the Casting of the Net and the Marriage Feast. Matthew 5:19 has Jesus saying, "Whoever therefore breaks one of the least of these Commandments, and teaches men so, shall be called least in the kingdom of heaven."

If Matthew thought stoning your fellow man was warranted for minor offenses, then eternal punishment for not visiting someone may not have been a stretch. Jesus did not tell this story as written because it goes against all of his other true teachings and his own character of loving and forgiving the sinners and wrong doers.

In contrast to the Sheep and Goats, the parable of the Prodigal Son is a story that Jesus told and it does reflect God's true nature. In the story, the son takes his inheritance and leaves his father's house. He squanders his inheritance and is left starving. He decides to return home to his father's house though he believes that he sinned against Heaven and his father. The father, who represents God, rushes out to meet him and forgives all of his son's personally declared trespasses. The father welcomes his son home with joy because the son is his father's treasure. This is truly how God in Heaven is and he continually welcomes his wayward children home, even the ones who are thoughtless, reckless, selfish, and do not visit the sick. We are God's treasure, not in this earthly form but in Spirit which is our true identity. Again, Jesus had to tell his stories as if we are here on earth because we think that we are.

The Sheep and Goats reveal a wrathful, vengeful, and judgmental King, while the truth is that Jesus is all forgiving and totally loving. God is patient and will wait until we repent (change our minds) and awaken to Him when we are ready. If Jesus told both the Sheep and Goats and the parable of the Good Samaritan, then virtually no Jews would make it to Heaven because the Jews would not help or even interact with other peoples. Another parable called the Good Shepherd contradicts the Sheep and Goats. Jesus says the shepherd leaves the ninety-nine sheep to go after the one, and all will rejoice when the lost one is found. The reason Jesus, as the shepherd, continually looks for and never gives up on the lost sheep, is because the Kingdom of Heaven is not complete without all of God's children, which is everyone. If the King sends away His children to everlasting punishment for whatever reason, then He would not be complete or perfect. Would the good shepherd leave any of his flock because they failed to visit the sick?

Jesus tells us to not be afraid and the absence of fear is a condition of perfect love. Would Jesus preach that we should fear not, and then drop the everlasting fire and punishment of the goats on us? The parable of the Sheep and Goats represents the epitome of fear because we will all come up short in some aspect of its requirements sometime in our life. Everything Jesus said was heard and interpreted through the human and Jewish lens of fear, guilt, unworthiness, and sin, based on the Old Testament. Would Jesus really judge us in the end for things that he would have forgiven everyone for while on earth?

Christianity, being based on salvation by grace through faith in Jesus, presents another problem. If Jesus told the parable of the Sheep and Goats, the culmination was either eternal life or everlasting punishment. Neither the righteous sheep nor the unrighteous goats knew Jesus personally or even who Jesus was. How can faith in, or belief in Jesus be part of eternal life if none of the two sides knew Jesus? Each group said Lord when did we see you? This means they did not know Jesus or know about Jesus. If the sheep didn't know or believe in Jesus but were rewarded with everlasting life, how can belief in Jesus be the only way to Heaven? Jesus either didn't tell the story as recorded or our Christian interpretation of salvation is not correct.

What could Jesus' message be if he told a story remotely resembling the Sheep and Goats? The lesson is that since we are all connected as one in Spirit, the way you look at any brother is the way you look at all of them including Jesus. If you can look at one brother with kindness and love, your unconscious mind knows that all brothers can and should be looked at with kindness and love, including yourself. As you begin to think loving thoughts and realize that you are love, you begin to act that way. The comparable psychological understanding might be that you become what you think about all day long. You don't show kindness to your brother because you will go to Heaven. You are kindness because you are love.

In typical Jesus-speak, the real message is that as you help the least of my brothers, you help Jesus because we are all one. Jesus himself rarely set up rules to follow and he didn't in this case either. The message is to treat your brother as yourself. How you treat your brother is a reflection of your thoughts about you and your brother, and that is what Jesus focused on. Additionally, if God made everyone in His image and likeness and they're His children, how can you love God if you don't love His creations?

To get out of this conundrum, Apologists might say this story is not exactly how salvation works and that it is symbolic or allegorical. If it is symbolic or allegorical, then are all the stories in the Bible about going to Heaven or hell symbolic or allegorical?

ACIM's Interpretation of the Sheep and Goats

Jesus was a teacher of love and forgiveness and that love and forgiveness extends to everyone, and that means everyone. Jesus sometimes taught on a mystical level that we don't fully understand. The part of this story where he wanted us to take care of our brother is because of the maxim, 'As you see him you will see yourself.' If you see your brother as worthy of love, kindness, and care, we will unconsciously see ourselves as worthy of love, kindness, and care. Like the self-fulfilling prophecy, we then become loving, kind, and caring. And when we do that, we will shed the negatives of anger, guilt, envy, fear, and judgment. In each moment of our lives, we can only be either love or hate, peaceful or fearful, forgiving or attacking. We make a decision in each instance of our lives which one to be and when we continually choose love, we will then be saved.

In this parable, Jesus talks about the Final Judgment or the Second Coming. This event is recorded in the Bible as a physical happening where Jesus comes back to judge the world and institute his Kingdom on earth. The thought of the Second Coming was misunderstood and not explained correctly in the Bible. The first was our fall into the dream state. The actual Second Coming is a description of the time when all minds are finally returned to the Holy Spirit, oneness is recognized by all, and Christ is restored to its one identity of love with God.

In short, it is when we realize the separation never happened and we awake to our home in Heaven. In the end, everyone will acknowledge that what is true is true and what is false never was. The Final Judgment is a judgment in the sense that we will look with the Holy Spirit on our lives and judge what comes up as not worthy of who we really are. As perfect children of God, our behaviors in the illusion were not who God made us to be because we are at home with Him. The Course says the Final Judgment on the world contains no condemnation as it sees the world as totally forgiven, as are you!

27. One Word Changes Everything

Biblical scholars say there are tens of thousands of discrepancies between all the fragments and full manuscripts of the New Testament. They could be copying errors or changes made deliberately. Even though we don't have any of the originals, Apologists say that with modern tools we can recreate what the original manuscript said with a high degree of accuracy. The example used to prove this assumption is that a verse with misspellings or missing words can be read and the reader can decipher what the original said or a very close approximation. Apologists believe the Gospel stories were written by eyewitnesses and/or inspired by God, and are therefore accurate, even inerrant.

Contrarily, many biblical scholars believe the Gospels were written by highly educated Greek-speaking foreigners, decades after Jesus' death. The earliest Gospel Mark is thought to have been written about 70CE or about forty years after Jesus' death. The Gospels were written in Greek and since Jesus' disciples spoke Aramaic and being itinerant laborers; they certainly didn't speak or write in Greek and most likely could not read or write at all.

Since the copies that exist are not exact copies of the originals, every one of us who relies on the Bible as a roadmap for salvation must decide if the words written are correct and are what Jesus actually said. I want to explore the fact that, even if we can approximate what the original manuscripts said using textual criticism and deductive reasoning, there are verses where one word or words are critical to its meaning. Can we be absolutely sure that one word from the writer is correct given we don't have the originals to verify? That is to say, can one word copied incorrectly, added, changed, misunderstood, misheard, or mistranslated from the original oration, fundamentally impact the meaning of what was said?

What follows are some examples of one word or words that can totally alter the meaning of Scripture.

The Catholics and a few other denominations believe the bread and wine that is consecrated during mass becomes the literal body, blood, soul, and divinity of Jesus. The term for this miracle is transubstantiation and it is a central part of the Catholic mass. The synoptic Gospels write about the last supper or Passover meal. Jesus says in Matthew 26:26, Mark 14:22, and Luke 22:19, this *IS* my body and this *IS* my blood…take and eat. John did not write about the Passover meal, yet has Jesus saying in John 6:54, "Whoever eats My flesh and drinks My blood has eternal life, and I will raise him up at the last day."

Many biblical scholars propose that Matthew and Luke used some of the material from Mark and a document known as Q from the German word *Quelle*, meaning source. Q is theorized to be a collection of Jesus' sayings. Given that many biblical scholars do not believe the synoptic Gospels were written by the Apostles, the Gospel writers heard from someone else exactly what Jesus said.

It's widely thought that Mark was writing for Peter so Mark's Gospel, and by extension Matthew and Luke, would be secondhand information if Mark got it from Peter. Looking at all the relevant information, it is clear Mark was not at the last supper and as a celebratory meal, all were drinking wine.

Consequently, the word 'is' looms very large in Catholic theology. It goes further than that as Catholics are the Christians who interpret that passage literally and replicate the taking in of bread and wine in their mass. The Eucharist, the Christian sacrament where bread and wine are consecrated and consumed, is the most important part of the Catholic mass. If the largest Christian denomination places such importance on the Eucharist and interprets it as Jesus' literal body and blood because of the word "is," why don't all Christians? Do other denominations think the word can be interpreted figuratively or that maybe the word was not the original word and as such is insignificant?

St. Paul saw such significance as he wrote in 1st Corinthians about eating the bread and drinking the cup. Since neither Paul nor the synoptic Gospel writers were at the last supper, what if they got the word 'is' wrong or it was later copied or translated incorrectly? Wouldn't we then have a major theological issue? What if the words spoken were this is *like* my body, or this *represents* my body, or this *equals* my body? If Jesus actually said this is my body and also said unless you eat my flesh, you have no life in you, then why don't all Christians take Holy Communion or some form of eating Jesus' flesh? Why don't all Christians who think the Bible is inspired and inerrant take Holy Communion?

Not all Christian denominations celebrate Holy Communion, possibly because they may have a different interpretation. Do they differ because they think Jesus used bread and wine figuratively, similar to when he said I am the door? Actually, Jesus' use of bread and wine was a symbol of the body to demonstrate the meaninglessness of the body. You would not eat something that is Holy; you would put it on an altar and revere it. If Jesus said something like this is my body, he meant that you must take in, imbibe, eat and drink up my teachings of love, peace, and forgiveness to awaken to eternal life.

Jesus was saying join with me, drink from my fountain of knowledge and certainty, partake or eat of my wisdom and you will see the light. Because Jesus knew we are all connected in Spirit, saying do this in remembrance of me means that in our remembrance of him and each other, rests our remembrance of God. Jesus often spoke figuratively or mystically, and non-spiritual practical people of that time almost always misunderstood his message.

Again, it doesn't matter as much what you do or believe in, it matters if you are extending love in what you do and believe. If you eat the communion host with loving reverence toward Jesus, then you are loving.

Another example where one word can change everything is in Mark 8:31 and Luke 9:22, where Jesus says the Son of Man *must* suffer many things, be rejected, killed and raised on the third day. One of the main tenets of Christianity is that God sent his only begotten Son to be killed and raised for our sins. In these Gospels, the word *must* conveys the thought that Jesus' suffering, death, and resurrection are part of God's divine plan to save His people. That is undoubtedly the way Paul understood the meaning. In technical theology, these several closely related thoughts and terms encompass substitutionary atonement, vicarious atonement, penal substitution, or the ransom theory. All are similar in that they proclaim that Jesus died for us, died in our place as a substitute for sinners, suffered the penalty due by God, and it was part of God's plan.

What if that specific word was misheard, misunderstood, mistranslated, written incorrectly, or just not said by Jesus? What if the word was *will* instead of *must*? Understanding the verse, the Son of Man will suffer changes the meaning Jesus ascribed to his death and resurrection away from God's master plan. Instead of Jesus being a pawn in his Father's one and only plan for salvation, Jesus, who knew his future from the Holy Spirit, said he will suffer because it was a lesson he was both teaching and practicing in his own awakening.

According to the Course, Jesus' death and resurrection taught that life and death are not real. How could death be real if people who died were raised again? In John 10:18, Jesus says, "I have the power to lay it down, and I have power to take it again. This command I have received from my Father." Jesus made the decision free from the Father's mandates and was a decision to teach forgiveness and the falsity of life and death. Jesus said we all have the power of resurrection and his death and resurrection was directed by the Holy Spirit to teach the eternal lesson of miracles and the illusion of death.

We have the same power as Jesus had, although our lessons to achieve enlightenment do not have to be as extreme as Jesus' were. Resurrecting the dead, like any miracle, takes a great amount of faith and becoming one with your brother and the Holy Spirit. Our lessons can be the everyday annoyances that come up, the negative emotions that we harbor and the grievances that we carry that need to be forgiven. We have the same power as some of Jesus' disciples, but it does take a great amount of faith and changing your thinking over to the Holy Spirit.

The crucifixion of Jesus was another lesson in forgiveness that Jesus was both teaching and living. That was his main message: forgiveness will get you home to God faster than any other religious or spiritual practice. If the word was *will* rather than *must*, the message changes from one of you needing someone else to die for you to get to Heaven, to one of follow my example. From a cruel God who sent His Son to die, to this is my lesson in forgiveness to attain peace when anyone seems to attack you.

Another example is when Jesus is reported in Mark and Matthew to have said that anyone who speaks against the Holy Spirit will not be forgiven. The use of the word forgiven in the negative contradicts Jesus' main message of forgiveness for everyone. It implies that some will not be saved and even subjected to eternal condemnation if they speak against the Holy Spirit. This goes against other verses where Jesus says that whoever believes in him shall not perish but have everlasting life.

Jesus didn't mention the blaspheming of the Holy Spirit as a disqualification when he talked about how to be saved in this and other passages. Instead of the word forgiven, Jesus probably said that anyone who speaks against the Holy Spirit will not be open to His guidance on how to awaken until he listens. To be saved, one must relinquish his own perception and rely on the knowledge of the Holy Spirit to help to clear out the deep unconscious guilt that our waking or conscious mind does not know about. The Holy Spirit is who God sent to help us with that. The Course says that its teaching of using forgiveness is not the only path to God, however it does say that everyone must turn their minds over to the Holy Spirit to be saved. All is Spirit including our right minds where the Kingdom of Heaven resides. When Jesus said, the Kingdom of Heaven is within you, he meant that literally.

Again, Apologists say even if the words are not the exact words used by the principals, we understand the general meaning. Except those words are symbols for things, and are relied upon for theology and salvation, and as such are critical. In the end, words and the things of this world cannot possibly describe God, Spirit or Heaven. Only revelation from God can come close to revealing the true message of God's love and how to get back home to Him!

28. Christianity Today

Has Christianity made the world better? Surely Christianity and the life and message of Jesus has touched countless individuals and positively transformed their lives. The example of living for others and the goodness that the religion instills has made many people better. Even so, most individuals still grapple with greed, envy, anger, violence, inequity, vengeance, etc. The Christian Church or body of believers has developed into a serving and comforting organization benefiting the needy, sick, and disadvantaged, along with offering the hope of eternal life. The Church is probably the most giving organization on earth, taking care of people in their local communities before governments began their social programs. Many hospitals, schools, and social organizations were founded in the name of Jesus and his saints to better all lives.

On the flipside, much violence and division has been perpetrated by individuals in the name of Christianity along with the claim of exclusivity touting Christianity as the one true religion. Sadly, the organized Church has been guilty of problems and even horrendous atrocities throughout its history including the crusades, inquisitions, infighting within the various denominations, sex scandals, witch trials, indulgences for money, and pedophilia. Apologists say if you are losing faith in religion because of the acts of men, then your faith is misplaced by not placing your faith in God. That is true enough, but evidently, faith in Jesus and God does not in itself make the world a perfect place or guarantee a place in Heaven. The Bible says to expect troubles and suffering, and we know how much the Jews suffered.

In ancient times, the worshipping of a God was not to secure the afterlife. It was to make the present life more tolerable and to gain favorable outcomes with war, crops, health, and fertility. Because of Jesus, Christianity has focused more on eternity with God. It's unfortunate that many of the New Testament's themes contain fear, guilt, and self-denial, especially regarding our sexual nature. Along with the traditional seven deadly sins, the Church continues to update sins for today's world. Are we getting better as a human race or is the world of the devil/ego getting the best of us?

If Christianity's main purpose is to get you to Heaven by making saints from sinners, it has failed as there are way more sinners than saints. If Christianity's purpose is to draw us closer to God, it has failed given the numerous biblical and Sunday sermons about the fear of hell and eternal punishment. If Christianity's purpose is to make disciples of all nations, it has failed given the small percentage of Christians in the world and the lagging growth compared to population growth. If Christianity's main function is to follow or imitate Jesus, it has failed as there are not many that come close to Jesus' love, peace, and forgiveness. If Christianity's main function is the fulfillment of God's work in the Bible, then Christianity has failed because the Jews don't follow Jesus and Christians are not His Chosen People. If God created the world for us to commune with Him, wouldn't God continue to talk to us through present-day prophets?

Does Christianity help us in the world to preserve our peace and protect our hearts from fear, pain, and loss? One of the most positive types of Christianity preached is the prosperity Gospel taken from the Gospels that say, ask and you shall receive. Unfortunately, the preachers of this feel-good experience are routinely vilified by the more conservative Christians in favor of the God of sacrifice and punishment. Can you imagine a loving God or Jesus being happy watching us struggle by not getting what we want or need to live happily? God's joy should be our joy but even Christians find themselves in a joyless world. Life is getting easier for some because of advances in science and technology, but everyone suffers pain and loss.

If the main purpose of Christianity is salvation, most people and many Christians will find themselves outside the gates. The Jews couldn't always follow the Law and Jesus said it is easier for a camel to go through the eye of a needle than a rich man to enter Heaven. If it's that hard to get in and the alternative is eternal punishment, wouldn't most people rather just cease to exist after death? If we have free will to sin against God, do we have free will to be annihilated rather than face eternal punishment? I sympathize with people who are ambivalent due to the fear of God's eternal punishment. I don't blame people who can't believe in a God who would allow His children to suffer forever.

Jesus in the Course says, "If God knows His children, and I assure you that He does, would He have put them in a position where their own destruction was possible?" (T-3.VII.3:6) Any Scripture that paints God as allowing the destruction of His own treasure is insane. Apologists say we choose our fate with our free will to deny God, but God would have had to set up that system knowing the outcome and that is not a totally loving God.

Apologists say the Bible and Christianity are the best answer and most reasonable explanation for the origins and nature of the universe and the humans who inhabit it. The evidence Christianity proposes is that the universe could not have sprang into existence out of nothing. The fine tuning needed to live on the planet must have had a divine hand, as every society believed in a master creator. Christians believe that the totality of the evidence is supported by the Bible's claim that God made this world and it is imperfect. This argument is usually used against atheists and is framed as: God as the creator versus an atheistic view of everything happening randomly out of nothing and then evolving. Neither position can answer all the questions or adequately reflect the way the world actually is.

A Course in Miracles proposes that God didn't make the world and the world didn't just appear out of nothingness. The explanation is that we are part of God in Spirit and share His infinite creative power. We made the world out of the thought of what it would be like to be other than God in Heaven. This is the cause of the big bang and the formation of the dream world. A question for all Christians is, are you afraid to go where the evidence leads?

We are on a journey of learning the truth and all earthly things can be relatively true until new information is discovered or revealed. Learning should not be to defend our position at all costs, it should be used to examine new information to see if our position holds up or we need to modify it. Human nature is such that no one wants to be wrong and having your set of lifelong beliefs open to critical analysis can be devastating. Unfortunately, Apologists today seem to have dug in so deep on the inerrancy of the Bible and rightness of Christianity that they are not open to the truth.

Apologists say there are three tests that any belief system must pass to be true, and Christianity should be under the same scrutiny. The first test is, is it logically consistent? This means, does it have contradictions? I have pointed out some of the theological contradictions; the most obvious is if God is all-loving, then He would not have anything that is not all-loving in Him.

Apologists argue that God is all-loving but also righteous, judgmental, and just, defined as morally justified. All-loving is all-loving and there is no room in that definition for anything that isn't all-loving. Would eternal punishment be loving if someone didn't follow God because of their culture, geography, upbringing, or innate character?

The second test is empirical competence. Is there proof of its validity? Christianity meets this test historically because there was a man named Jesus who lived two thousand years ago, performed miracles, taught followers, was crucified, and rose after three days. However we don't have the original texts of the New Testament or know with certainty who all the writers of the Gospels were, therefore, we can't prove that the text is exactly what Jesus said and did. The proof points to the fact that he probably said and did some of the things that are attributed to him. But the contradictions in theology deny Jesus said exactly what the text says.

The third test is experiential relevance. Does it work in real life and will it get us to Heaven? After two thousand years of Christianity and a lifetime of devotion to the religion, we still have a lot of problems in society and personally experience anger, envy, sadness, anxiety, etc. Also no one who has died has come back to confirm that belief in Jesus, or following the Jewish Law, or being a good person is the way to Heaven. Most Christians believe in salvation by grace through faith in Jesus, but that is a belief, because there is no real proof. I have submitted the argument that if Heaven is perfect love, peace, and joy, you will not fit in unless you have become love, peace, and joy. Jesus promises in the Course that if you diligently practice forgiveness of yourself and your brother, you will become loving, peaceful, and joyous in your life on earth no matter what is happening around you.

A comparable self-help teaching is that it doesn't matter what's happening in the world or in your life. What matters is what you think about what's happening in the world and in your life. That is where your peace of mind lies. Jesus had this mindset which made him so different from anyone else, and a threat to the status quo.

When you think everything is someone else's fault, you will either suffer yourself or attack someone else. But when you know you have made it all up with your divine powers, you will have peace. One could say that Jesus was peaceful because he was the Son of God and knew he was going back home. They would be right, but Jesus' message that was not communicated very well was that we are all the Sons of God and we will all be going back home to our Father in Heaven. Follow me, means follow the same unattached mindset I had.

The Christian theology is clear that only through belief in Jesus can you be saved. Some Apologists say that even if you have a different religion or no religion at all, everyone is responsible in their hearts to respond to God as He revealed Himself to us in the created order. The created order might be the universe and nature, and this allows those non-believers to be saved by responding in their own way to God. This is similar to purgatory and is used to appease the faithful who can't believe a loving God would banish His own children. If God is revealed through the natural world, we must be honest that the world is not always so great to induce us to worship its creator. It's difficult for someone suffering, or just struggling in life, to praise the maker of these circumstances. There must be another answer to this world.

Would Jesus be a Christian today? Jesus wasn't a Christian when he walked the earth. He was born a Jew, lived as a Jew, and died a Jew. He followed most of the dictates of Judaism his whole life. He knew it didn't matter as much what you did, it matters what you think. Your thoughts determine your actions therefore loving thoughts produce loving actions. Jesus believed he was divine and knew we were all divine, religious or non-religious. Jesus knew we were an equal part of the Trinity, the same as Jesus being the Son of God. Therefore, Jesus would have stayed in the religion he was born into. Regardless of what religion he found himself in, he would have done the same thing he did with Judaism. He would play his role in his religion and society, finding truth while reinterpreting some of the incorrect doctrines. He would teach as his function and he would spend his time with his connection to God or Spirit and practice love and forgiveness to overcome the world.

Apologists recommend finding a good Bible-based Church. Since the Bible is full of fear, guilt, judgment, and condemnation, it may be more helpful to find a good Church of love and forgiveness. Or go to a Bible-based Church as a place to practice forgiveness.

ACIM's Reflection of Christianity Today

The Course says the world is not good or bad, it is neutral. Similarly, any religion including Christianity is not good or bad, but is helpful if it teaches us to extend the love of God to our brothers and facilitates an inner connection with the Holy Spirit. To the question of Christianity making the world a better place, in the big picture, it doesn't matter. The Course says, "[…] seek not to change the world but choose to change your mind about the world." (T-21.in.1:7) You change your mind to look on the world as a tool to get you home through forgiveness. Given that we are thinking creators like God and we created the world with our thoughts, the world is an effect of our thoughts.

Leo Tolstoy said, "Everyone thinks of changing the world, but no one thinks of changing himself." By changing our thoughts to loving thoughts, the world will become more loving. The world will never see peace until the people of the world have inner peace. The world is the domain of the ego, which is our wrong mind. As more people become enlightened and shift their thinking from identification with the ego to identification with Spirit, the physical world will soften until it disappears altogether at the end of time.

Christianity will absolutely help you get to Heaven if you focus only on its teachings of love and forgiveness. The realization of the unity between God, Jesus, and all of humanity is the key to perceiving that all the children of God are innocent and guiltless. And since you are one with them, you are innocent and guiltless. What is Heaven except the awareness of perfect oneness and nothing else? Once you truly understand this concept and accept it for yourself you will begin to awaken to your true home in Heaven. Just as Jesus used the Law to teach but did not teach all of the Law, he would use Christianity to teach but not teach all of Christianity.

The human relationship is where the real work of salvation takes place and it can be done in any religion or culture. The Course says, "The holiest of all the spots on earth is where an ancient hatred has become a present love." (T-26.IX.6:1) Therefore any religion or no religion at all is holy only to the degree that it fosters loving relationships.

29. Sin, Repentance, and True Prayer

Sin is one of the main themes running through the Bible and it goes hand in hand with the repentance preached throughout both Testaments. With the writer's biases and translation issues, was sin and repentance understood, interpreted, and written down correctly? Jesus spoke in parables and they were heard and interpreted by the Jewish sin and sacrificial mindset. The word sin is generally translated from the Hebrew and Greek as missing the mark or transgression. Sin is a condition which needs to be corrected and not the cause of eternal damnation. Sin goes with repentance because when you miss the mark, you try again. Because of a fearful, wrathful, judging depiction of God, we have elevated sin into a supernatural offense against God. Believing in sin's condemning power is the root of our fear of God. It demands that we see God as other than totally loving. Biblical laws, once violated, cause us to think we have sinned.

When we think we have sinned, we believe we are guilty. When we are guilty, we believe there will be punishment. When we think we will be punished, we are fearful of the judge and punisher. When we are fearful of the judge and punisher, we cannot love Him with all our hearts and minds. Sin should be viewed as a lack of love, but we have turned our non-loving behavior into the positive presence of evil rather than a lack that needs to be filled. Sin is just a failure to love unconditionally; except we gave it the power to defeat us and it demands our guilt in defeat.

With all the possible sins of commission and omission, is it even conceivable to not sin? If we can't help but sin, then what does that do to our self-concept, emotions, and our will to be better? Is there a comprehensive list of all the sins that we must avoid? The Catholic Church divides sin into two types: mortal sin, which destroys the grace of God in our heart; and the less serious venial sin, which does not cut us off from Christ. Catholics have a historical list of seven deadly sins: lust, gluttony, greed, sloth, wrath, envy, and pride.

Recently, they have added to that list keeping up with the times. The new sins include genetic modification, experiments on humans, polluting the environment, social injustice, causing poverty, becoming obscenely wealthy, and taking drugs. St. Paul also had a healthy zeal against sin in his letters, and included adultery, fornication, uncleanness, lasciviousness, idolatry, witchcraft, hatred, lewdness, sorcery, emulations, wrath, strife, seditions, heresies, envy, murders, selfish ambitions, strife, deceit, maliciousness, drunkenness, and evil mindedness. It's even believed that you can sin by doing good things for the wrong reasons. Are these truly what God is judging us on? How do we know that Moses, Paul, and Church leaders received these directly from God? It is written that if we turn to God, we will be forgiven; even so, there are damaging and demoralizing effects of being a dirty rotten sinner.

In early Christianity, the emperor Constantine converted to Christianity on his deathbed as did other Christians. They did this because they knew they would sin in their lives and the deathbed conversion was the most expedient way to guarantee they wouldn't sin much more. Constantine had a point about how hard it is to not sin. The Catholic Church also has a point about the severity of certain sins because they can't all result in eternal damnation. Can sins that are built into our nature by God like envy, pride, greed, sloth, and lust send us away from God forever? The Holy Spirit doesn't see us as sinning, He sees us as making mistakes or acting in non-loving ways in the dream world. Since God is eternal, He has all the time in the world for us to correct them.

The Course is clear that it's not whether you sin or not, it's how long will you hold onto the attack thoughts or your grievances with another or yourself. The Course says it's not that you should not have impure thoughts; it's that you should not keep them. It's your job in forgiveness to look past the faults of yourself and others because that's what the Holy Spirit does. When you see others as pure Spirit, that's how you also assess yourself. Regarding sin, Martin Luther King Jr.'s analogy helps, "You can't stop a bird from landing on your head, but you can keep it from building a nest."

Jesus' message from the beginning of his ministry was repent, which was the Greek metanoia, and originally meant to change your mind. The Church Fathers interpreted repent to mean to turn away from sinful behaviors and feel guilty about your sins or your inability to follow God's laws. Jesus spoke about repentance from a more spiritual place. When he said repent, he meant leave behind or change your way of thinking over to the Holy Spirit's guidance. Jesus only used the word sin in order to communicate with the Jews. Jesus taught that thought was more important than behavior by interacting with the sinners who, as tax collectors and harlots, would enter the Kingdom before the Jewish elite. The Pharisees said and did all the right things but in their hearts and minds they judged and were not expressing love.

Sin as a mistake or a lack of love only needs to be replaced with love. We don't need to look back with guilt and self-condemnation on it or us. We only need to use our missteps to know that in each and every present moment we have the opportunity to choose differently this time. Once love becomes your nature, everything you do will be right because your actions will be from a place of love.

Jesus was a Jew in first-century Palestine and knew it would take a very long time to shake our cultural conditioning so he didn't hit us over the head with his message. He knew that we are guiltless or sinless, not in the illusion of time, but in eternity in Heaven where real life is. We think that sin can cut us off from our relationship with God, although we could never lose our connection to the voice for God, which is the Holy Spirit. God sent the Holy Spirit to help us awaken and His will cannot be thwarted. We only have the free will to decide when we will listen. The judgment, condemnation, guilt, and fear that sin causes were not part of Jesus' true teachings for he knew that we could not hate or guilt ourselves into a version of ourselves that we could love.

God does not forgive sins because He has never condemned. Since the world is not real because it is not part of God, God does not recognize sin. Jesus healed two paralytics, addressed the woman who anointed him with oil, and said your sins are forgiven. He did not say I forgive your sins or if you repent your sins will be forgiven. He said your sins ARE forgiven, which he knew they were by God who has never condemned his loved creations. In essence, the thought of sin is letting illusions take the place of truth. The truth is that we are at home in Heaven, in God's loving grasp dreaming that we are here on earth. All of our problems and so-called sins are the result of our thought of separation from God.

The correct understanding for all encounters with others is to realize that they are either expressing love to us, or not expressing love to us. If they are expressing love, then our response should be to love. If they are not expressing love, then they are calling for love and our response is love. Therefore, in all interactions our response is love. Jesus did this throughout his life and even on the cross. He recognized that the Jews were expressing fear as a result of his total love. Since fear is the opposite of love, in their unconscious, Jesus' crucifiers were calling out for love by displaying a lack of love. He forgave them and sent them his love, knowing they were his brothers. Jesus knew that every loving thought was true and everything else was an opportunity for healing and help regardless of the form it took.

Our belief in sin is one of the reasons that we don't have a more intimate relationship with God because we feel unworthy and fearful. How can we open up to God and be our most vulnerable when we fear punishment? Prayer is the usual method for communication with God, yet there are a lot of misunderstandings about what true prayer is and what it can do. In the synoptic Gospels, it plainly says that if we pray for something, it will be given to us. Matthew 7:7–8, "Ask and it will be given to you…For everyone who asks receives." Mark 11:24, "Therefore I say to you, whatever things you ask when you pray, believe that you receive *them,* and you will have *them*." Luke 11:9, "So I say to you, ask, and it will be given to you."

These verses clearly say that if you pray for anything it will be granted you. There are no conditions, qualifications or fine print. There are countless people who pray fervently every day and what they pray for does not come to pass. There are some prayers that do come true but not with any regularity and certainty. Apologists say your prayers may not be part of the divine plan, what is best for you, or that they are all answered but it may be a no. Those are possibilities, although the Scriptures do not carry that caveat. These are examples of Jesus saying something in Scripture that seems straightforward but has a meaning that we don't understand.

According to the Course, true prayer is communing with God and asking for his love. After that, a secondary benefit may be the specific answers to our requests. Jesus said that your Father knows the things you need before you ask Him. We know that God is not a giant vending machine, although we ask for things anyway. If we continually pray for our earthly needs instead of communing with God, we make those things into our lesser gods. Putting earthly needs before our relationship with God is how we make them our false idols, which is the first Commandment. Since God did not make the world, would He be more concerned with our earthly problems or our awakening from the thought of separation from Heaven where there are no problems? Seek first the Kingdom.

God did not leave us helpless; He gave us the Holy Spirit to answer our prayers. In life, we often make decisions using our own knowledge and wisdom and then we pray to God to bring those things to fulfillment. Rather, what we should do is pray for inspiration as to what decisions to make before we make them. Who has the knowledge of everything that has and will happen except the Holy Spirit? Wisdom is not that you are smart and know things; real wisdom is knowing that you can't know the thousands of variables that are in play when you make a decision. Sometimes we ask in prayer for things that are not good for us and the Holy Spirit will never answer a prayer with something that will increase our fear. As parents, we think we know what's best for our kids, and can generally give them solid advice. Even so, we really don't know what's best for each individual since they are so different and the variables in play are almost limitless.

Regarding our specific needs, they should become gifts to God for they tell Him that we have no other gods before Him, no love but His. This is so crucial to prayer that the first four Commandments direct us to put God first in our lives. We feel that we lack something in our lives because we think we are here and not in Heaven. The Course is quite clear that, "A sense of separation from God is the only lack you really need correct." (T-1.VI.2:1) If we are in Heaven, then we have no needs, no problems, and no desire except for God's love. When we forgive our brother and begin to love like Jesus, we become purified and the channels of communication between us and God begin to open up and we can hear the voice for God more clearly. When we know we are not separate from God in our true nature, then we can do all manner of wonders like Jesus did. Miracles will become natural for us to give and to receive. Jesus declared this in John 14:12, the works that I do, you will do also and greater works than these you will do.

The Holy Spirit, which is the voice for God, is the intermediary between you and God. Prayer in its truest sense is God's gift to you at the alleged separation where He gave us the Holy Spirit to help us find our way home. True prayer really asks for nothing because in God's mind, we are with Him in Heaven where there are no needs. Therefore prayer is a song of love and thanksgiving between the creator and the created. There is also an echo of the song that is the answer to our earthly needs. God's answer is first and foremost your remembrance of Him. True prayer asks to receive what is already ours: the love of God and help in accepting it. Healing in the form of prayer is only the returning of your mind to God, thereby being whole.

When you are whole, you can lack nothing and must be healed. To be whole is to practice forgiveness because it will demonstrate that you know we are all one, which is the definition of being whole. Do your forgiveness work by becoming a being of love and peace. Spend your prayer time in the classroom of silence bathing in the love of God. Once you have God, you really need nothing else.

An example of one of my prayer sessions follows. I pray several rote prayers and continually lose my place and find myself thinking about a thousand things for that day. When I get back on track, I see Jesus and we embrace and I tell him how much I love him and he tells me how much he loves me. I chuckle and say, geez you love everyone! I thank him for the lessons that he taught. I see the Holy Spirit and we do the same. I ask the Holy Spirit to help me hear His guidance more clearly. They are both like beams of light but then I see them in physical form as they take my hand and lead me to God, who is an all-encompassing light like the sun.

I try to tell God how much I love him, but I have to work through the unworthiness and lack of closeness I experience. Sometimes I'm not feeling it with Him; He is like an absentee father. Where has He been in my times of need, or even my moments of joy? I realize that to know and love God is to love all of His creations, my brothers. This is difficult because I am not totally loving and some people still get under my skin. Sometimes it's hard to love the flesh and bones person, but I try to look past that and see them as Spirit, or a smaller light. Jesus tells me to continue in the world and express to my brothers the same love that I felt from him. He says go forth and love you good and faithful servant, because love is what you are.

30. The Body, World, Spirit, and Ego

This chapter embodies the quote from the French theologian, Pierre Teilhard de Chardin, "We are not humans having a spiritual experience. We are Spirits having a human experience." Expressed another way, we are non-spatial beings having a spatial experience and timeless beings having a time bound experience. The mind that we all share is outside of time and space. Just like we have been wrong or ignorant about so many things throughout history, we are mistaken about our nature. Since we think we are here on this planet as humans, we tend to ask what our purpose is. A more revealing question might be why are we even here?

Our understanding of everything is continually evolving. We are limited because we can see the past and live in the present, but we cannot predict the future and its revelations. This makes us somewhat myopic; we think we are the smartest evolutionary beings, and that's true for now, yet future generations will think we were the equivalent of the caveman.

Let's look back in order to put us in a position to look forward. The discovery of fire and tools like the wheel were enormous advancements for the first humans. Early man had no idea of why it rained or even why it got dark. In biblical history, most everyone prayed to their gods and had festivals for everything that was critical to them including crops, fertility, health, and war. Everybody in the past thought the earth was the center of the universe and everything revolved around us. This view was held by the Church because of the Bible and our own prideful thoughts that we were special to God.

During the Renaissance, Nicolaus Copernicus proposed a heliocentric model of our universe where the planets revolved around the sun and it turned the world upside down, including a prohibition against Copernican theory by the Church. We have since discovered that the universe is so much more vast than anyone could have imagined. As advanced humans, we have learned about germ theory, chemicals, energy, medicine, and other various disciplines.

We are also continually trying to understand the mind, but still have very limited knowledge of how the mind works, why we do what we do; what causes psychological behaviors and disorders. We have been wrong and ignorant before; and we are wrong now about the body, world, Spirit, and ego.

Let's start with the fact that we think we are physical bodies, why we think that, and what the Bible and religion have to say about this aspect of who we are. We think that we are physical beings living on planet earth separate from other physical beings. Some of us also think we have a spiritual component or soul and there might be an unseen world that our senses cannot detect. We think everything is form because that's all we've known. Our physical laws point to the fact that we as bodies are real and the world is real.

Didn't we learn in physical science class that what we thought was solid in our environment was, in fact, not solid? The teacher said knock on your solid hard wooden desks. While it feels solid, it is made of vibrating molecules or atoms, and at the atomic and subatomic level it is not solid. The objects around us look and feel solid to our basic senses, but physicists are using quantum mechanics to prove that some physical laws are not absolute.

Another reason we think we are physical bodies is because of religion and the Bible. Some eastern religions have varying beliefs about the reality of humanity and the world, some saying the world of form is an illusion. The Judeo-Christian religion believes that we were made by God in his image and likeness. With the influence of the great Greek thinkers, the philosophy of some early Church Fathers and Jesus, the thought of the immortality of our souls separate from the body known as Spirit, began to take hold.

Jesus gave numerous teachings about the Holy Spirit and the Kingdom of Heaven as a goal rather than just staying alive and following the Law. The tradition of sacrificing animals to God in His temple morphed into the understanding of Jesus as the sacrificial lamb. This evolved into the importance of our bodies as the temple of God. Biblical laws obligated the faithful to sacrifice our wicked and lustful desires to keep the body temple pure as the carrier of the soul. Now, the body is the prized creation of God and we must keep it virtuous, especially in the area of sexual misconduct.

As Paul writes in 1 Corinthians, that your body is the temple of the Holy Spirit who is in you and you are the temple of God and the Spirit of God dwells in you. Paul gets specific in 1 Corinthians 6:9, "Neither fornicators, nor idolaters, nor adulterers, nor homosexuals, nor sodomites, nor thieves, nor covetous, nor drunkards, nor revilers, nor extortioners will inherit the kingdom of God." The ego's grand plan comes to fruition convincing us to think we are a body and it is the temple to God, with the body doing most of the sinning against God.

The Bible says God made the body, although it has natural desires like greed, lust, indulgence, and sexual gratification. If the needs of the body are so abominable, why would the Spirit of God dwell in such an iniquitous place? How could it be a temple if it is so wicked and unclean? How could the body be so important to God if He killed so many bodies in the Old Testament? Why does the body suffer with disease and accidents, and then die of old age? Jesus' resurrection convinced the early Christians that Jesus' body was very important. Why did he let it be brutalized and killed? His last words in Luke were, Father into your hands I commit my Spirit. Jesus did not commit his body or protect it as if it was the sacred temple of God.

The existence of the world is also confirmed by our senses and the laws of physics. The Bible says that God created and so loved the world, so He must think it is special and, therefore, we think it is special. Most people also believe we have a soul or Spirit which means we must somehow be eternal. If we are really eternal and these bodies are temporary, then we had to be somewhere before we were born into this world. We have to assume that we, as Spirits, were with God in Heaven. If we were in Heaven, then were born on earth as bodies with a Spirit, do we then spend the rest of our lives trying to get back to Heaven? Why did we leave the perfection of Heaven to come to this suffering world in the first place?

On top of that, Christianity says most of us will not get back to Heaven, rather we will suffer eternal punishment. With that scenario, did we have free will to not come here? Why would anyone choose to leave Heaven? If we didn't consciously choose to leave Heaven, why are we held responsible for our behaviors while trying to get back? Should we be accountable for offending God if we didn't make an agreement to come here?

The Spirit is a common theme in the Bible which the writers got mostly right. The Spirit is part of an unseen world which cannot be realized with the five senses. The Trinity is Spirit including the Son which is the Spirit individual to us. I think of how we are part of the whole Spirit like the ocean. Spirit consisting of the Trinity, (God, Son, and Holy Spirit) is the ocean. We, as individuals, are like a drop of water in the ocean, separate but the same and an equal part of the whole. Another way to say this is, that all minds are joined, or we all share the same mind.

In John 4:24, Jesus said, "God is Spirit, and those who worship Him must worship in spirit and truth." He solidifies it in John 14:20 with, "I am in My Father, and you in Me, and I in you." Jesus is saying that everything, all of us must be Spirit. We think we are bodies although we are really Spirit dreaming that we are bodies. We don't hear the Holy Spirit communicating with our Spirit nature because we are totally immersed in the world and the needs of our bodies. Can we go one day without thinking about the needs of our body?

Jesus also had a body but knowing he was Spirit, he focused on that part of his being that was true Spirit. He accessed the part of his mind that was Spirit to transcend the physical laws of the world with miracles. He was in the world but not of the world. When we absolutely understand what Jesus did, we will be free. We limit ourselves by believing that Jesus is the only begotten Son of God, and as such, is special and we are not. Jesus says in the Course that we are the same as him. He has love and we have love, the only difference now is he doesn't have anything else. His state is only potential for us now. We will not be fully open to the Holy Spirit until we realize we are Spirit. Jesus couldn't fully teach this so he gave us hints and left the Holy Spirit to teach us all things.

People throughout history could not fathom that anyone could be the same Spirit as God. The Apostles could eventually hear the voice for God more clearly since their hearts had been opened from the love and teachings of Jesus. The body is not the temple of the Holy Spirit, the mind is. The mind is not the brain, which is an organ of the body. There is another level that is beyond the level of the thinking brain; it is the universal mind that we all share. When you notice yourself thinking, you need to ask who was it that noticed me thinking. This is the unseen mind that is the thought that created everything. The Course says that a loving relationship is the holiest thing on earth and that relationship is in the mind, not physical. The command to love your neighbor is not always in deeds, it is in the mind.

If God created the world and exists everywhere, and Jesus came to save the world, why is there a Holy Spirit? The function of the Holy Spirit is to be the mediator or communication link between God in Heaven and the split minds of people who think they're bodies and living on planet earth. The Holy Spirit was given to us by God at the moment of the alleged separation, to help us wake up from this dream. The Course says that the means to wake up are set, only the time that you decide to learn your lesson is voluntary. The Holy Spirit reminds us of the means but we need to do our part. The fastest way to remember God is through forgiveness of our brothers.

Jesus is clear how vital the Holy Spirit is when he says in Luke 11:13, "[…] how much more will your heavenly Father give the Holy Spirit to those who ask Him!" The Holy Spirit has the answer to all of our questions and directs us home when we are open to Him. How much effort we spend listening to the Holy Spirit will ultimately determine when we will be saved.

The ego in the Course is like the devil in the Bible. Neither the ego nor the devil are real, they're both thoughts in our minds. The ego is the false self we created as a replacement for the true self God created. As a thought, the ego is the belief that we are separate and completely on our own. The ego is only a part of your belief about yourself, while your real life has continued in Heaven. Our ego minds made bodies that seem to be separate and no longer one with God. Thinking it is separate from God, the ego promotes the things that are not of God, including sin, guilt, and fear. The ego uses the illusion of time to convince us of its story by continually telling us that we have sinned in the past, resulting in guilt in the present, culminating in the fear of future punishment, and this punishment will ultimately come from God.

The ego, like the devil, is not something to defeat, only something to dismiss. You always give power to what you focus on, positive or negative. This wisdom is reflected in the story of the two wolves. The elder tells his grandson that there is a battle inside of us between two wolves. One is anger, envy, greed, guilt, and superiority. The other is love, joy, peace, hope, and generosity. The grandson asks which wolf wins and the elder replies, the one you feed. With the ego, you do not have to fight or overcome it, you just remove your attention and fuel from its negative urgings and it will slowly fade away and die. The ego mind is part of your wrong mind and every day you need to decide if you want to feed it.

We suffer on earth because the ego can be petty and vicious as a twisted replacement for the punishment we think we will get from God for disobeying and separating from Him. Since I am a dog lover, I like to think of the ego and the Holy Spirit this way: The Holy Spirit is like the family dog, always excited and willing to see you no matter what you have done or how long you have been gone. If you locked your dog and your girlfriend (ego) in your car trunk, when you open the trunk after a few hours, which one will be happy to see you? Your ego will never give you peace. Throughout all time, regarding the ego, the world, and this life: it's always something, and if it's not something, it's something else! With Spirit, it is only love.

We believe that God is perfect but created an imperfect world. We believe that God is Spirit, but His children on earth are form. We believe that God is perfect love, yet this world is full of hate, fear, and anger. We believe that God loves us and wants to take care of us, yet we all suffer. We believe that God wills that none shall perish, and sent Jesus to die for our salvation, but most will perish. A perfect God cannot be lacking anything, and yet Christianity's teachings result in most of God's creations being separated from Him forever. We believe that God gave us free will to reject Him on earth, but not the free will to come here.

We don't understand most of our world; however, we think we understand what God wants from us. We really want God to love us in the world, to add meaning and purpose to this life, but there is no true meaning in an illusion. Only by going to the classroom of silence and listening to the one who knows, will we hope to gain the understanding and knowledge of the divine. Some say our purpose is to know God and make him known, and that can only be done with intentional effort.

ACIM's Take on the Body, World, Spirit, and Ego

God is eternal, perfect, Spirit, and did not and would not create the body or the world. God creates only that which is exactly like Him. He created us perfect in Heaven where we still are, dreaming that we are here. The body and the world are projections of our ego mind meaning we made the dream world when we had the thought of what it would be like to be different from God. Since God is everything, we could not be different from Him. Since this tiny mad idea of separation could not and did not occur, a world of unreality was the only thing that could have grown from it.

The proof that this happened is that we think we are here in a body and can't really explain how and why we got here. The world in itself is not evil or bad, it is neutral. The Course says to renounce the world and the ways of the world and make them meaningless to you. Renouncing the world is not to withdraw or despise it, only to not become too attached to it. To make the ways of the world meaningless to you is to put your attention first on the Kingdom of God. Your investment in the world gets in the way of seeking the Kingdom. You cannot serve two masters or revere the world and know God at the same time because only one is true. Just like you cannot overeat and diet at the same time.

The body is not the temple of the Holy Spirit but it is used by the Holy Spirit to build a holy relationship. The proper use of the body is to express and receive love. If you use the body to bring God's love to those who have not experienced it, then the body becomes a holy instrument. The body, including the brain, is just a machine, and will respond to your thoughts, even the thoughts outside of your physical being. Loving thoughts produce loving actions. Relationships are where you apply the practice of forgiveness. Seeing your brother as sinless and at one with Spirit is the way to salvation.

Jesus, being born a man, had an ego. The ego world of form is ruled by perception, which is variable and can be wrong, as opposed to the Holy Spirit's knowledge which is constant and true. Because of perception, we don't see things the way they are, we see things the way we are. The ego uses the body to attack and the Holy Spirit sees the body only as a means of communicating the truth of love. Therefore, listening to the Holy Spirit is the way to be in communion with God.

31. Forgiveness Is the Way

A Course in Miracles is not The Course in Miracles. It does not claim to be the only way to God, merely one of the thousands of ways. It does claim to be the fastest because it uses the practical application of forgiveness to demonstrate to our minds that we are one with our brothers and ultimately one with God. Forgiveness removes the blocks to the awareness of us as love. The Course says that it does not aim to teach the meaning of love, for that is beyond what can be taught. Its direction then, is to remove the blocks to the awareness of love's presence. If Heaven is perfect love, then you need to become love to fit in.

The practice of true, meaningful, unconditional forgiveness is the functional thought system that will most quickly and effectively remove the blocks to us as beings of love. Christians strive to imitate Jesus, and Jesus became only love through the practice of forgiveness. Through forgiveness, you begin to realize that only love is real and nothing else exists. When you forgive, you can't judge because you are forgiving. The Course says we will keep coming back to the world in some form until we learn our lessons, and the lesson the Course teaches is forgiveness. Even with thousands of ways to Heaven, everyone must use the Holy Spirit to lead us home, even if it takes many lifetimes to do it.

Relationships are the laboratory of the Holy Spirit and through forgiveness we learn that there is no path to God that is separate from our path to each other. We can only listen to two competing thought systems, the ego's and the Holy Spirit's. The ego always wants to make it someone else's fault. It is the other people who are separate from us that are the cause of all our problems. We become victims or combatants and the result is defensiveness or attack, both of which are reactions and/or actions without love.

Forgiveness becomes a gift to ourselves. Because we are all one, when we forgive our brothers we are also forgiving ourselves. When we see our brother as sinless and guiltless perfect children of God, then through our unconscious minds, we begin to see ourselves as sinless and guiltless perfect children of God. The next logical step in our unconscious is that we see ourselves as only love and we begin to act that way.

The Holy Spirit doesn't see you sinning; He only sees that you're making mistakes which can be corrected. The correction of those mistakes is not always behavior oriented; they are corrections of your thought processes. Because the world is based on cause and effect, the Holy Spirit works with you on the cause of your misperception of who you really are, and that cause is always your thoughts. The cause of all our problems is always the thought of separation from God. The correction of that thought is called the atonement.

In the Course, the atonement is the undoing of the wrong thought system of separation and re-remembering the right thought system of oneness with God. We undo the mistaken thought that we are separated from God by forgiving our brothers to the realization of our connectedness as Spirit. The Course says, "No one who learns to forgive can fail to remember God. All blocks to the remembrance of God are forms of unforgiveness, and nothing else." (P-2.II.3:1–3) The whole Course is based on dismantling the thought system of fear and guilt and accepting the thought system of love. Each and every moment, you either think love and forgiveness with the Holy Spirit or you think fear and attack with the ego.

Sometimes these thoughts are in the forefront of our awareness and sometimes they're buried deep in our unconscious mind. Since all behaviors stem from our thoughts, salvation begins with our thoughts. Everything that Jesus and the Bible tell us about being saved is dependent on our thoughts. Thoughts change when you watch your thoughts and ask for help from the Holy Spirit. Becoming aware of your thoughts is the first step for any modification.

Judgment or condemnation is the opposite of forgiveness. Judging others is the hallmark of separation. We only judge others if we think we are different or separate from them. These are condemning judgments that judge others as unworthy sinners who are separate from us. When we think we are separate, we judge others as not part of the Kingdom of God. Regarding relationships, notice that we inherently feel a connection with and are more apt to forgive family members, friends, similar groups, and our geographical identifications.

We instinctively fear the people we don't know because we think we are separated from them. Judging puts our assessment of the person's value at other than the value God put on them as His treasure. Because we are all one, when you judge someone and find them sinful and not worthy of salvation, your unconscious mind sees it as you judging yourself sinful and not worthy of salvation. In traditional forgiveness, where we declare that the other person has sinned and we forgive them anyway, this is really judgment and not true forgiveness. When you relinquish the judgment that promotes separation, you recognize we are all the only begotten Son of God.

The Course says that forgiveness and salvation are the same in that they both imply that something is wrong. You need to be saved from something or forgiven for something, hence you are not whole. The only thing you really need to be forgiven for or saved from is your thought that you could be separate from God. All of our problems are caused by the thought of separation, because without that thought, we wouldn't be here. Therefore, forgive what you thought you made (form) that is separate from God and you are saved. We judge when we do not forgive because we must justify our failure to forgive. The beauty of forgiveness is that if you forgive, you cannot judge because the mind can only hold one thought at a time.

The reason Jesus saves and his teachings lead us to salvation is because the thoughts of fear, guilt, and anger are buried in the unconscious mind. You need supernatural help to uncover what you can't understand and correct yourself. "Jesus saves" means that Jesus' love heals the mind. If you don't believe in or follow Jesus, the Holy Spirit's love works the same. Jesus is one with the Holy Spirit in Heaven as are other great spiritual masters that have awakened. As long as we identify with negative feelings, it is very difficult to hear the voice of the Holy Spirit and to give and receive miracles. The miracle understood from *A Course in Miracles* is a divine intercession of love from a thought system beyond our own, disseminated by the Holy Spirit to us in our thoughts.

We think we are forgiving beings, but oftentimes it is not true unconditional forgiveness because it is based on getting something in return or possibly unconscious superiority. Some of our true motives, though unconscious, might be something like the following. I'm religious or spiritual and I forgive you because I'm right and you're wrong. I'm better than you are therefore I will forgive you. I don't want to be a dirty sinner like you so I will forgive you. Or I want to go to Heaven so I will forgive you to assure my place at the table.

The true forgiveness practiced by Jesus and espoused by the Course has one very important element that we don't think to include because of our traditional Christian upbringing. True forgiveness recognizes that what you thought your brother did has not occurred. How could it have really occurred if we are dreaming this life? Judging in the world is like holding someone responsible for something they did to you while you were dreaming. The sin or offense that you judge or blame him or yourself for has not happened because all form is an illusion. The Course says, "It (forgiveness) does not pardon sins and make them real. It sees there was no sin. And in that view are all your sins forgiven." (W-PII.1.1:2–4)

True forgiveness does not pardon sins because that would make sin real. It merely sees there is no sin because this is an illusion. All forgiveness really does is remove in our minds everything that prevents us from loving. There is real peace in knowing that what you think someone has done has not occurred because the world is not real.

There is no sin because there is no world of form. This is communicated in John's Gospel when he said, "In the beginning was the Word, and the Word was with God, and the Word was God." The word is thought, God is thought, Jesus is thought, Spirit is thought, we are thought. God created us with thought and He only creates exactly like Him, therefore we are thought or Spirit. God creating us in His image and likeness can be clarified as image is thought and likeness is of like quality.

Our current situation arose because we are free to think that there might be something other than God and Heaven. Once this tiny mad thought happened, our creative power created the world of form in our minds. This is the biblical creation story including the fall. The thought and the interruption were over in an instant and Heaven continued on as usual. Heaven is still as it always was, only a part of the mind of God's children is asleep and dreaming that we are here. God noticed a slight difference in communication and sent the Holy Spirit into the dream with us to be here until we all seem to awaken. There is only one dream but we each see it from a different perspective like the pieces of a hologram.

Forgiveness is the recognition of the truth of our innocence rather than a pardoning of transgressions. Jesus' healing miracles were a shift in perception of the sick mind of separation, fear, guilt, and denial over to the Holy Spirit's pure love and oneness. Jesus shining love into the person's mind made them whole and if you are whole, you cannot be sick. Again from the Course, "A sense of separation from God is the only lack you really need correct. This sense of separation would never have arisen if you had not distorted your perception of truth, and thus perceived yourself as lacking." (T-1.VI.2:1–2) This sense of separation is corrected by forgiving what you hold against or think is wrong with your brother. All that is left is non-judgmental love and a realization that we are all one. The lack is replaced by knowing complete oneness and wholeness, where there is nothing lacking.

It's okay if you fail to forgive your brother, because another similar opportunity will present itself until eventually your lessons are complete. The early Church was diverse and some Christians believe in reincarnation. The Church generally was against it because it conflicted with bodily resurrection. Hebrews 9:27 says that man was appointed to die once. As you have read, Hebrews is one of the disputed Pauline letters and its teachings regarding reincarnation should be questioned. Reincarnation is believed by other major religions including Hinduism and Buddhism. Reincarnation answers the problem of how a loving God could relegate us to an eternal hell after a very short time on earth. The true answer is that He couldn't and didn't.

There is great hope in knowing that we will continue to reincarnate until we are purified and can return our minds to Heaven. Reincarnation is actually an illusion like space and time. It does not matter how long it seems to take to learn our lessons because God is eternal and knows not of time. In the divine plan, it is not up to you what you learn; it is only up to you to learn either through joy or pain, but you will learn. The only worthwhile question is how long do you want to suffer in this world before you decide for Spirit?

The path you choose is up to you but the one thing that is not under your control is that you cannot be saved alone. We need each other if we are one. We also need the Holy Spirit because we really think we are a body and everything in our life points to the reality of the world. Indeed, it will probably take some convincing for you to believe that we are not real. When Jesus said, of myself I can do nothing, he was giving up all specialness and counting on his true power from the Holy Spirit. He could not perform miracles or wake up totally by himself. He was so committed to listening to the Holy Spirit, that love and peace became his one and only true nature.

It had to be frustrating to go through what Jesus did and keep his peace and display love and forgiveness to all. We naturally assume he was special and not like us. Jesus just learned most of his lessons in previous lifetimes and used his last lifetime to teach us forgiveness and the meaninglessness of earthly life and death. If anything, he was just way ahead in the learning curve. Admittedly, it's really difficult to be like Jesus. Forgiving is hard while fighting back or attacking is easier. Trying to prove we are right has become second nature to us. By going on the offensive, we display our weakness. One way to think about forgiveness that may make it easier is if you believe that you are forgiving someone for what they haven't really done. Why hold an imaginary grudge against an illusory act if none of it is real? Jesus knew this to be true, and as a result had access to divine power and comfort.

When we were young, our parents said that walking away from a fight was harder than getting into a fight. They were right, and forgiveness is the same. Forgiveness looks weak but demands strength and is usually hard for us to offer. Forgiveness is sometimes a solitary endeavor and is for you first. When you forgive, it frees you from the burden of judgment, anger, and retribution. The person being forgiven may not even know about it. If you don't forgive, you can suffer the effects of what the other person has said or done forever. You are, in effect, letting the person control you. Forgiveness can also remove the sense of strain, hurt, guilt, anger, and fatigue from your mind, and restore your sense of invulnerability. When you forgive, you fulfill Jesus' admonition to turn the other cheek, by showing them that they cannot hurt you. The Buddha said it well: holding onto anger is like drinking poison and expecting the other person to die.

Forgiveness can restore your peace. Whenever anything happens, big or small, that causes anger, fear, or guilt, it has taken away your peace. Whenever you have a fight, grievance, problem, or have been wronged by a brother, it can take away your peace. It doesn't matter if the situation happened in the past or even if the person has died, all can be forgiven. Time is an illusion so forgiving something in the past is just as helpful for you as forgiving something in the present. If you can forgive, but it has taken you years, next time try to do it in months. If it takes weeks, try to do it in days, hours, or minutes. Try to shorten the time it takes to forgive until you can forgive immediately or automatically, as Jesus did. Wear forgiveness as a badge of honor knowing that very few of us can forgive everyone for everything.

Family members are a great place to practice forgiveness because of the sheer volume of opportunities and the importance of forgiveness to keep the relationships alive and healthy. Spouses seem to be an ever-present river of forgiveness opportunities. Forgive your spouse and your relationship will blossom into the holiest of encounters. With practice, you will eventually forgive immediately and forgiveness will not be needed as you will have learned not to judge because you and your brother are one, and in that moment you are saved. And don't worry, no one is getting away with anything because none of this is real…so forgive with reckless abandon!

Do not become attached to being perfect or to practicing perfect forgiveness. Demanding perfection will make you feel guilty and sad. Do the best you can and forgive yourself for your imperfections. The good thing about forgiveness as a means of salvation is that your brothers are everywhere and you do not have to seek far for an opportunity to save or be saved. You are saved through giving forgiveness and you save by teaching forgiveness to your brothers when you forgive them. Forgiveness is an earthly form of love.

Forgiving yourself is the same process as forgiving others. It's normal to have problems and act in unloving ways, the trick is to forgive yourself for having them and try again. When you forgive, you remember creation as one and therefore you remember your creator. You cannot love the creator while judging and condemning His creation, which includes you.

32. Choose Again

I could not cover everything I wanted to in this book and certainly did not probe the deep waters of *A Course in Miracles*. I feel like a seeker searching for truth, who finds a treasure which is more than I can imagine, and I rush out to show other seekers what I have found. My intention is to be a catalyst for questioning the status quo and to point you to the truth. Questioning religion, the Bible, or Christianity doesn't mean you are questioning God or Jesus. Their truth remains intact regardless of what anyone says about them. You are questioning man's interpretation of God and Jesus and their perceived directives and actions in the world.

One thing we can know for sure is that man is fallible and his interpretation and understanding of almost everything can be faulty. It doesn't matter if you believe what I have said or believe the Course, what does matter is through some form of introspection or personal awareness you realize that you are a perfect child of God and you begin to ask the Holy Spirit for guidance to think truly.

The probable rejection of *A Course in Miracles* by the religious establishment reminds me of the Hungarian physician Ignaz Semmelweis, who in 1847, unwittingly discovered germ theory. He noticed that midwives had a much lower mortality rate for delivering babies than medical doctors who delivered babies but also worked on cadavers. He instituted hand washing with chlorinated lime to prevent the decayed flesh smell and mortality rates dropped dramatically. Dr. Semmelweis and his methods were largely ignored and often ridiculed by the doctors who could not believe that unseen germs transferred from cadavers or patients could infect healthy people and cause death. His dismissal by the medical community was so disturbing that he was later confined to a mental hospital where he died after two weeks. He could not back up his theory with evidence because germs were relatively unknown, although he was later proved right by Louis Pasteur and others. Science will catch up to the theory of connectedness and the illusory nature of form; however many will never believe it is the truth. Sometimes, it is too painful to acknowledge, even to ourselves, that what we have truly believed is not so.

All theologies and religions demand that you have faith. Even living a normal life requires faith that you will return home safe, or you wouldn't ever leave your house. However, blind faith in religion is how many of us have operated because we have not asked questions, explored explanations, or dared to look outside our traditional religious upbringing. We have traditionally viewed our Christian faith as either belief in Jesus as salvation or belief that Jesus taught salvation, and both require faith. *A Course in Miracles* states Jesus' teaching as the way to salvation.

ACIM is an alternative to blind faith in orthodox Christianity or an agnostic/atheistic belief. However, better than blind faith is understanding. Even better than understanding is knowing. Not knowing about God or Jesus but knowing them directly through communing with them in the classroom of silence. Having a connection, an experience, a deep understanding, or even a revelation is far more impactful than someone telling us about their understanding or experience. Hence, religion is following someone else's experience and spirituality is having our own experience. We don't have Jesus the man, and can't be sure exactly what he said, therefore, the Holy Spirit, the guide promised by Jesus, is our way, truth, and life. The Holy Spirit will not force himself on us. For this reason, you must ask for His help. The Holy Spirit cannot be heard by an unwelcoming host. The Course asks, "Would you be hostage to the ego or host to God?" (T-11.II.7:1) I invite and encourage you to have your own experience with the divine.

A Course in Miracles is a self-study course where we, with the guidance of the Holy Spirit, reorient the mind from fear to love using forgiveness. It makes sense that the Course cannot be the only way because Mother Teresa did not have the Course and she exemplified the saintly traits of love, peace, and forgiveness. What sets her apart is how she ministered to all faiths and no faiths. Her mission was to help the poorest of the poor. She was a Roman Catholic nun but saw the face of Christ in all people. She loved everyone unconditionally and was a person of peace. Mother Teresa said her spiritual philosophy was that when she encountered anyone, she simply saw them as Jesus in all of his distressing disguises. Through her works, she demonstrated her beliefs that we are all connected in Christ and are all worthy of love and kindness. She may not have needed to practice intense forgiveness because she learned that lesson earlier and did not appear to judge.

Blaise Pascal, the seventeenth century philosopher, theologian, and mathematician, postulated *Pascal's Wager*. He proposed that humans wager their lives on whether God does or does not exist. The wager calculated what someone would lose by picking one or the other. Believing that God exists might cause someone to lose some earthly pleasures, receiving instead eternal rewards. Not believing in God might give you some earthly pleasures but at the cost of eternal separation from God. Everyone must pick a belief and you have to have faith to be on either side. The wager seems like another form of fire insurance.

If you don't go by blind faith, then faith in the evidence is what you are left with, either atheistic or orthodox. As with everything, even evidence needs to be interpreted. I and *A Course in Miracles* are proponents of a third alternative that there is a God but not the God described in the Bible. I would like to review some of my evidence or proofs of the Course's explanation of true life.

I call these statements proofs, albeit they are not all provable or not provable similar to many of the Bible's theological claims. They make sense to people who are open-minded and are searching for a better explanation. To support my point, I offer a quote from St. Thomas Aquinas, "To one who has faith, no explanation is necessary. To one without faith, no explanation is possible." Congratulations on coming this far; you are open to the truth, which means you are on your way to awakening.

- God is perfect and made us in His image, therefore, we must be perfect, not in time and space, but in eternity in Heaven.
- God is perfect and perfection by definition cannot need anything nor lack anything. Therefore, God cannot be without us, not in physical form but in our true form as Spirit.
- If we will have everlasting life or eternal punishment after death, then we must be eternal and nothing of form is eternal. Therefore, our true selves are neither bodies nor form of any kind, only Spirit.
- Time is limited and eternity is unlimited. Another way to say this is: eternity is no time. Hence, time and eternity contradict each other;

therefore, one must be true and the other false. Eternity must be true since God is eternal.

- God created everything with His word which is thought. When thoughts are shared, they go out to others and are still part of their source. Therefore, as creations of God made from His thoughts, we have never left our source, which is God.

- Just as a tree is known by its fruit, a God of perfect, limitless love could not have created a world with such suffering where death and eternal punishment is possible.

- If miracles are possible and they invalidate the laws of the physical world, then the laws of physics must not be real or true.

- The thought that we need salvation means we need saving from something. Something is wrong that our perfect God created and that scenario cannot be. Salvation is just undoing our false personal thoughts of separation from the perfect.

- The Bible says God gave us free will, but we are not free if we are trapped here in a body and separated from God in Heaven. We are not free to spend eternity with God; therefore, we do not have free will to sin or follow God in our temporal form.

- God wills that none shall perish and God's will is absolute because there is only God. Therefore, we cannot suffer eternal separation from God and there must be another explanation.

- If we are created by God in His image and likeness, then we also have His power to create with our thoughts or rather to miss-create this world of illusion and then dream that we are here.

- Jesus said to love God with all your heart, soul, and mind. Fear is the opposite of love and the Bible is full of fearful passages, therefore it is inconsistent with Jesus' Commandment and cannot be God's word.

- We all know that we can look at or become aware of our own thoughts, therefore there is another part of us that is aware of our mental thoughts and that part is who we really are – Spirit. We are not the brain or body, but the unconscious part of the universal mind that is still unknowingly connected to God in Heaven.

- The evidence that the Course is true is that we think we are here and not with God.

Salvation, according to these proofs, is undoing our thoughts of separation. Since we created this illusory world with our thoughts, when we withdraw our thoughts from the world and seek the Kingdom, the world will cease to exist in our minds because it is not real. As stated earlier, all of our earthly problems stem from our thought of separation from God, because if we didn't have that thought, then we wouldn't think we are here.

Jesus preached about light and darkness. The light represents the truth and darkness is the opposite which would be anything not of God. Darkness cannot obliterate light, but light can shine away the darkness. Similarly, in our lives we focus our religious or spiritual practice on bringing darkness to the light. The Bible conditions us to focus on sin and evil (darkness), rather than focusing on the truth of perfect love (light). Do not bring sin and evil to God; bring God's love to the dream of sin and evil. Studying sin and evil does not lead to correction; rather overlooking these errors is the aim of *A Course in Miracles*.

As Socrates said, "The secret to change is to focus all your energy, not on fighting the old, but on building the new." The Course is clear that you cannot see two worlds. Light and darkness cannot coexist. There are two worlds: the world of form that includes sin, evil, pain, suffering, loss, and death; and the world of Spirit which is the loving God. With your right mind, you must choose what you want to see, and you will see it.

The Course says, "Temptation has one lesson it would teach, in all its forms, wherever it occurs. It would persuade the Holy Son of God that he is a body, born in what must die, unable to escape its frailty, and bound by what it orders him to feel. It sets the limits on what he can do; its power is the only strength he has; his grasp cannot exceed its tiny reach. Would you be this, if Christ appeared to you in all His glory, asking you but this: Choose once again if you would take your place among the saviors of the world, or would remain in hell, and hold your brothers there." (T-31.VIII.1:5)

Temptation is from the ego/devil, tempting us into thinking that we are different from God. Hell is not a place; it is the thoughts that seem to keep us separated from God. Our purpose on earth is to receive the love of God and to extend the love of God to our neighbors. In doing this, we will fulfill the will of God on earth as it is in Heaven. And by doing only this, we will experience true happiness and the peace that passeth understanding. The way to determine if a religious or spiritual path is valid is to judge whether the path is making you more loving and peaceful.

Are you more at peace, less fearful, and happier even during hard times? Do you not fiercely defend your positions and not attack others for theirs? Do you blame others less, forgive more quickly, and feel guided to make decisions that benefit everyone? Do you delight in the occasions to experience the love God is offering you? The Course says, "You have one test, as sure as God, by which to recognize if what you learned is true. If you are wholly free of fear of any kind, and if all those who meet or even think of you share in your perfect peace, then you can be sure that you have learned God's lesson, and not your own." (T-14.XI.5:1–2)

Here is a useful mantra similar to the Thomas Merton quote about love – our job is to forgive others without stopping to inquire if they are worthy. If we don't forgive our brothers, another interaction will present itself and we will have the opportunity to make a different choice. During those encounters, Jesus whispers in our ear: choose again my brother! Thankfully, God's love is always and forever there for our choosing.

I will finish with one of the most beautiful and hopeful sayings in the Course.

"This is God's Final Judgment: You are still My Holy Son, forever innocent, forever loving and forever loved, as limitless as your Creator, and completely changeless and forever pure. Therefore awaken and return Me. I am your Father and you are My Son." (W-PII.10.5:1–3)

References

All ACIM quotes are from *A Course in Miracles,* copyright 1992, 1999, 2007, by the **Foundation for Inner Peace**, 448 Ignacio Blvd., #306 Novato, CA 94949, www.acim.org, used with permission.

Scripture taken from the New King James Version. Copyright 1982 by Thomas Nelson, Inc. Used by permission. All rights reserved.

Acknowledgments from Related Books:

Renard, Gary R. (2002) *The Disappearance of the Universe*, Carlsbad, CA: Hay House.

Renard, Gary R. (2006) *Your Immortal Reality*, Carlsbad, CA: Hay House.

Renard, Gary R. (2013) *Love Has Forgotten No One*, Carlsbad, CA: Hay House.

Geisler, Norman L. and Howe, Thomas (1992) *The Big Book of Bible Difficulties*, Grand Rapids, MI: Baker Books.

Funk, Robert W. and Hoover, Roy W. (1993) *The Five Gospels*, New York, NY: Harper Collins.

Wapnick, Kenneth (1983) *Forgiveness and Jesus*, Roscoe, NY: Foundation for *A Course in Miracles*.

Ehrman, Bart D. (2009) *Jesus Interrupted*, New York, NY: Harper Collins.

Ehrman, Bart D. (2007) *Misquoting Jesus*, HarperOne.

Ehrman, Bart D. (2018) *The Triumph of Christianity*, Simon and Schuster.

Ehrman, Bart D. (2016) *Jesus Before the Gospels*, HarperOne.

Kushner, Harold S. (2004) *When Bad Things Happen to Good People*, New York, NY, Anchor Books.

Korte, Chris R. (2016) *I Wish I Knew Then,* Amazon KDP.

CITATIONS

[i] Gary R Renard, *Your Immortal Reality*(Carlsbad, California: Hay House, Inc, 2006), 166
[ii] Gary R Renard, *Your Immortal Reality*(Carlsbad, California: Hay House, Inc, 2006), 167
[iii] Gary R Renard, *Your Immortal Reality*(Carlsbad, California: Hay House, Inc, 2006), 167
[iv] Gary R Renard, *Your Immortal Reality*(Carlsbad, California: Hay House, Inc, 2006), 171

9 7 9 8 8 9 1 5 5 0 8 3 4